IMAGES
of America

SANTA CRUZ WHARF

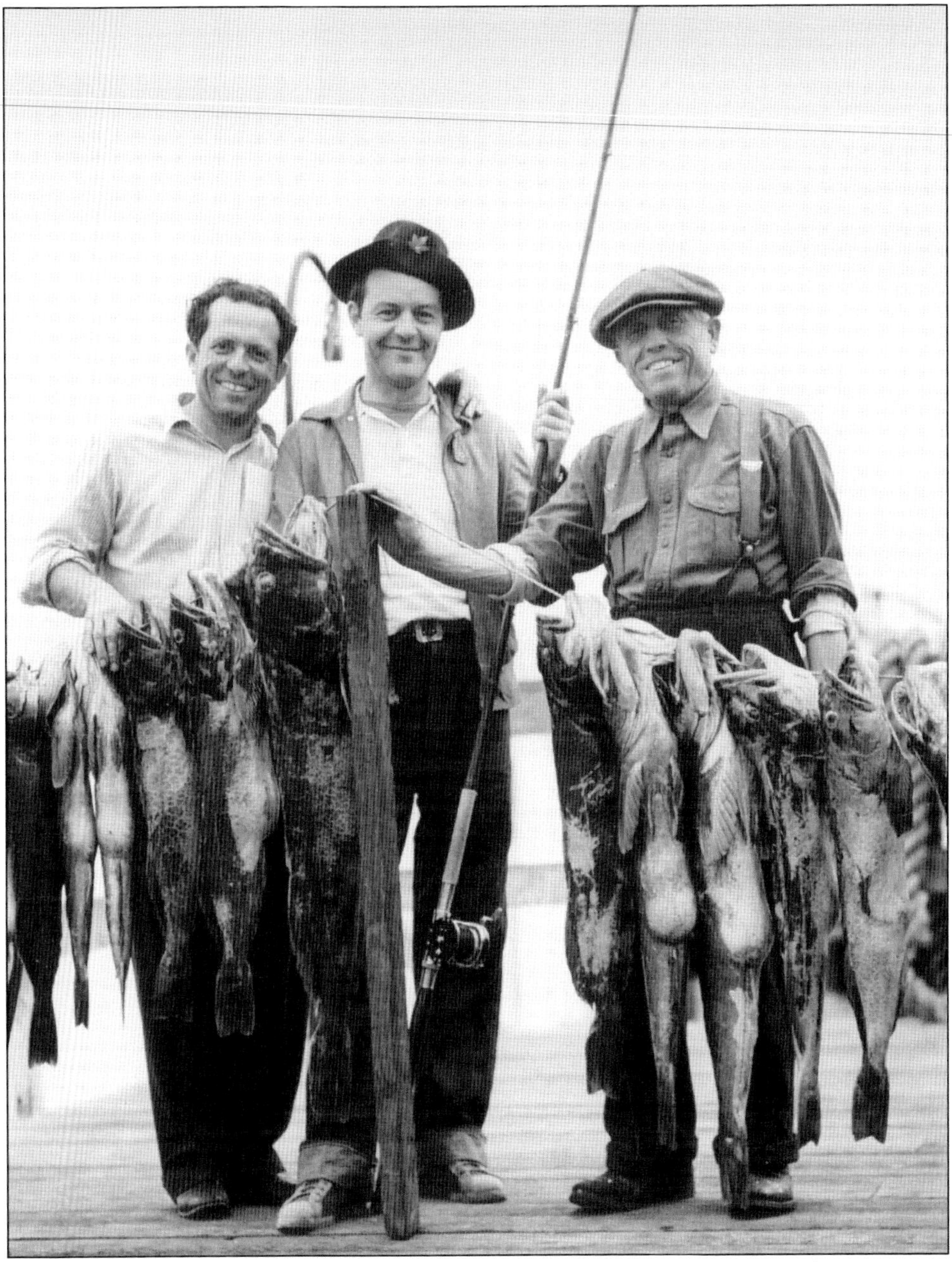

This large string of lingcod was caught off the coast of Santa Cruz and displayed in Santa Cruz publicity around 1938. Brothers Malio J. Stagnaro (left) and Cottardo Stagnaro II flank famed West Coast cartoonist Moyer Sinclair "Thommy" Thompson, who often drew cartoons and sketches of the Santa Cruz waterfront for the *San Francisco Call-Bulletin*. (Author's collection.)

On the Cover: This 1,000-pound sunfish, or *Mola mola*, was caught off the Santa Cruz coast near Natural Bridges, on March 17, 1939. The fish was caught on a C. Stagnaro sportfishing boat, the *Marie*, and was displayed, along with three salmon, on the main Santa Cruz Wharf for several days. *Mola* in Latin means "millstone" and describes the ocean sunfish's somewhat circular shape. The woman is unidentified. (Author's collection.)

IMAGES
of America

SANTA CRUZ WHARF

Geoffrey Dunn

ARCADIA
PUBLISHING

ISBN 978-1-4671-3393-7

Published by Arcadia Publishing
Charleston, South Carolina

Printed in the United States of America

Library of Congress Control Number: 2016950347

For all general information, please contact Arcadia Publishing:
Telephone 843-853-2070
Fax 843-853-0044
E-mail sales@arcadiapublishing.com
For customer service and orders:
Toll-Free 1-888-313-2665

Visit us on the Internet at www.arcadiapublishing.com

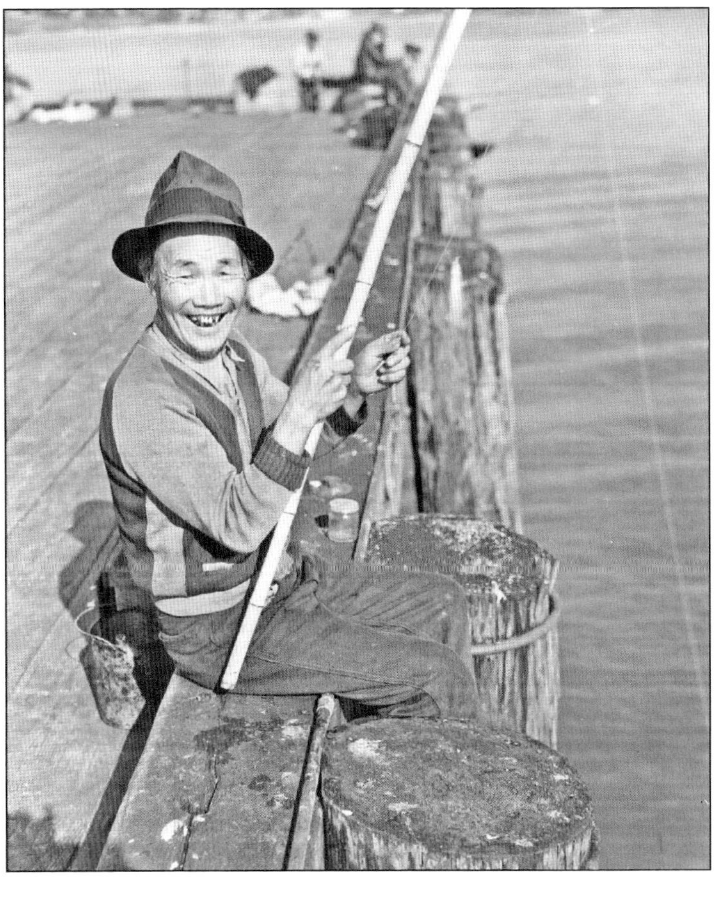

Legendary Santa Cruz fisherman Ah Fook, a native of Canton, China, lived in the last Santa Cruz Chinatown. This image was taken during the 1940s at the end of the wharf. Warren "Skip" Littlefield writes in a 1941 edition of the *Sunday Sentinel-News*: "Ah Fook was born to fish. . . . For Santa Cruzans not to know [Fook] is comparable to a mountaineer spending a lifetime within five miles of Yosemite Valley and never taking the trouble to view the wonders of its waterfalls." (Santa Cruz Seaside Company.)

Contents

Foreword and Acknowledgments

I have had a lifelong love affair with the Santa Cruz Wharf. It's a romance that dates back to my earliest childhood, when I would spend carefree days with my cousins roaming around various landings and catwalks, fish houses, and storage sheds. During the first half of my life, I worked in various capacities on the wharf—rolling newspapers at a young age for nickels, then advancing to fish cutting and dish washing and serving as a deckhand on fishing barges and cruise boats. I cannot imagine a more delightful childhood playground, every bit as colorful as Mark Twain's Mississippi River, and I count my blessings for the gift of the wharf as the social and cultural setting of my formative years.

My roots in the Santa Cruz waterfront stretch back to the late 1800s—the date is not quite certain—when my great-grandfather Cottardo P. Stagnaro I jumped ship and eventually settled here. During the late 1890s and early 1900s, he helped to bring many members of his extended family from the small coastal village of Riva Trigoso, Italy, to the Santa Cruz waterfront. I thank each and every *Rivani*, past and present, who contributed to Santa Cruz Wharf history. In particular, I want to acknowledge those who formed the nucleus of my family from the 1950s into the 1980s, including my grandmother Batistina Stagnaro; my great-uncle Malio J. Stagnaro; my aunts Mary Stagnaro Herman and Stella and Gilda Stagnaro; my uncles Batista "Dodie," Malio "Stago," Joe, and Robert "Big Boy" Stagnaro; my great-uncles Robby and "Risho" Ghio—all of whom have now passed away—and who assumed their share of childcare responsibilities for my sister, cousins, and me during our early days on the wharf.

In addition to my own family, I also want to thank members of the Cardinale clan—especially brothers Frank and Joe—for whom I worked in the 1980s and who have always treated me like family. My cousin Kenneth Lamb, a poet and fish cutter, also taught me many things about life and fish cutting during my coming-of-age years. I was always particularly close to three other wharf families: the late Robby, Dante "Danny," and Auggie Canepa; Batista "Lily," Stefano "Ghighi," and Victor Ghio; John and August "Jocko" Carniglia; and their still-living brothers, Aldo Canepa, Victor Carniglia, and Johnny Ghio. To them, my heartfelt love and gratitude always.

During the wharf's 100th anniversary, I served on the Centennial Committee with a host of wharf aficionados, including Josh Clevenger, Norm Daly, Mauro Garcia, Larry Jackson, Rachel Kaufman, Rose Ann Mazzone, Camille Nava, Susan O'Connor Frazer, Carol Scurich, Vince and Maggie Tuzzi, Lisa Uttal, and Tiffany Wise-West. The centennial also brought me closer to Jon Bombaci and Danny Buecher, who in their capacities as wharf supervisor have expressed their love of the wharf in many ways. My longtime friend and the director of the city's parks and recreation department, Dannettee Shoemaker, was an absolute jewel to work with. Mark Gilbert, the owner of three restaurants and a gift shop (and there are, apparently, more on the way) has been a visionary on the wharf over the past decades. My friendship with Donha Lee Dunderdale dates back to her days as a waitress at Gilda's in the 1980s, and her business, Made in Santa Cruz, has added a new dimension to wharf history. Lisa McGinnis, a longtime member of the city's parks department, got us off to a good start and was an early promoter of this book. Charles Prentiss and Nikki Silva have been longtime comrades in all things historical and cultural; they not only played a critical role in encouraging this book but also served as consultants on the 2014 Santa Cruz Wharf Master Plan.

I am also grateful to the Santa Cruz Seaside Company for use of several images, and I especially want to thank company archivist Jessie Durant, along with Kris Reyes and Charles Canfield, for their assistance. They love the history of the waterfront as much as I do, albeit it from a slightly different perspective from the beach. I especially want to thank Darlene Stagnaro Dyer for providing me with family photographs. Nina Simon and Marla Novo of the Santa Cruz Museum of Art and History have also been helpful and supportive—in this book and in a variety of historic and artistic endeavors.

My title manager, Jeff Ruetsche, has been an absolute jewel to work with again in helping to guide what is now a second Arcadia project through to the finish line. Friends and local historians Sandy Lydon, Stan Stevens, Frank Perry, Dan Model, Rex Walker, George Ow, Barry Brown, and Kim Stoner have always been there when I needed an assist. The late Harold Van Gorder gifted me several of the photographs in this collection. To all those others who have lent a hand along the way, my heartfelt thanks.

This book is dedicated to Siri, Tess, and Dylan, and to my late mother, Yolanda "Lindy" Stagnaro Dunn.

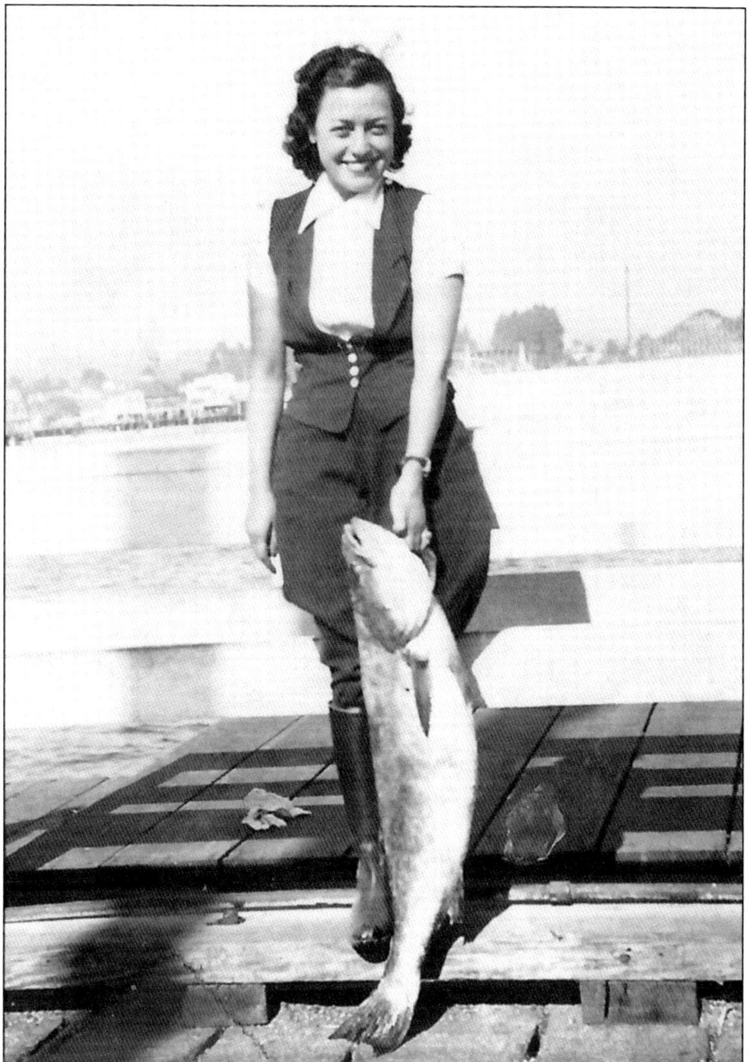

Yolanda "Lindy" Stagnaro Dunn (1915–2014), the mother of the author, is dressed in a horse-riding outfit on the Santa Cruz Wharf in the 1930s with a large California sea bass. Lindy worked on the Pleasure Pier, serving as a ticket taker and hostess for her family's speedboat rides, but never worked in the family fish businesses. She did, however, work as a hostess at Malio's restaurant in the 1960s and 1970s. (Author's collection.)

INTRODUCTION

For the past century, the Santa Cruz Wharf has been an iconic structure on the California coast, serving not only as a gateway to the Monterey Bay National Marine Sanctuary but also as a primary destination point for millions of visitors to Central California.

With a rich and fabled fishing and shipping legacy, the wharf continues to serve as an important economic engine in the region, hosting a wide array of fine restaurants, fish houses, gift shops, and recreational outlets for visitors and locals alike.

Today's Santa Cruz Wharf is actually the sixth pier on the Santa Cruz waterfront. In the aftermath of the Gold Rush and California's ascension to statehood, these earlier wharves served critical roles in the export of a variety of regional resources and products: potatoes, hides, tallow, lime, gunpowder, redwoods, and later, fish.

The current wharf was built a century ago primarily to accommodate large steamships, hence its extension a half-mile from shore. With the addition of davits—small hand-cranes used to lift fishing boats out of stormy seas—the wharf served as home to the Santa Cruz Italian fishing community for nearly 50 years. You will find a significant portion of this waterfront history covered in the following pages.

At 2,745 feet, the Santa Cruz Wharf remains the longest wooden wharf on the Pacific Ocean and in the coastal United States. Its views of the bay and the surrounding coastal mountain ranges are truly magnificent and panoramic, from the peaks of the Santa Lucia Range to the south to those of the Santa Cruz Mountains northward. You can encounter—quite literally, if you aren't careful—marine life in abundance, most notably hundreds of California sea lions, which now claim the wharf's crossbeams and landings as their own.

And, I would argue, it's a place where you can also find yourself. The Santa Cruz Wharf—and all the 4,528 wooden piles that compose it—provides both external and internal vistas simply not to be found anywhere on land, a place for contemplation, reflection, and quietude.

As the wharf celebrated its 100th birthday in 2014, we were all reminded of what a great gift it is, not only for those of us who are fortunate to live in California but to the entire world. May it reign another 100 years.

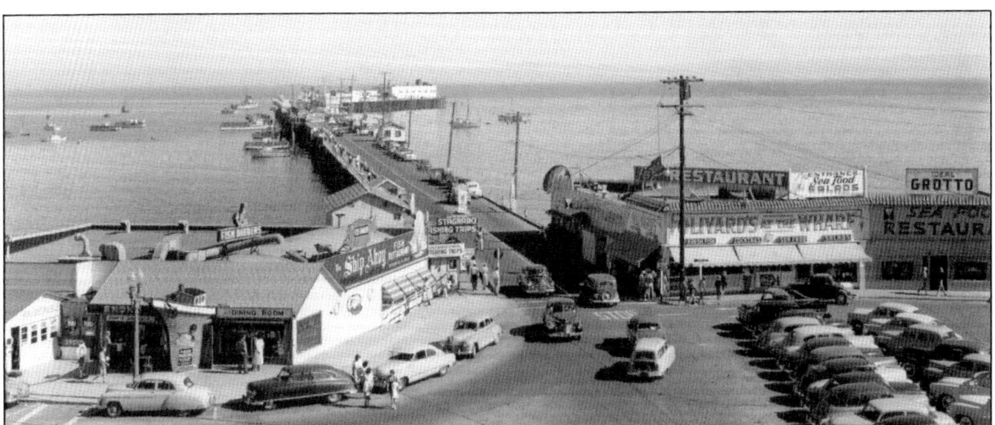

Seen here is the entrance to the Santa Cruz Wharf around 1949. (Author's collection.)

One

EARLY WHARVES

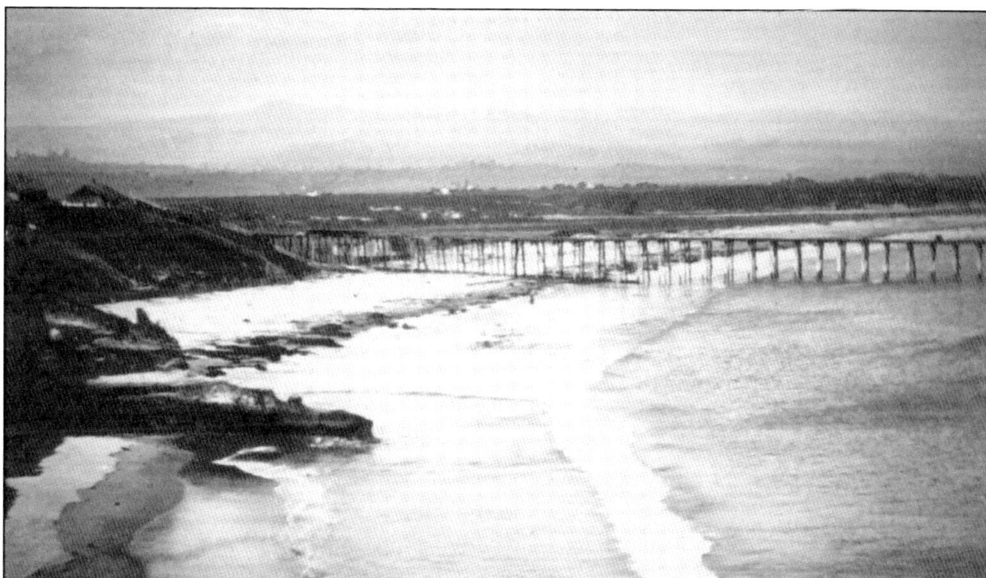

The first known pier on the Santa Cruz waterfront, built by Elihu Anthony in 1849, was little more than a ramp or chute coming off the end of Bay Street to ship potatoes from Santa Cruz during the Gold Rush boom. In 1854, the ramp was expanded by the Davis & Jordan lime operation, and it was purchased by Henry Cowell in 1865. Since the 1940s, it has been mistakenly asserted that the wharf built by David Gharky in 1857 was located near the site of today's wharf, but it was actually constructed farther east, at the foot of present-day Main Street (pictured). In 1865, the wharf was taken over by the California Powder Works for the shipment of various explosives and the receipt of saltpeter and sulfur. (Author's collection.)

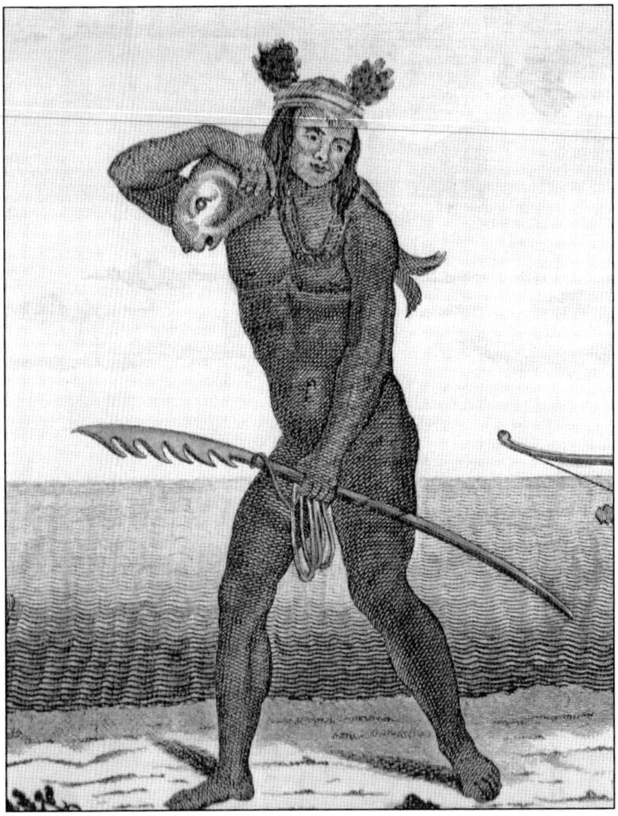

It is important to note when chronicling California waterfront history that indigenous peoples lived in the region for millennia before the arrival of European explorers and Spanish missionaries. Archaeologist Robert Cartier has asserted evidence of Paleo-Indian hunters dating back as far as 11,000 years. Archeological evidence indicates that fish and other marine staples provided protein for coastal communities throughout the Monterey Bay region. This image is from Charles Theodore Middleton's A *New and Complete System of Geography*, published in 1778. (Santa Cruz Museum of Art & History.)

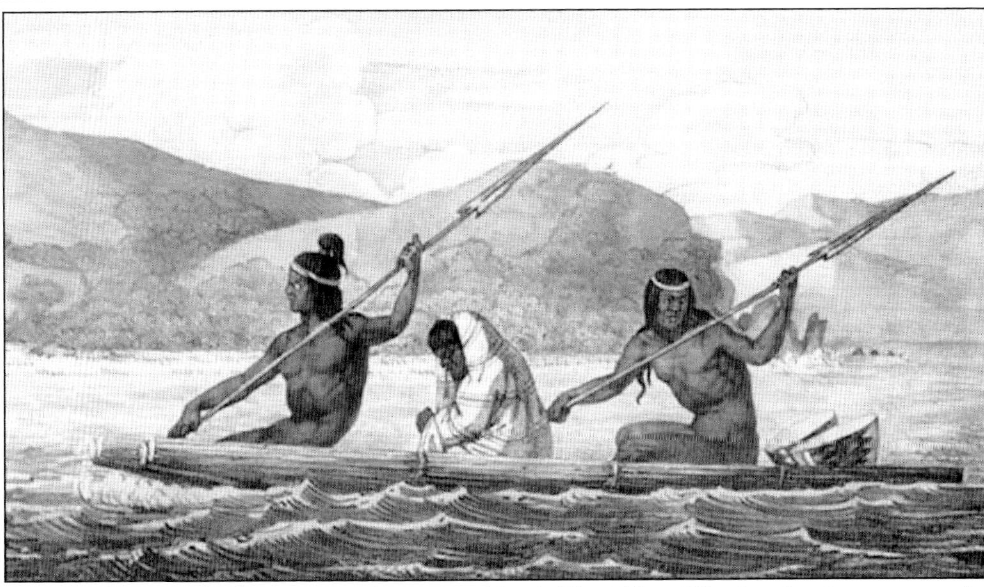

As Malcolm Margolin has noted in his seminal book *The Ohlone Way*, local indigenous peoples were "nearly amphibious." Small vessels made of tule and balsa were lashed together with cordage made of grass or hemp. Paddles were double-bladed. This image, a hand-tinted lithograph, was drawn by Russian explorer and illustrator Louis Choris of San Francisco Bay around 1822. (Santa Cruz Museum of Art & History.)

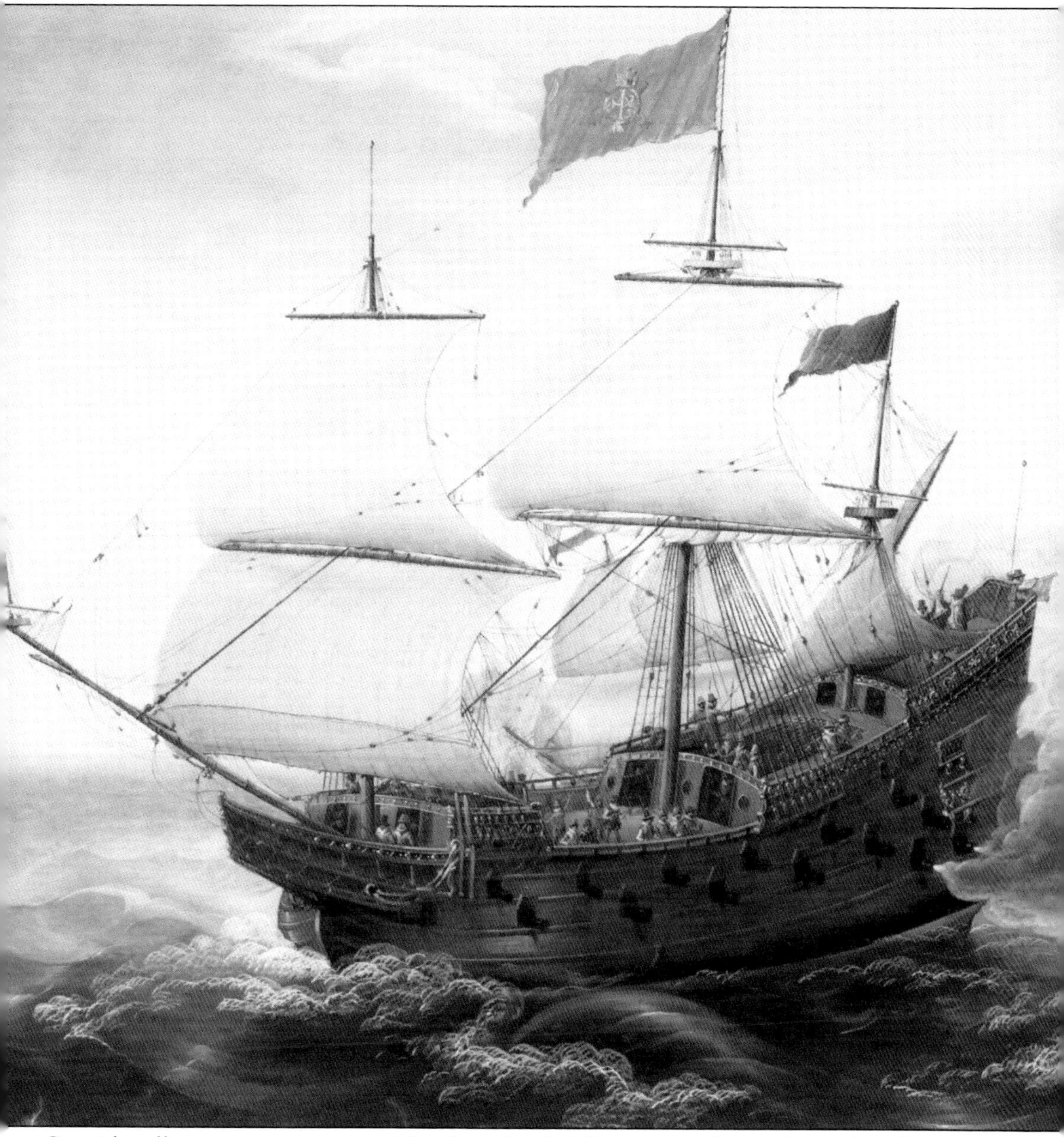

Spanish galleons were a common sight along the California coast during the 18th and early 19th centuries. While Santa Cruz served as a port for such vessels, there were no known piers or wharves constructed by the Spanish in the region. They anchored in deep waters and brought tenders onto shore. This detail of a galleon is from a larger painting by Cornelis Verbeeck, *A Naval Encounter between Dutch and Spanish Warships*. (Author's collection.)

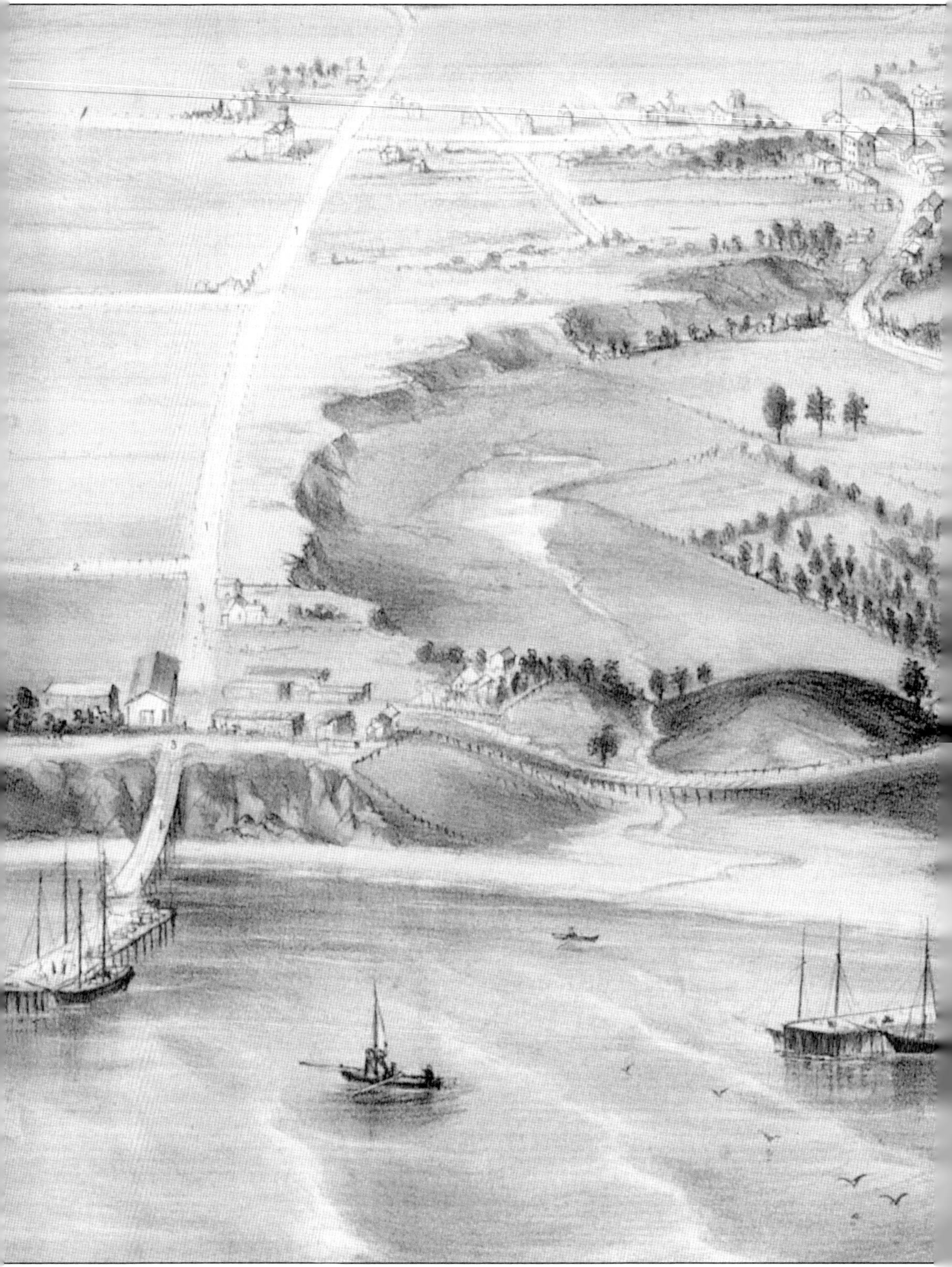

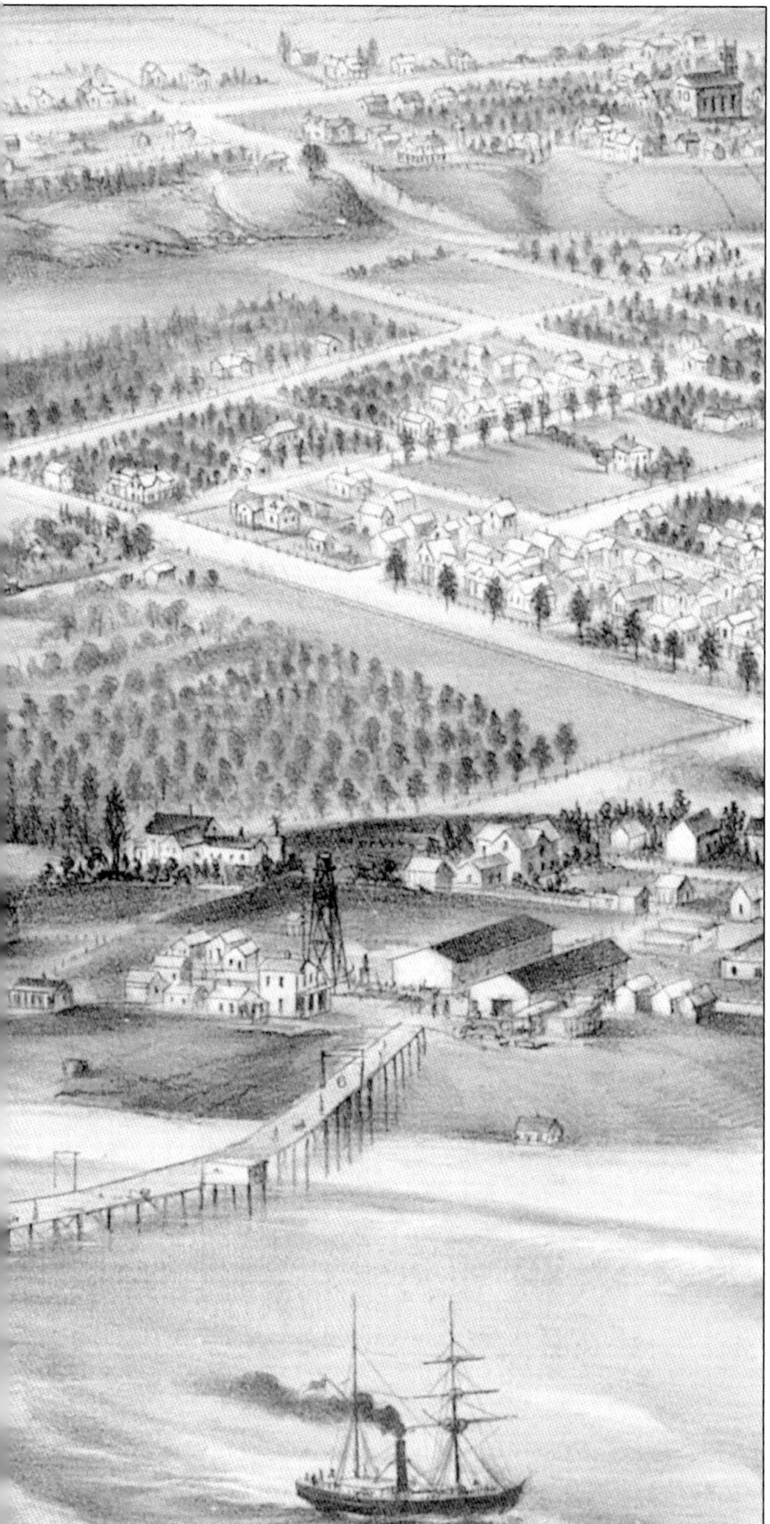

This is one of the first known images of the so-called Cowell Wharf (left), emerging off the end of Bay Street (between what is today the Sea & Sand Hotel and the Dream Inn). Neary Lagoon is in the center of image. The first known pier or wharf in Santa Cruz was the so-called Potato Chute wharf built by Elihu Anthony to ship potatoes grown in Santa Cruz to San Francisco. Pictured is a detail of the lithograph *Bird's-Eye View of Santa Cruz, Cal.*, by Charles B. Gifford, published by A.L. Bancroft & Company around 1870. The author owns one of the few known copies of this lithograph. (Author's collection.)

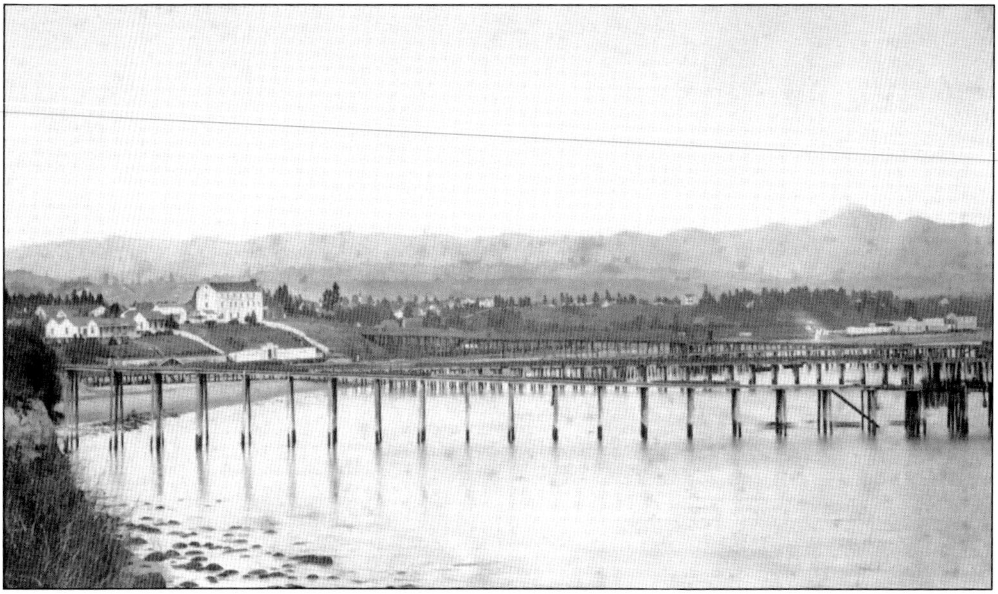

This rare panorama, showing four wharves in the early 1880s, was taken from what is now West Cliff Drive on the Santa Cruz waterfront. The closest is the Cowell Wharf; next is the Railroad Wharf, midway along which is the Connecting Wharf or S Wharf, which linked to the Powder Works Wharf. Early Santa Cruz hotels can be seen on Beach Hill, along with the incipient saltwater bathhouse industry that eventually became the Santa Cruz Boardwalk. Loma Prieta is in the background. (Santa Cruz Museum of Art & History.)

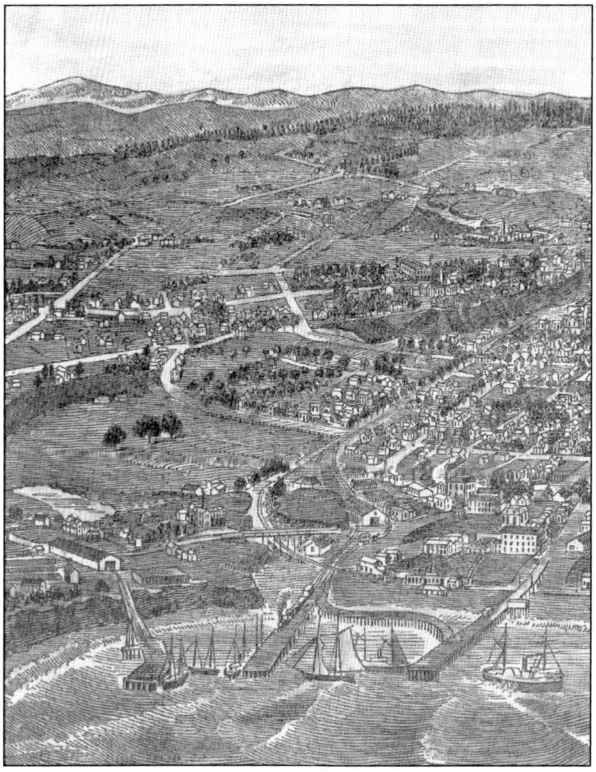

Another rare panorama from the early 1880s shows four wharves on the Santa Cruz waterfront (albeit with some artistic license), this time in a woodcut from an unidentified Swedish-language periodical. Note the steam train on the second pier from the left. What is important in this rendering is the direct link between the downtown neighborhoods of Santa Cruz and the waterfront. (Author's collection.)

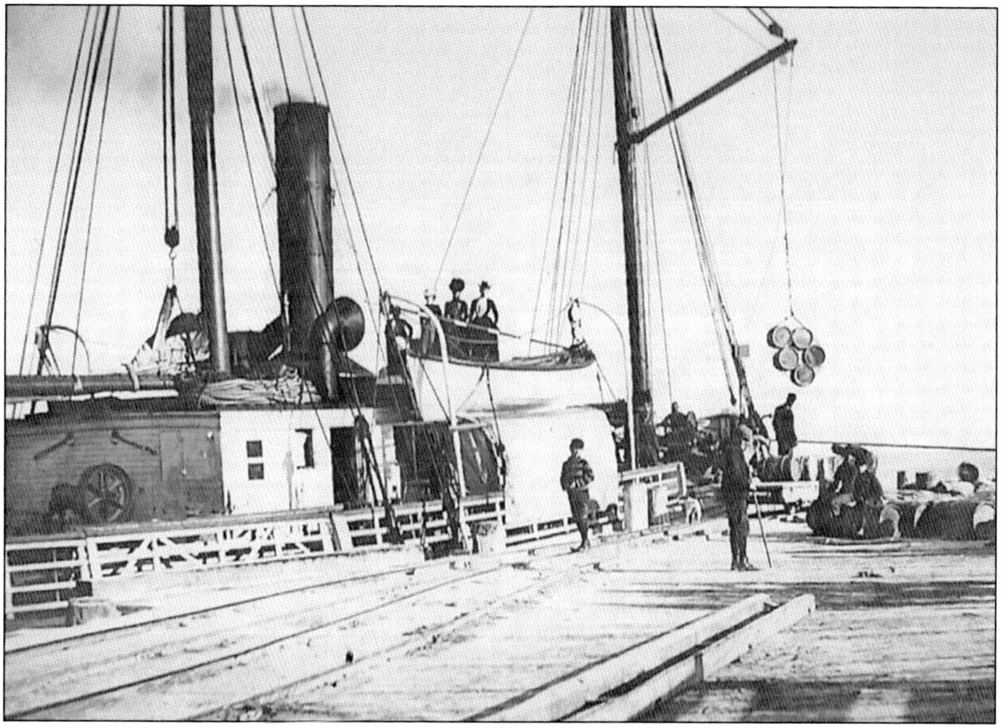

This magnificent c. 1890s photograph of Cowell Wharf shows a steamship loading barrels of lime for export to the San Francisco Bay Area. Note the women aboard ship behind the tender. They are possibly passengers. The rails on wharf are not for steam trains but for horse-drawn shipping cars that brought the lime barrels down the relatively steep angle of the pier for shipping. (Santa Cruz Museum of Art & History.)

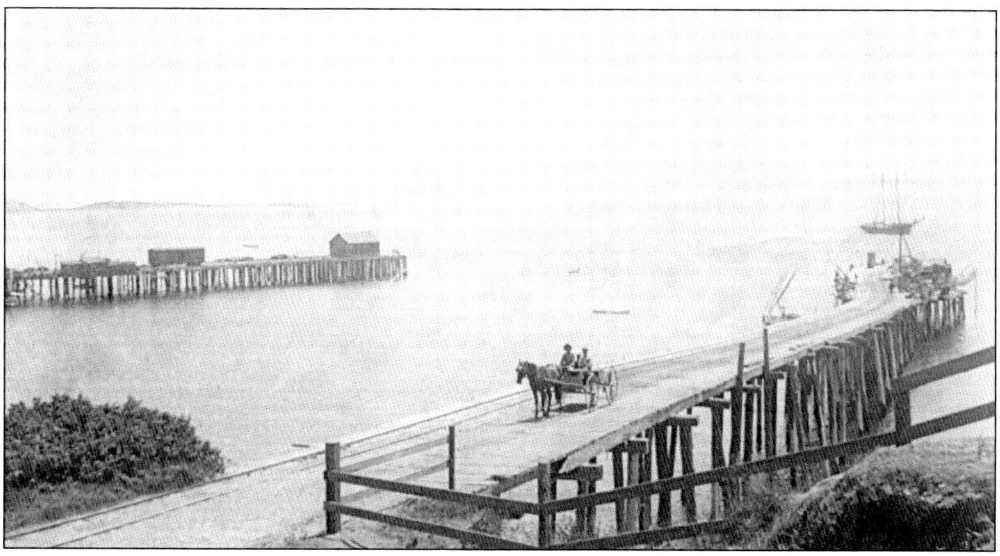

Here is another view of the Cowell Wharf from the cliffs. The horse-drawn wagon appears to be for passengers and small shipments only. To the left is the Railroad Wharf (note the railroad car in the middle). Also note the small lateen sailboats used by early Italian fishermen, who docked their boats at the Cowell Wharf. (Author's collection.)

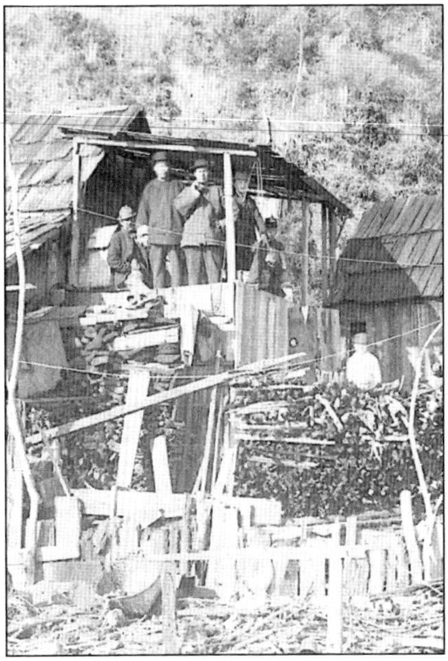

Contrary to popular conception, it was Chinese immigrants—not Italians or Portuguese—who first established the commercial fishing industry in California, including Santa Cruz. No known image of the Santa Cruz Chinese fishing village exists, but the US Census of 1880 indicates that 29 fishermen were living at this ramshackle driftwood village in Capitola (pictured at what is now New Brighton State Beach), ranging in age from 16 to 48. (Capitola Museum, courtesy Carolyn Swift.)

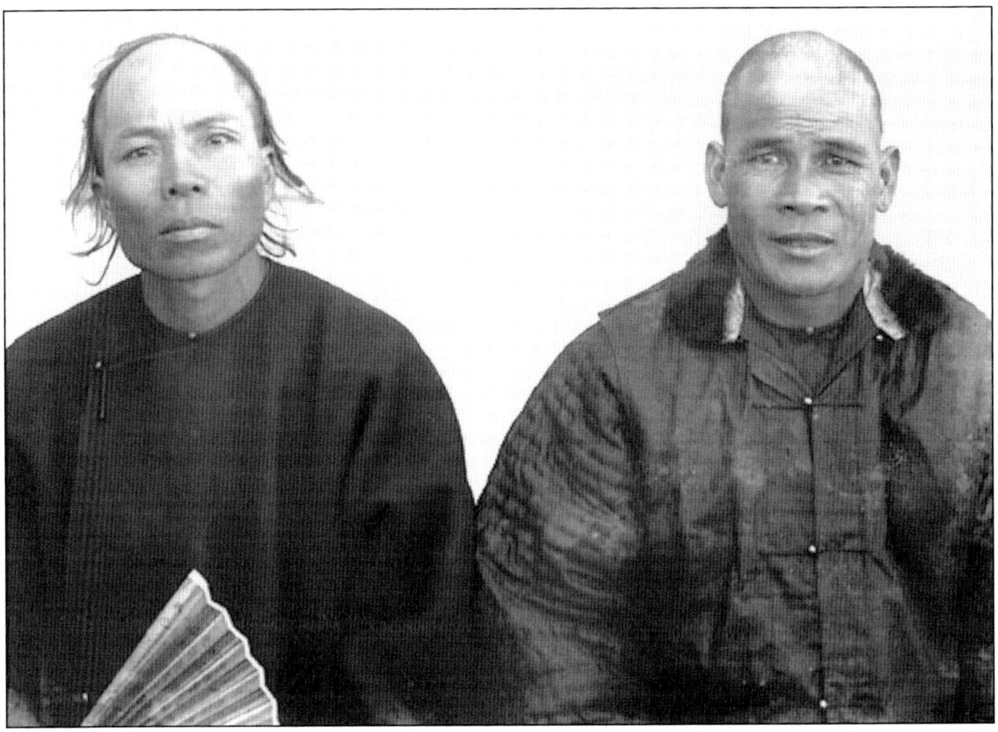

Chinese fishermen first entered the fishing industry in the region by harvesting abalone in the 1850s, then gradually expanded to other fisheries once the railroad opened up markets in the San Francisco Bay Area and inland valleys. As historian Sandy Lydon notes in his landmark work, *Chinese Gold: The Chinese in the Monterey Bay Region*, "over half of the fish caught in Santa Cruz County [in 1879] were caught by the Chinese near Capitola." Here are two members of the Monterey Bay Chinese fishing community, including Jung San Choy (right) of Pebble Beach. (California Views, Pat Hathaway Collection.)

While Chinese fishermen worked all angles of the local fishery (including collecting seaweed to export back to China, pictured), by the late 1880s, the fishermen from Capitola were pushed farther east toward Aptos and eventually all the way to the Pajaro River. The anti-Chinese movement in California was particularly virulent in Santa Cruz. By the early 1890s, the Chinese had been driven from the local commercial fishery entirely. (Author's collection.)

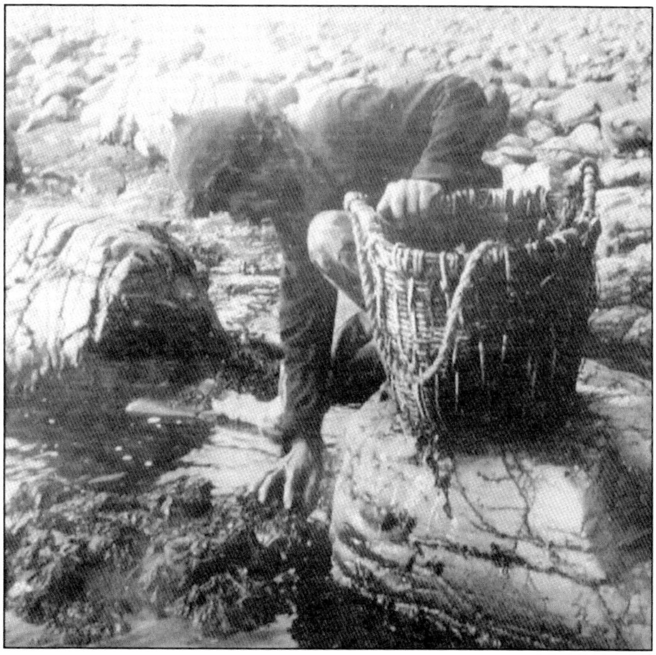

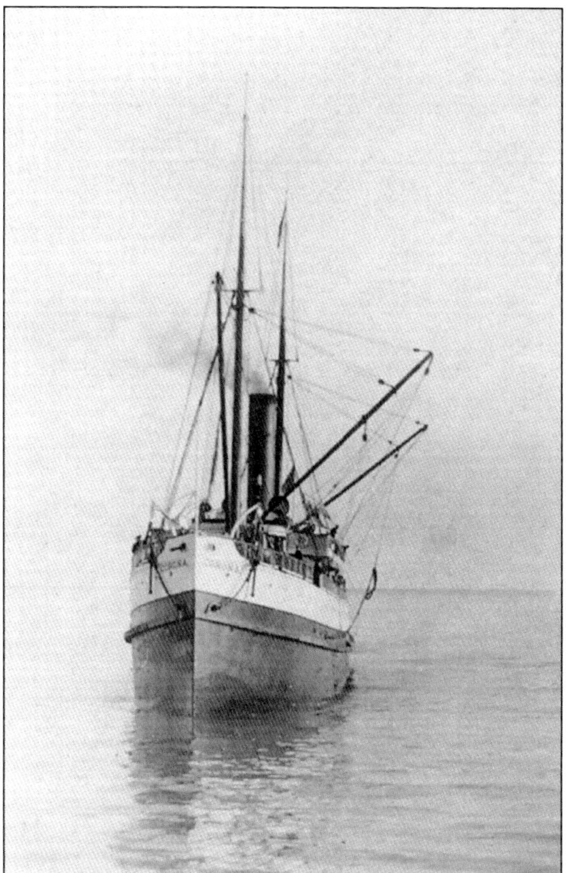

To fully understand the development of the Santa Cruz waterfront, one needs to understand that steamship traffic along the California coast was extensive in the 19th century and that Santa Cruz was a major port for steamship lines—for supplies, mail, and passengers. The steamship *Corona* (pictured near Santa Cruz) ran from San Diego to Puget Sound and occasionally as far north as Alaska. In 1898, the ship ran aground off Lewis Island in Alaska but was saved from extensive damage by a large blackfish wedged in the hole of its damaged hull. (Author's collection, photograph by Lillian Howard.)

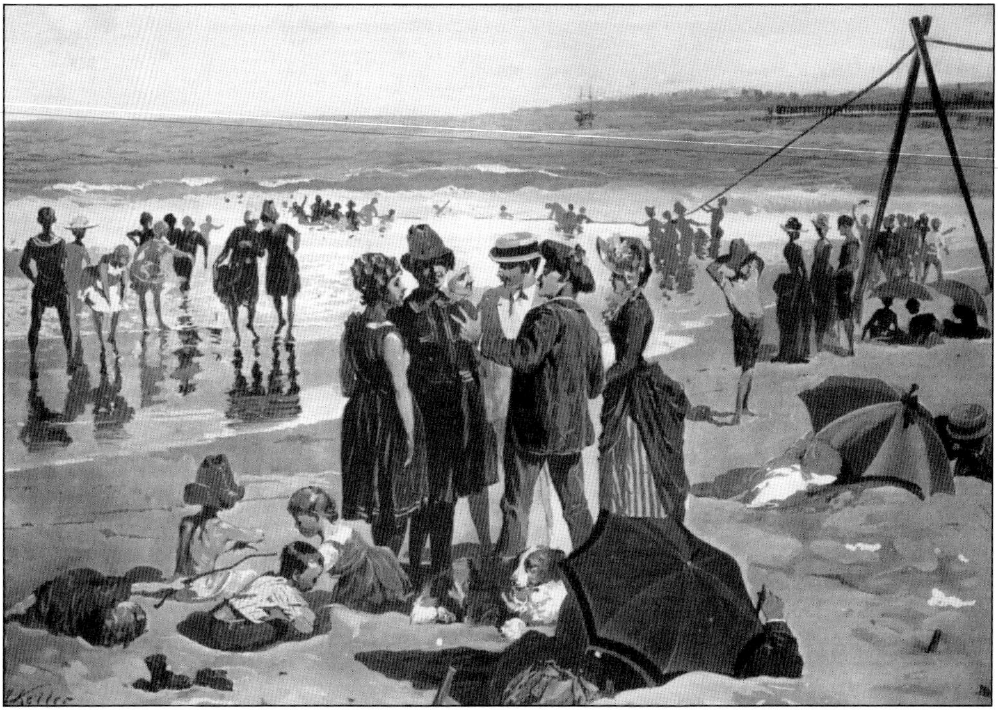

This rare, hand-colored lithograph was rendered by noted graphic artist Arthur Ignatius Keller (1867–1924) in the late 1880s. Keller's work often appeared in East Coast magazines and newspapers. Note the swim-line extending out into the water. Because of the heavy steamship traffic, swimmers on the Main Beach were forced to use the beach and break-line farther east toward the San Lorenzo River. (Author's collection.)

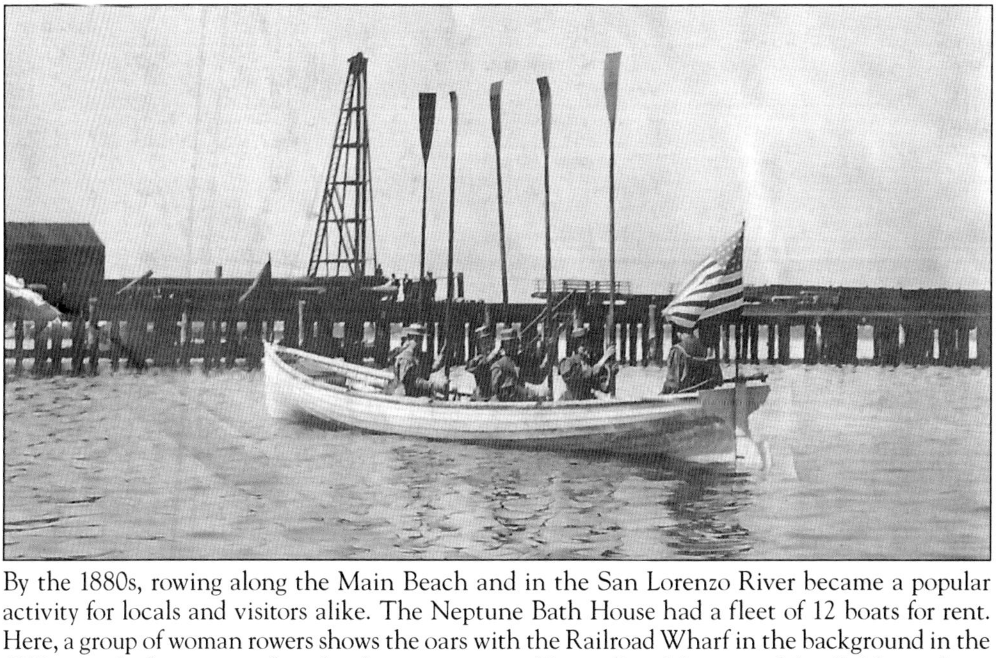

By the 1880s, rowing along the Main Beach and in the San Lorenzo River became a popular activity for locals and visitors alike. The Neptune Bath House had a fleet of 12 boats for rent. Here, a group of woman rowers shows the oars with the Railroad Wharf in the background in the 1890s. A pile driver is on the wharf issuing repairs. (Santa Cruz Museum of Art & History.)

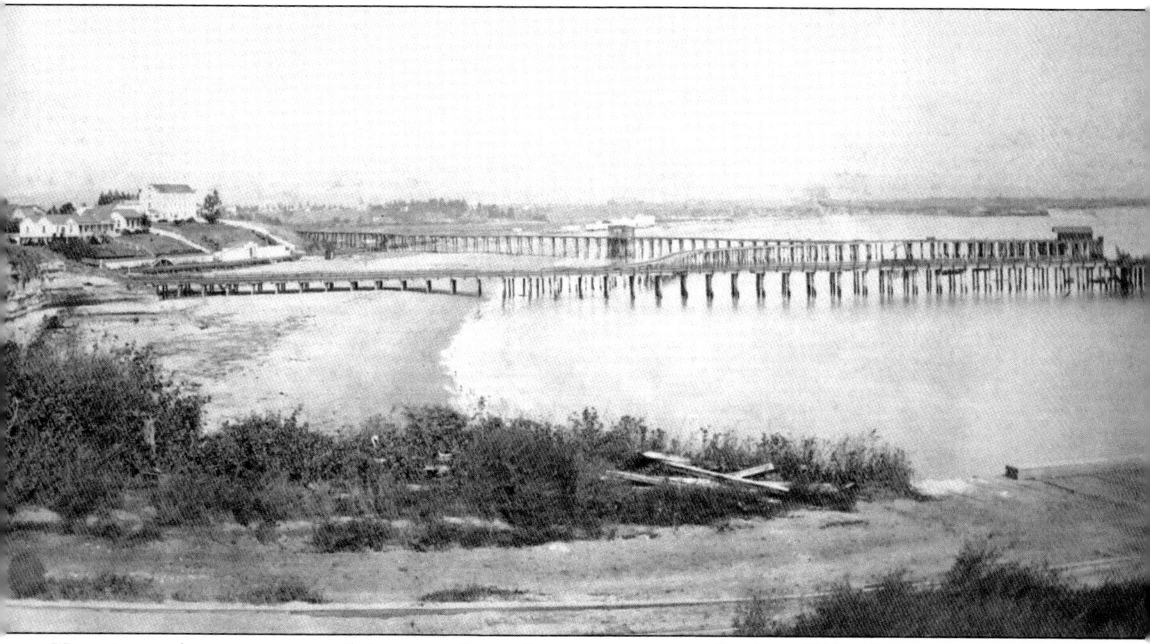

Here is another panorama of the waterfront showing more clearly the S Wharf connecting the Powder Works and Railroad Wharves. The ramp going down to the Cowell Wharf is at lower right. After it ceased being used in 1883, a portion of the Connecting Wharf was cut to water level and served as a swimming platform for visitors to the Main Beach. (Author's collection.)

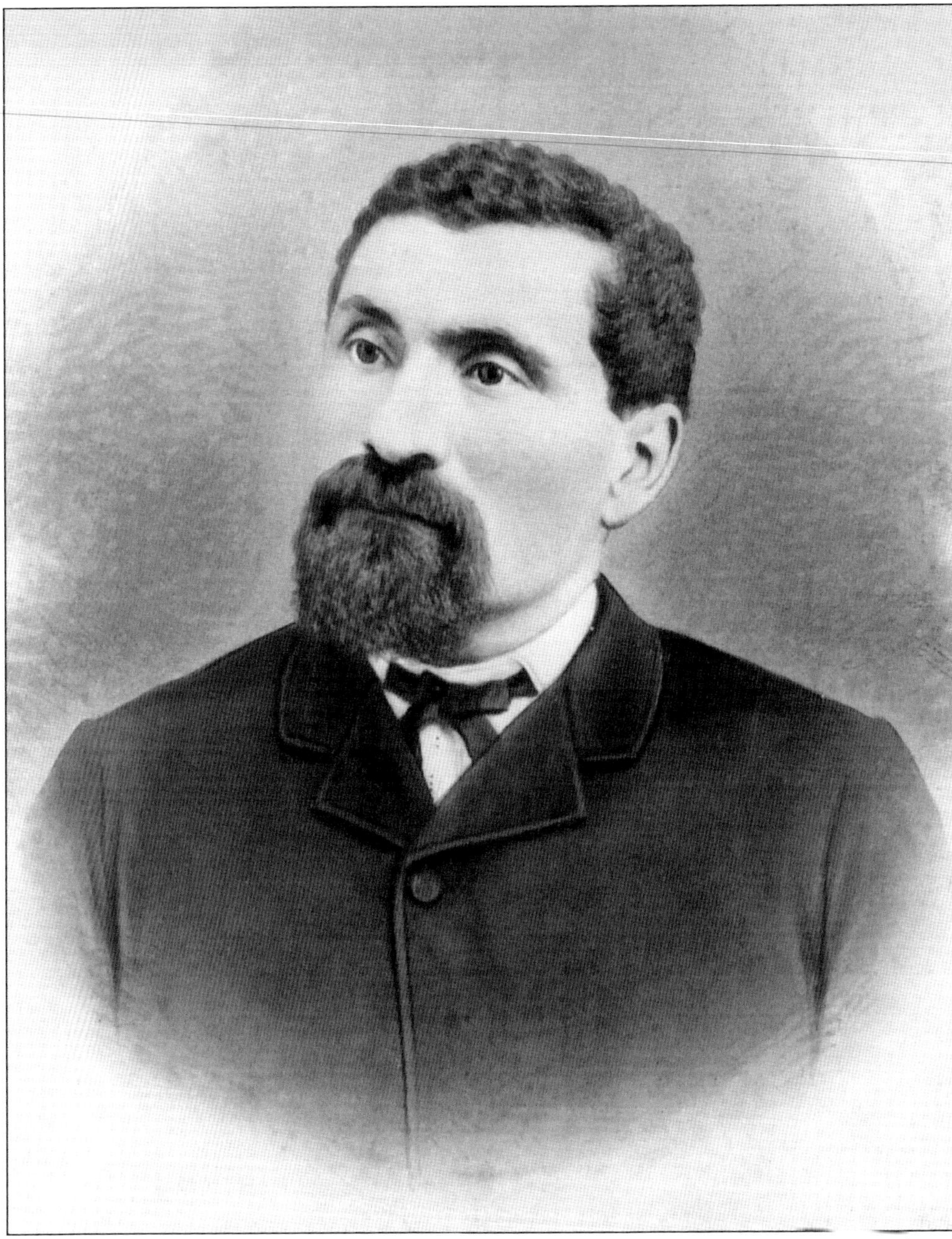

Fred Perez Sr. was one of the first successful large-scale commercial fishermen and fish merchants on the Santa Cruz waterfront. A descendant of several early Branciforte families—Soria, Amaya, and Perez—he was born in a family adobe under Mexican rule in 1847 and later fished primarily off the Cowell Wharf. He was killed in July 1906 when he was hit by a switch engine at the Southern Pacific Depot picking up fish boxes. His three sons—John, Abel, and Louis "Big Jim" Perez—continued the family fish business. (Santa Cruz Seaside Company.)

Two

The Santa Cruz Railroad Wharf

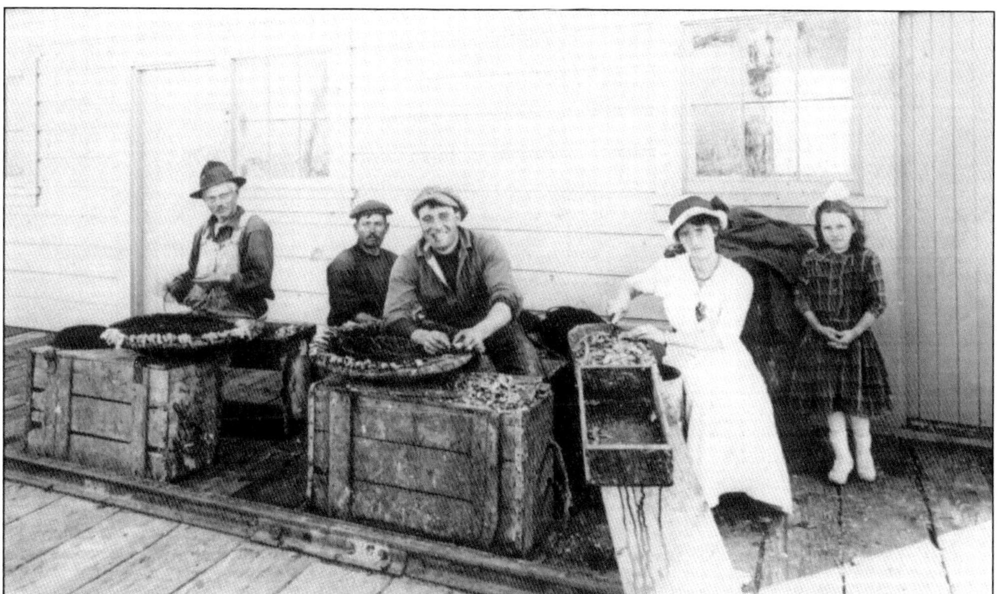

The emergence of railroad transportation in the western United States led to the completion of the Santa Cruz & Felton Railroad in 1875 near the present-day juncture of Front and Beach Streets, which included a rail line leading out to the end of the pier. In later years, it became the home of Santa Cruz's first large-scale commercial fishing industry and sportfishing fleet. Here, fishermen bait Portuguese long-line fishing baskets around 1913 on the Santa Cruz Railroad Wharf (note the iron rail at the base of the image). From left to right are Giovanni Bregante, Agustino Olivieri, Ernesto Canepa, Lina Righetti Canepa, and Margarita Canepa. (Author's collection.)

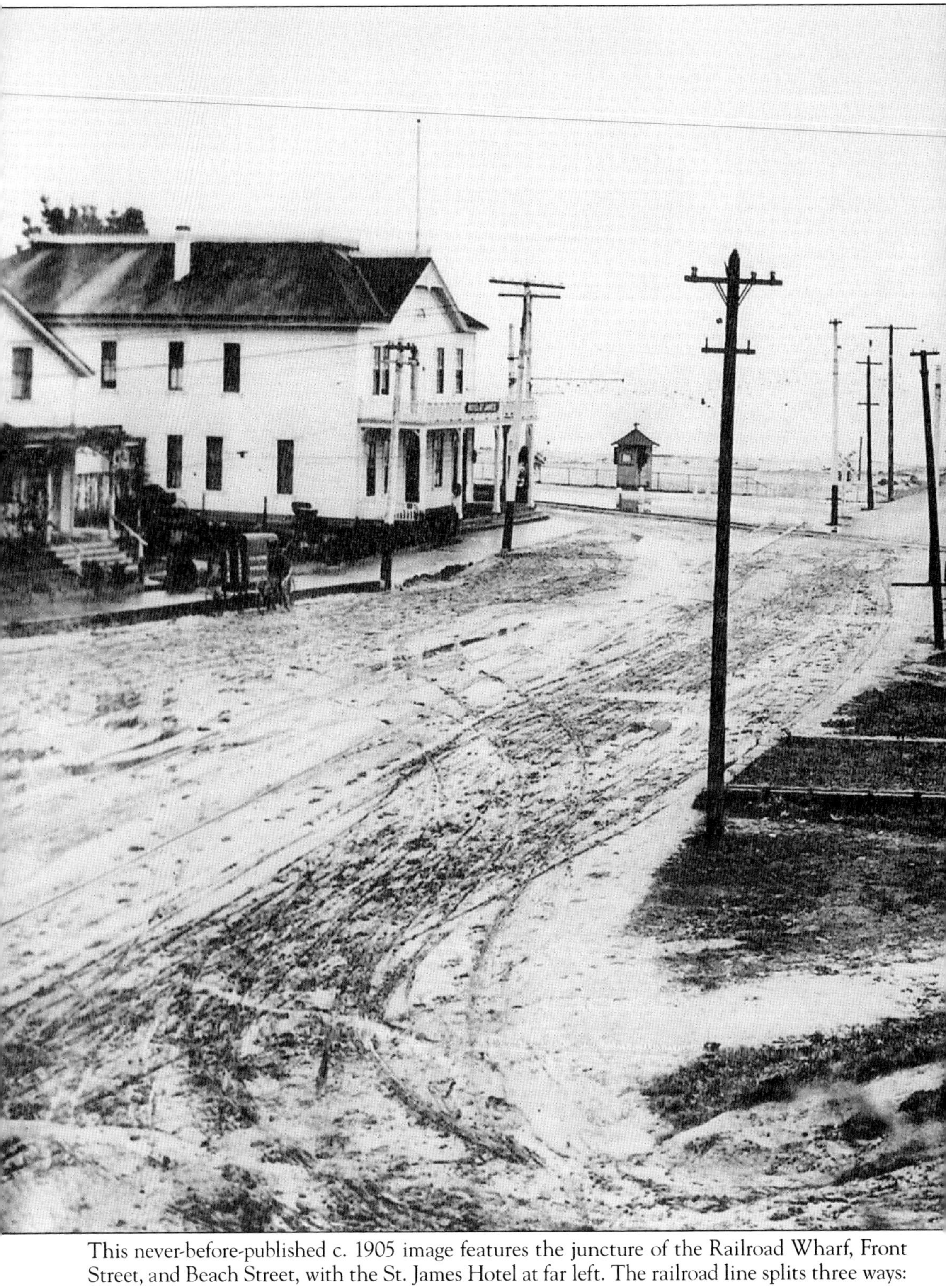

This never-before-published c. 1905 image features the juncture of the Railroad Wharf, Front Street, and Beach Street, with the St. James Hotel at far left. The railroad line splits three ways:

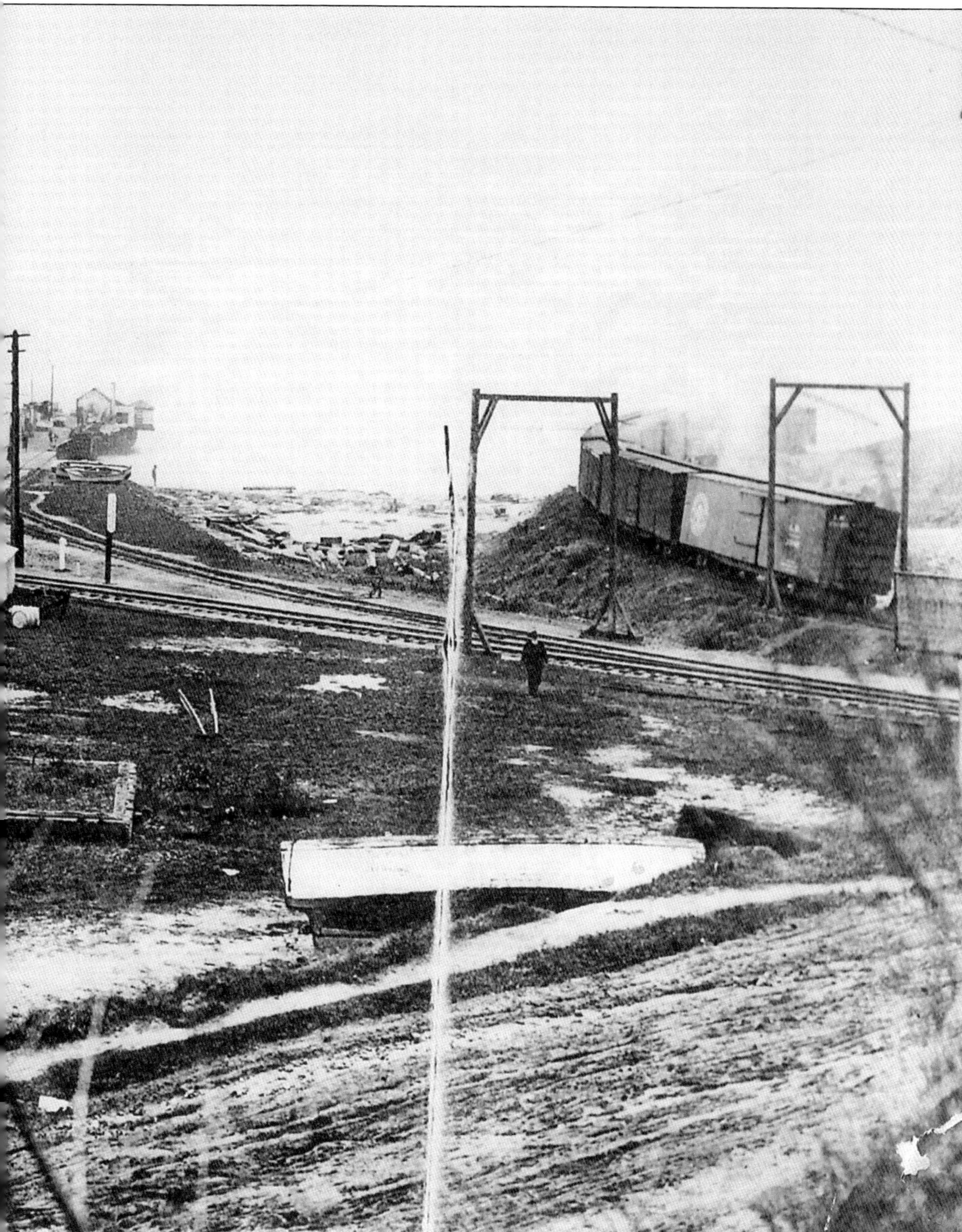

along Beach Street, out to the wharf, and a short spur west curling around the site of the present-day Dream Inn. (Author's collection.)

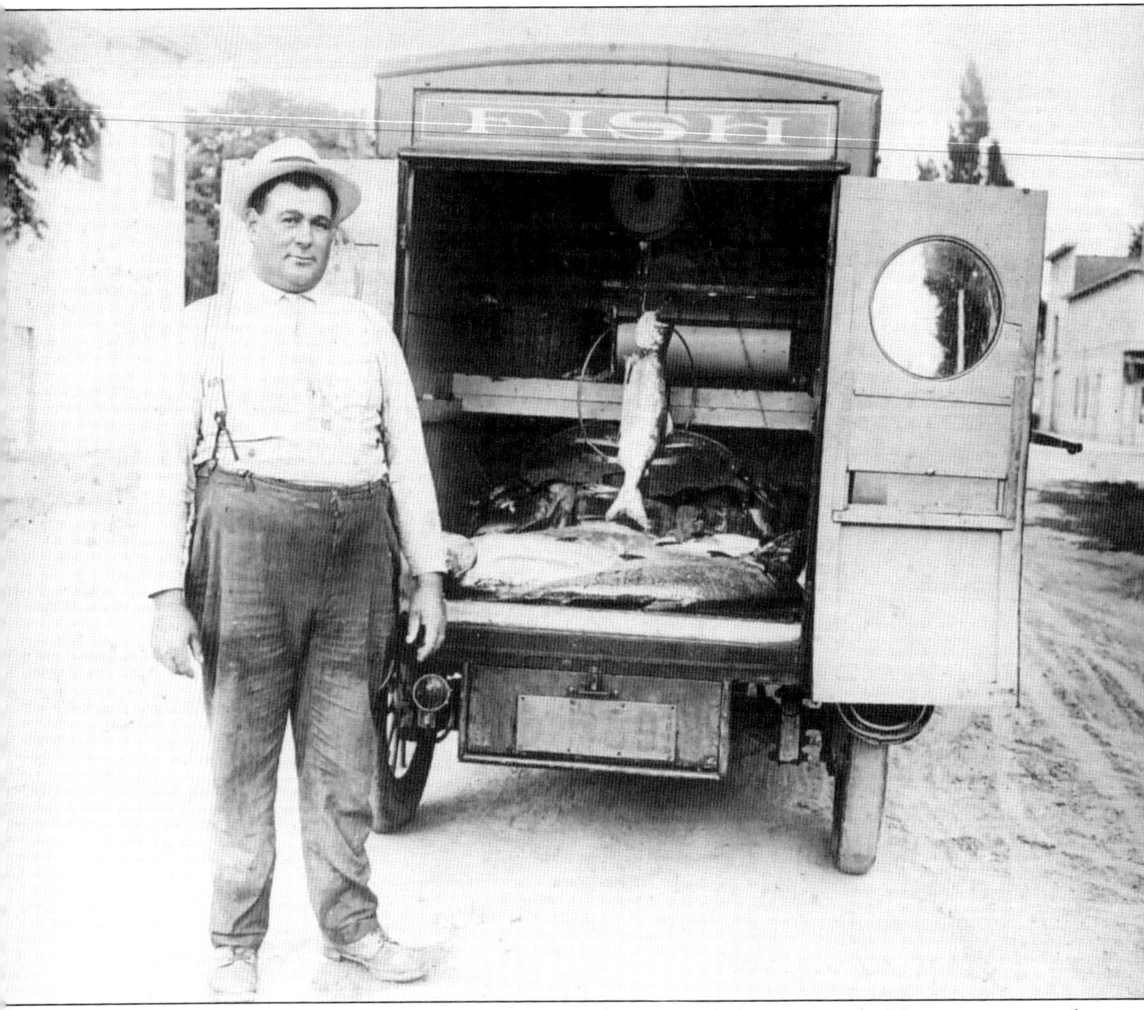

"Big Jim" Perez, son of Fred, is pictured around 1915 with his ice truck. He was a giant of a man—six feet five inches tall and 300 pounds. A small salmon is hanging from the scale. (Author's collection.)

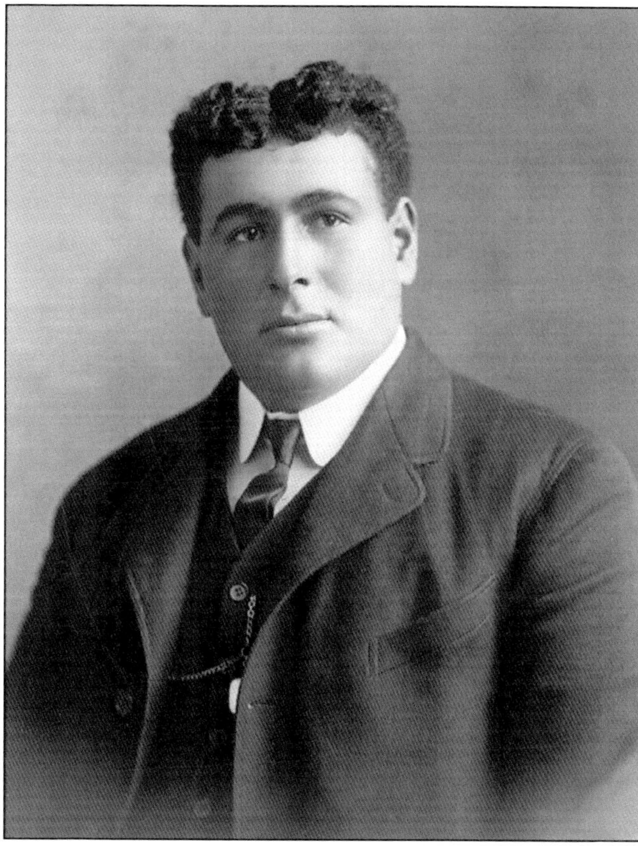

"Big Jim" Perez poses in his Sunday suit. All the Perez brothers were renown pugilists who, according to Malio Stagnaro, reached their degree of fistic proficiency "fighting amongst themselves." Big Jim reportedly once challenged heavyweight champion Jack Johnson to a bout and was a close friend of former heavyweight champion Jim Jeffries. In spite of his size, Big Jim was also an accomplished handball player. (Santa Cruz Seaside Company.)

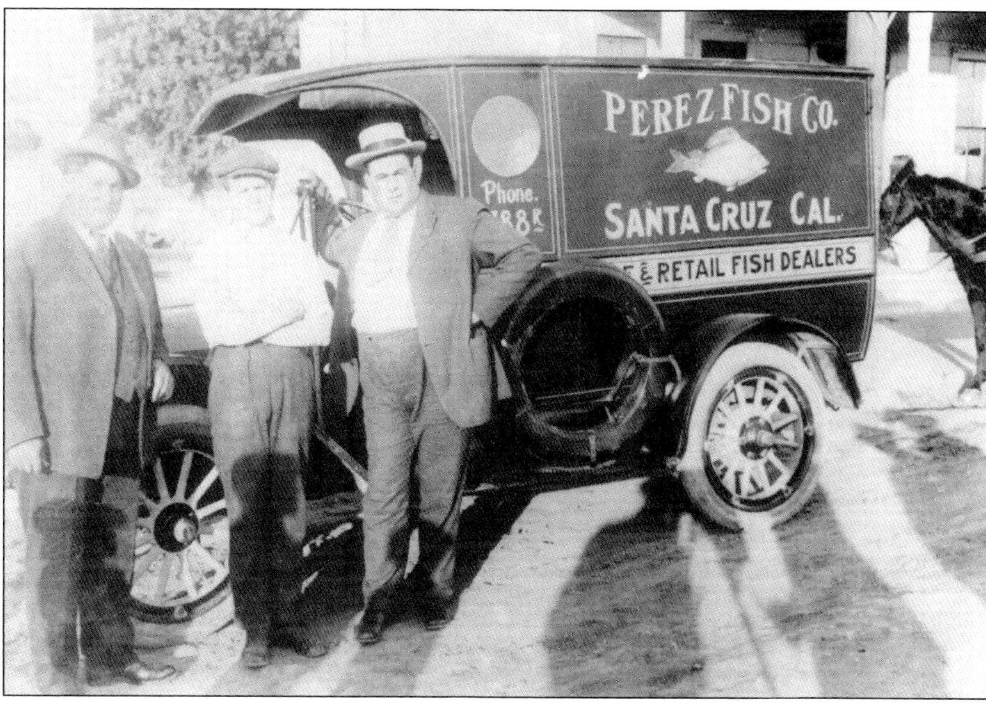

Abbie Perez (left), Louis Beverino (center), and Jim Perez are pictured 1918. Their fish wagon was considered the state-of-the-art delivery vehicle for its day. Note the horse attached to a carriage immediately behind them. (Santa Cruz Seaside Company.)

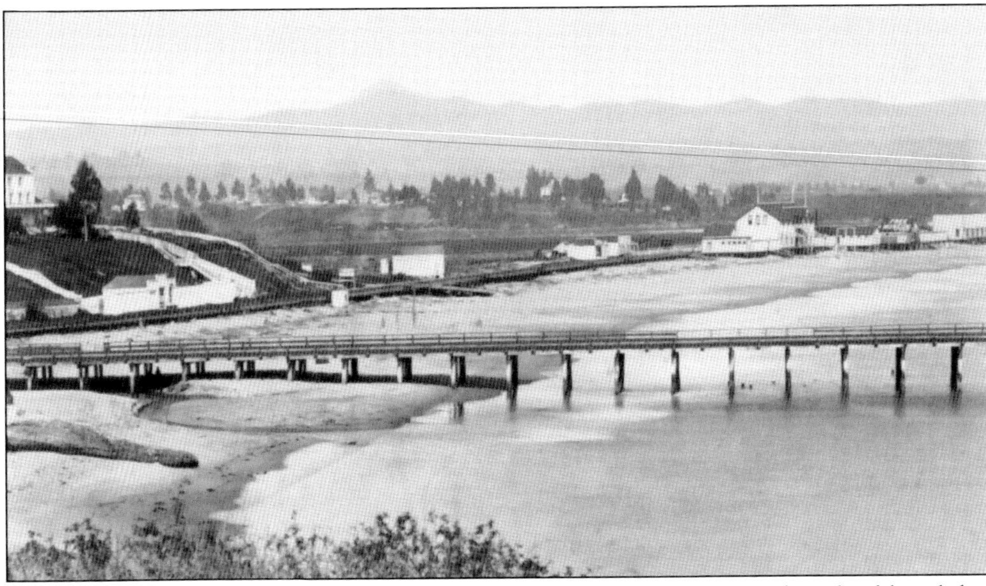

The refurbished Railroad Wharf is pictured around 1900 with the Powder Works Wharf demolished and before the building of the first casino. The Neptune Bath House and Free Museum are located on the beach. The middle-distant ridge is the eastern bank of the San Lorenzo River, and the first mansions are visible on Ocean View Avenue. (Author's collection.)

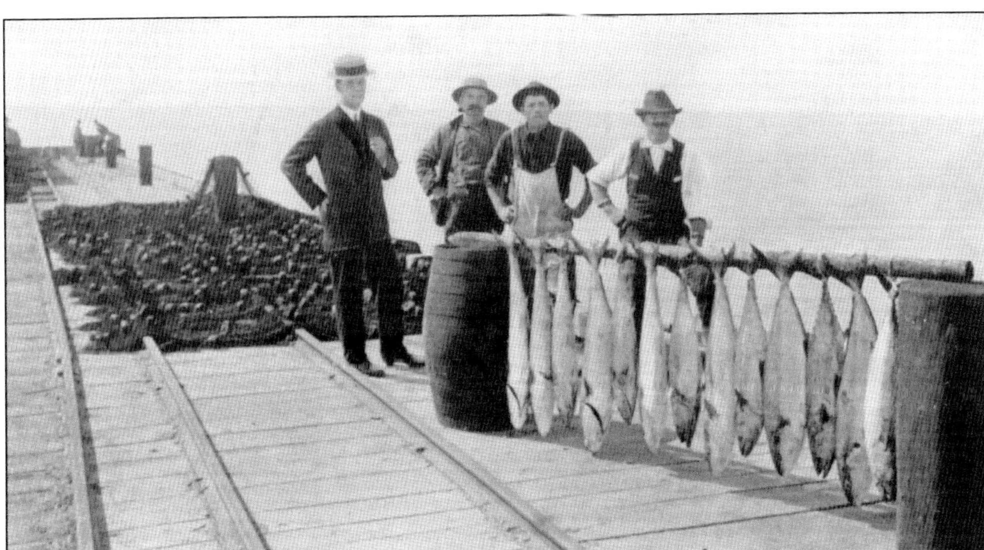

Albacore are hanging on the Railroad Wharf around 1904 with the author's grandfather Cottardo Stagnaro II second from right, dressed in overalls. Paranzella nets are stretched out over railroad tracks to dry. This particular image was turned into a popular postcard. (Author's collection.)

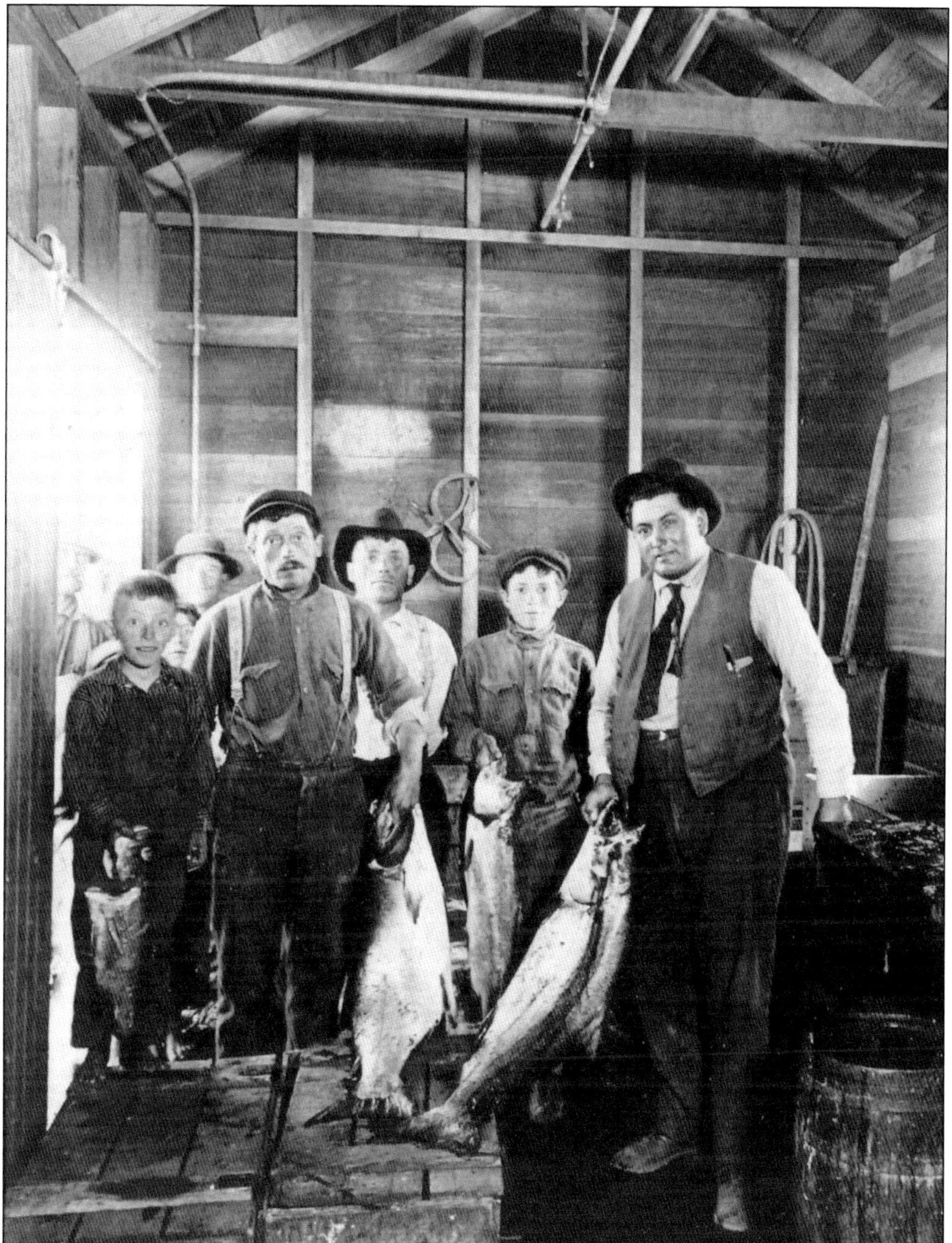

This is a rare interior photograph of a wharf fish market, the Perez Fish Company, in 1914. In foreground are, from left to right, seven-year-old Cottardo "Babe" Stagnaro, Cottardo Stagnaro II, Joe Loero, Malio Stagnaro, and one of the Perez brothers. In background, at left, is Domenico Castagnola. The fish boxes read C. Stagnaro & D. Castagnola Fish Company. An article in the *Santa Cruz Sentinel* notes that the pair had bought new fishing launches in October 1914. The men were partners in the years leading up to World War I. (Santa Cruz Seaside Company, Malio Stagnaro Collection.)

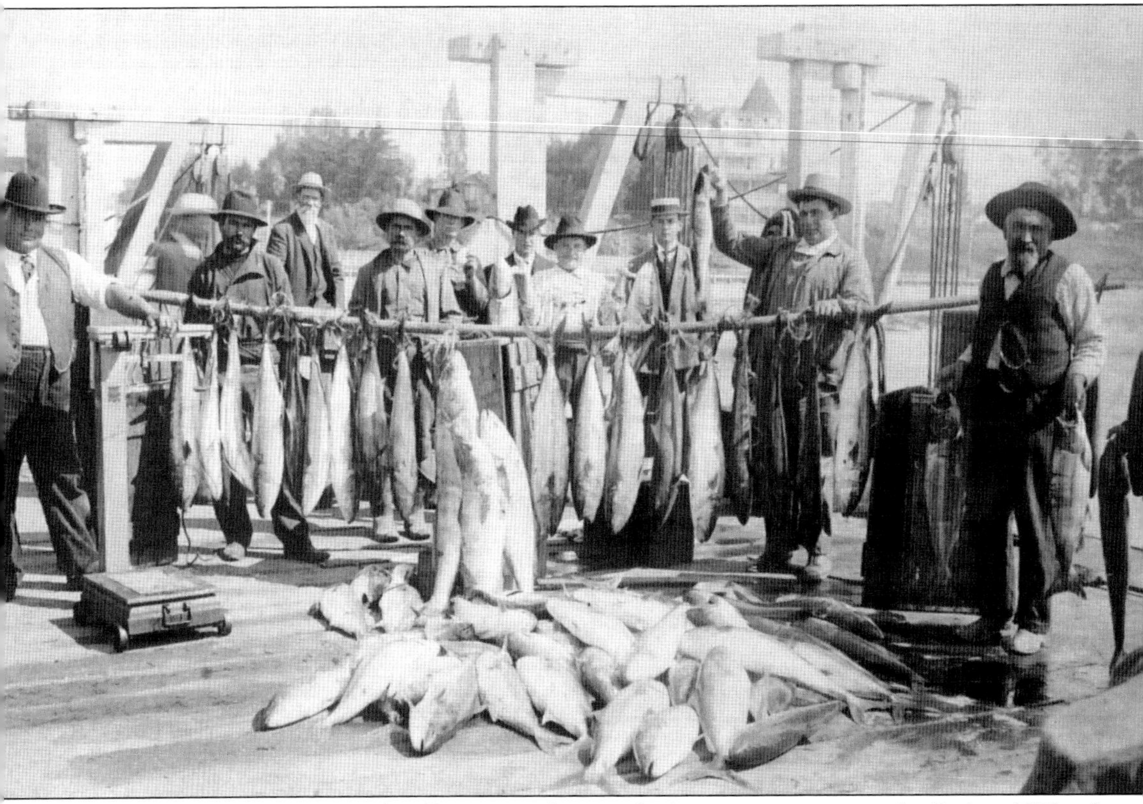

A catch of what appears to be albacore, sea bass, and salmon is strung across the Railroad Wharf around 1905 with John (far left) and Abbie Perez (third from right) flanking the author's great-grandfather Giovanni Batista Loero (second from left), and to the right is Fred Perez, shortly before his death. Albacore are not common to Monterey Bay but arrive sporadically during El Niño conditions, when a band of warm ocean water develops in the central and east-central equatorial Pacific and moves northward, occasionally to the Monterey Bay and beyond. (Santa Cruz Seaside Company.)

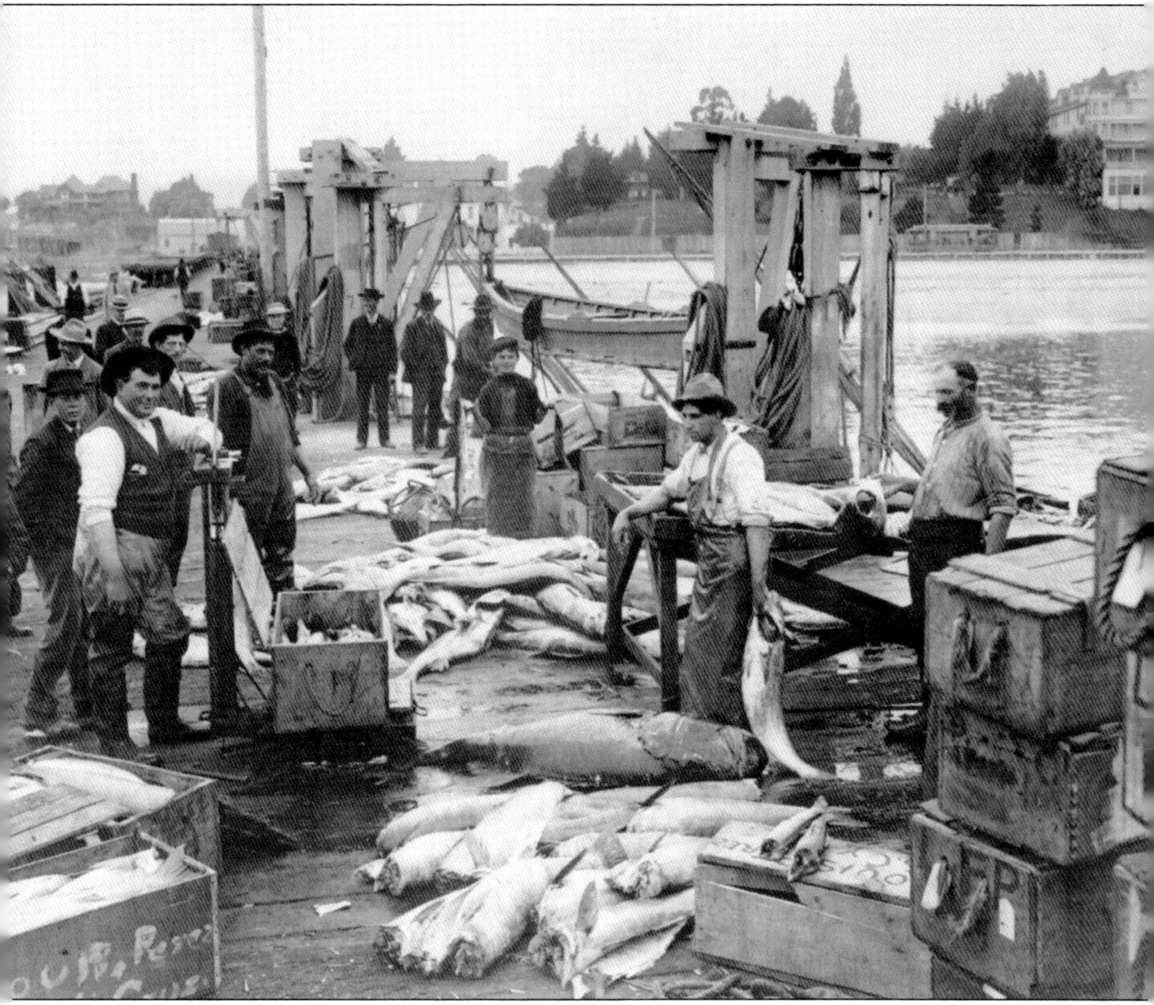

This classic c. 1908 photograph is of a large catch of fish sold to Louis "Big Jim" Perez (left, with his arm on a scale) after his father's death. Sea Beach Hotel is in the background. A giant sea bass (*Stereolepis gigas*) is lying on planks in the middle of the image. Again, this is likely an El Niño catch, as the giant sea bass was more common to Southern California (although identified as far north as Humboldt Bay). During the late 19th and early 20th centuries, they were commonly caught by commercial fishermen and sport anglers alike, with some fish weighing as much as 560 pounds. Presently threatened with extinction, they are now a protected species. (Author's collection.)

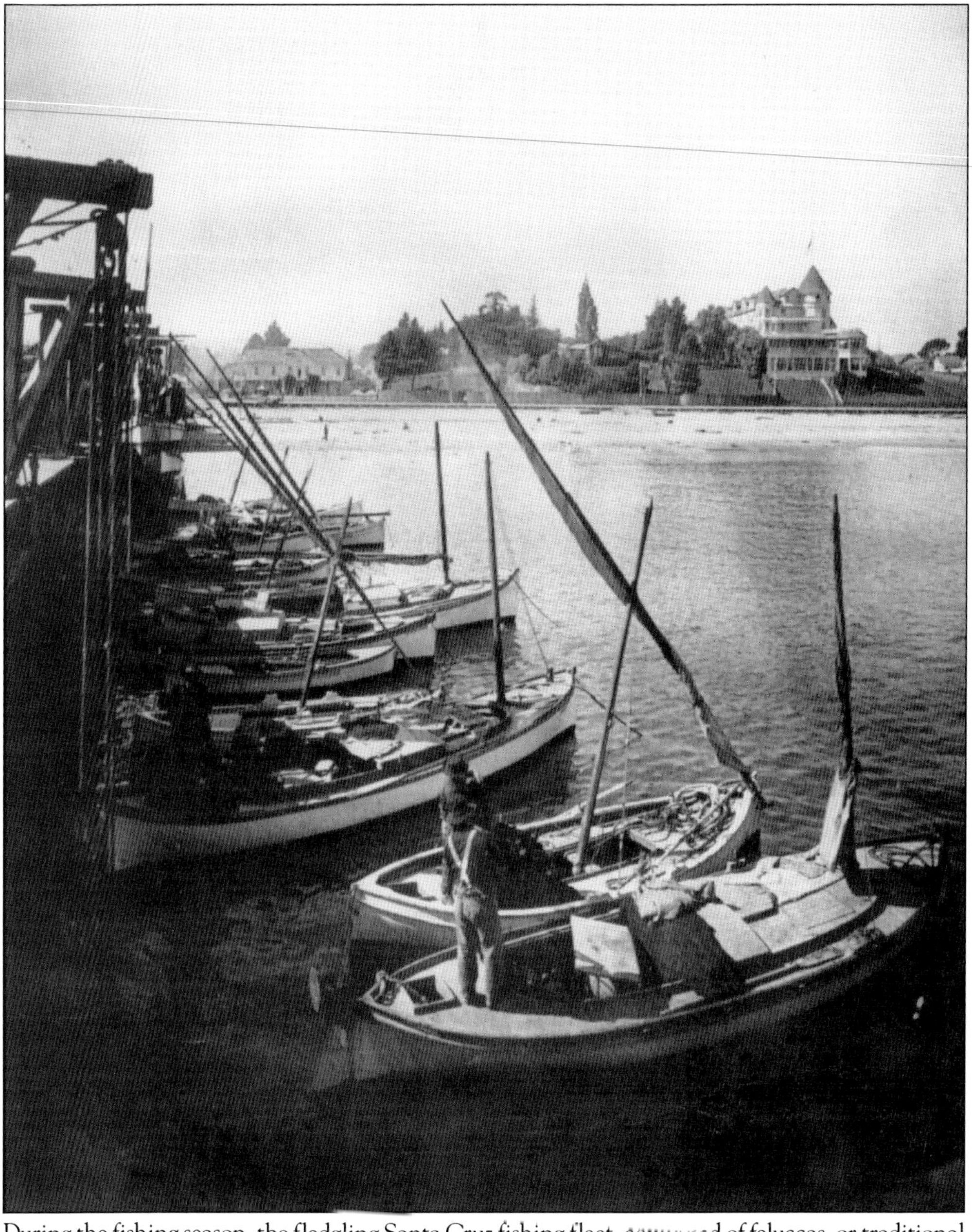

During the fishing season, the fledgling Santa Cruz fishing fleet, composed of feluccas, or traditional lateen sailboats (without engines), were tied to the east side of the Santa Cruz Railroad Wharf, where the south-flowing Pacific current pushed their sterns away from the piles. Feluccas were common in California seaports during the late 19th and early 20th centuries. Using triangular sails on a titled mast, they allowed fishermen to tack against the wind—a necessity in coastal waters. (Author's collection.)

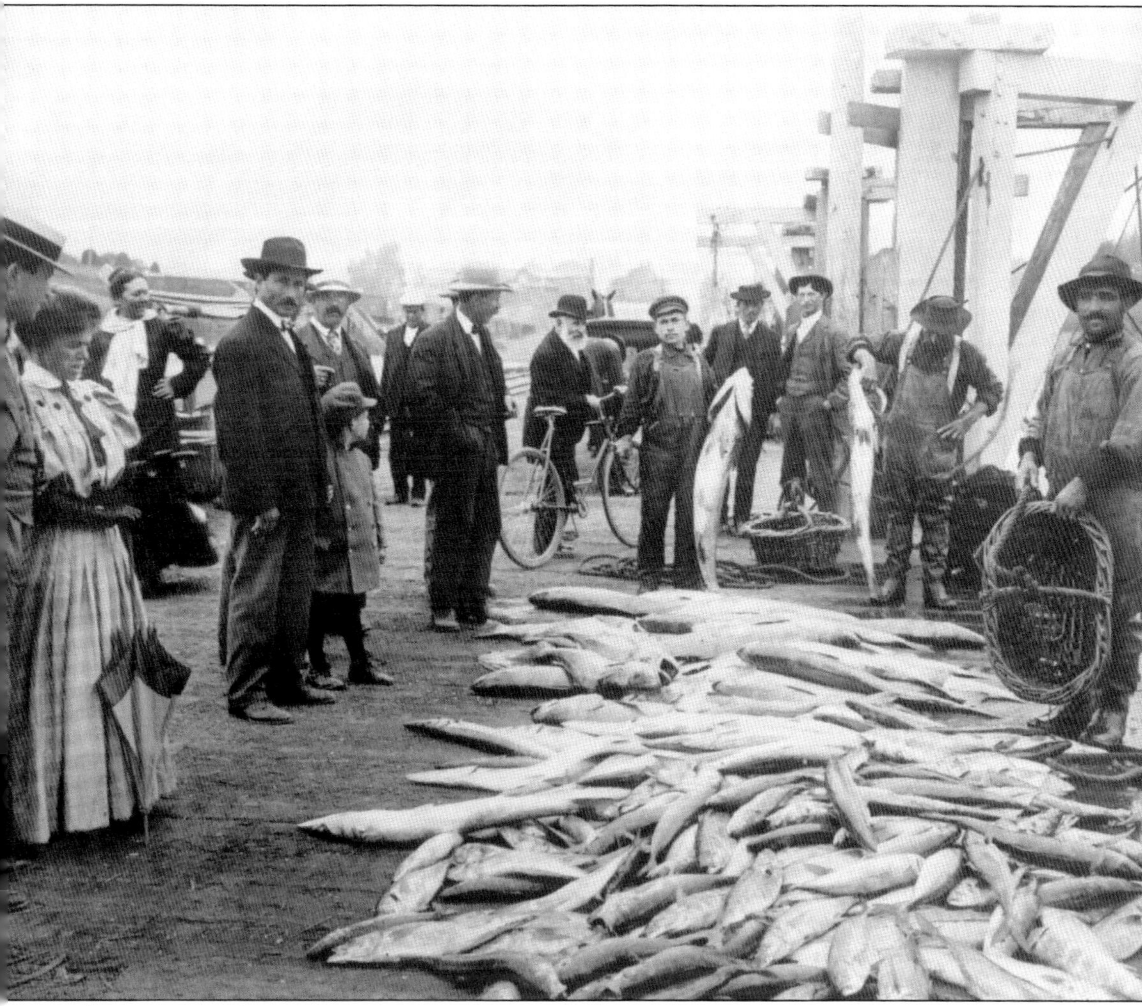

Stefano "Steve" Ghio (center with overalls and cap), patriarch of the Ghio fishing family, holds a large sea bass as part of the same catch pictured on page 29, closer to the entrance of the wharf. A large catch of barracuda is at his feet. A horse-drawn buggy is located directly behind Ghio. A native of Riva Trigoso, Liguria, Italy, he originally fished in San Francisco Bay before joining family here following the 1906 earthquake. (Author's collection.)

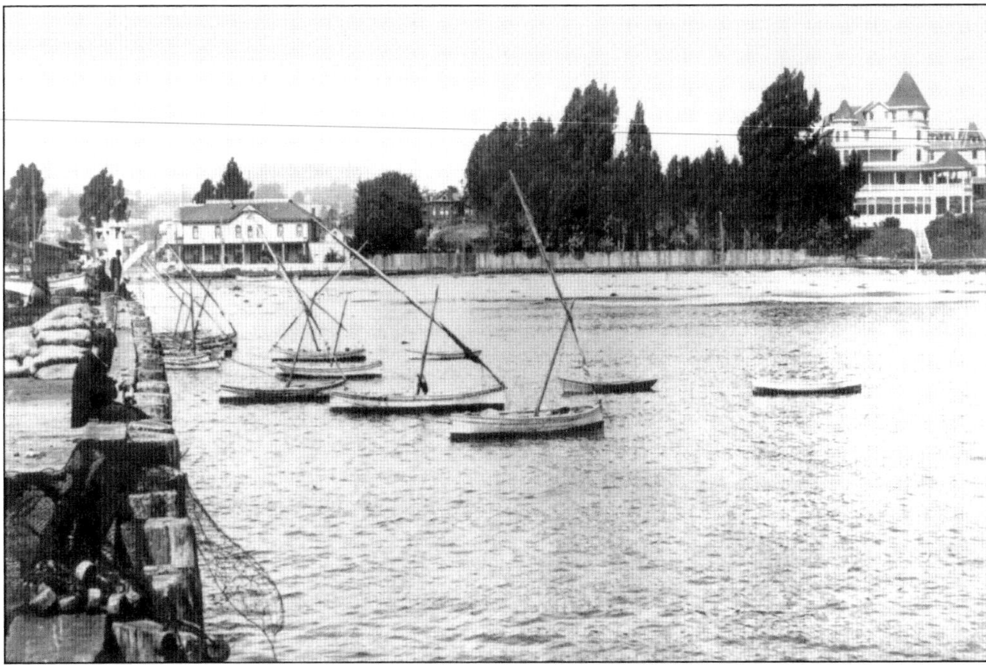

On a quiet day on the Railroad Wharf, feluccas are anchored in shallow water just off the Main Beach. The famed Sea Beach Hotel is located at top right. The hotel was considered one of the finest on the Pacific Coast and served as the queen of the Santa Cruz waterfront. Although ultimately assembled with a unifying Queen Anne architecture, it was a bit of a hodgepodge in terms of construction. Various buildings were brought together to form it. Some of it was constructed from the remnants of the warehouse at the base of the Powder Works Wharf. Two days before it was to open for the summer of 1912, the hotel burned to the ground. (Author's collection.)

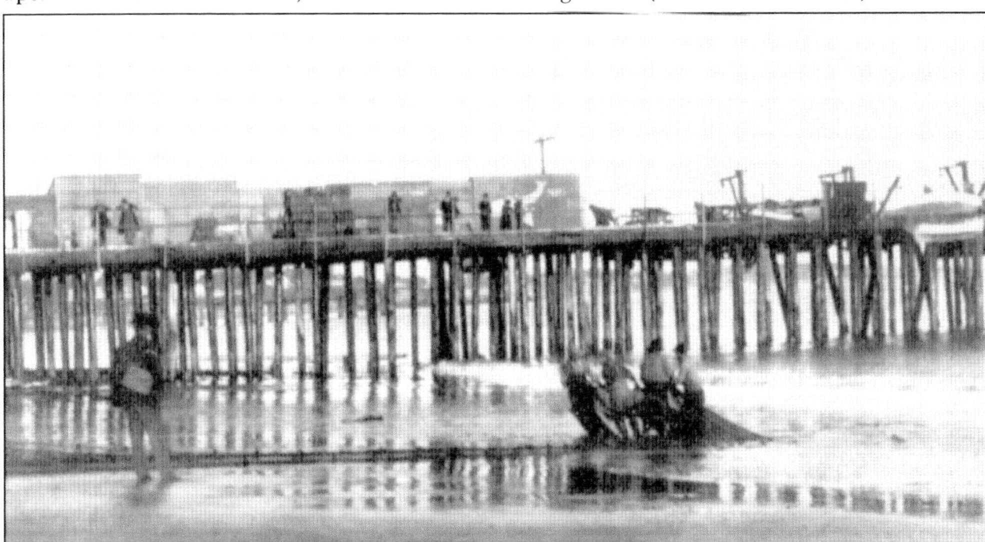

Here is a rare c. 1910 image of Italian fishermen hauling in a beach seine net at Cowell Beach with the Railroad Wharf in background. Seine nets are placed vertically in the water with cork floats on top and weights on the bottom, then circled by a small boat around schools of fish and pulled into shore. The Pleasure Pier can be seen through the piling. (Author's collection.)

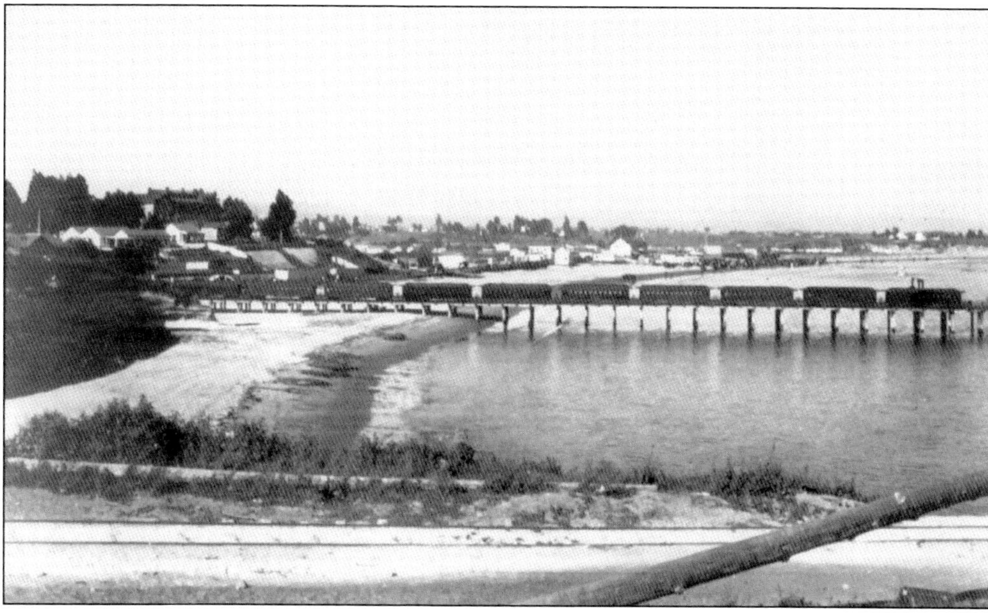

This very rare image shows the Railroad Wharf with approximately a dozen boxcars stretching its full length. The cable in the right foreground is from the entrance to the Cowell Wharf. (Harry Mayo collection.)

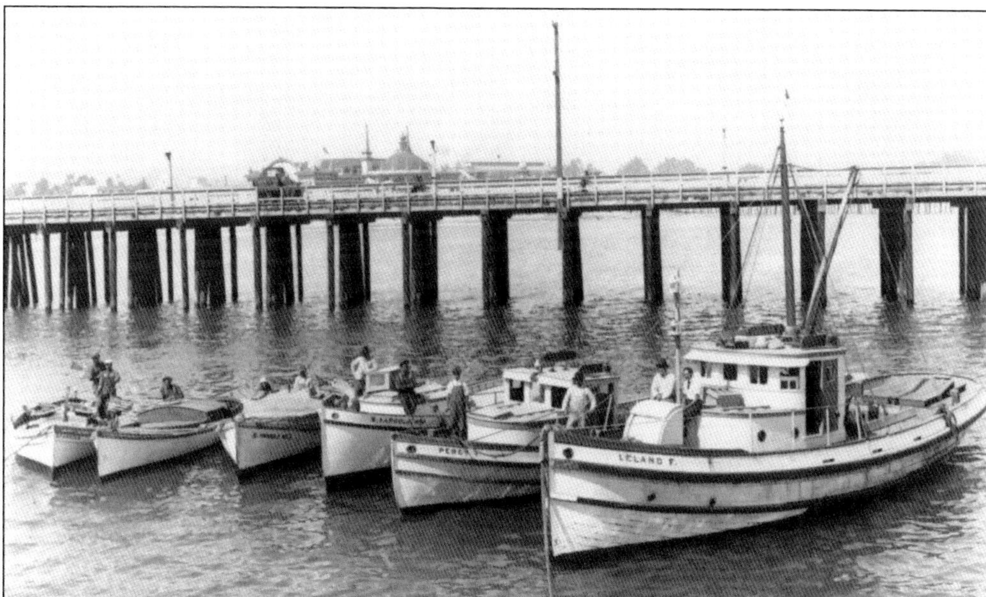

In 1902, John and Sunday Faraola, whose father immigrated to California in the 1860s, established a commercial fishing company on the old Railroad Wharf. The Faraolas were cousins of the Perez family. Their fleet grew to six launches and used paranzella nets in north-coast fishing grounds, with two boats required to pull both ends of the net. Primary catches of the paranzellas (or drag nets) were bottom fish, including sole, flounder, and sand dabs. (Santa Cruz Seaside Company, Lee Faraola Collection.)

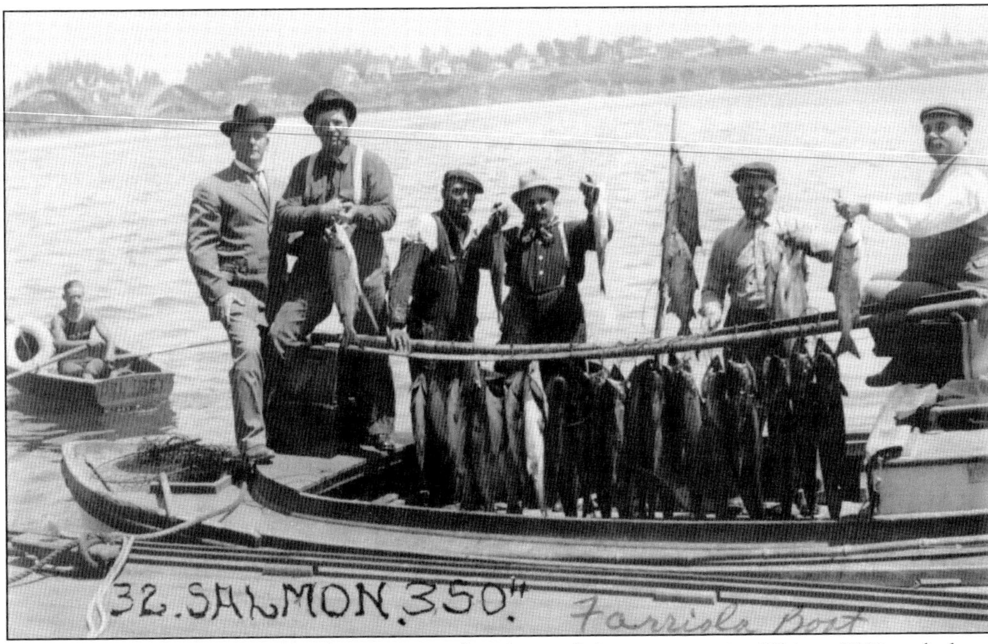

The Faraola fleet facilitated both commercial and sportfishing categories. This c. 1910 real-photo postcard of the Santa Cruz waterfront depicts visitors from Bakersfield, Oakland, and Los Angeles aboard a Faraola launch skippered by Lorenzo Zolezzi (third from left), with 32 silver salmon weighing in at 350 pounds. The little dinghy is called the *Del Rey*. The fishermen are identified on the back of the card as "Dr. [August Francis] Schafer, Judge Creeley, C.C. Bain, H.S. Bain, and Dr. [Frederick J.] Crease." (Author's collection.)

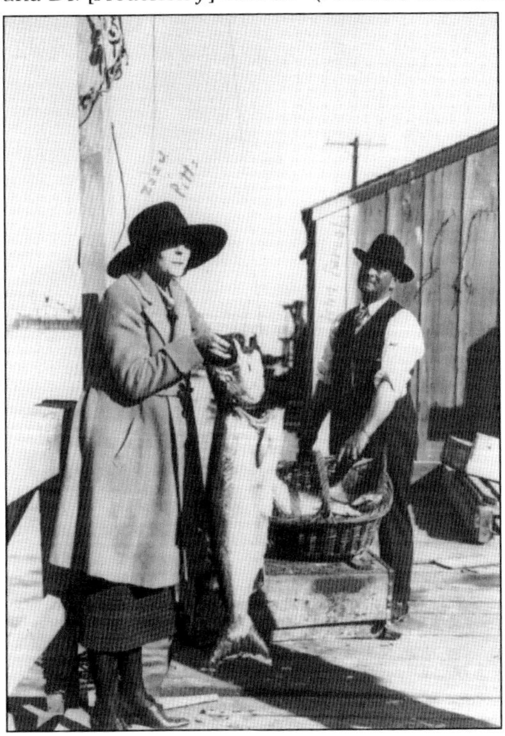

Actress Zasu Pitts (left) holds a salmon with John Faraola around 1920 on the Railroad Wharf. A star of early silent films and, later, talkies, Pitts was a talented comedienne raised in Santa Cruz who graduated from Santa Cruz High School in 1914. By 1917, she was starring with Mary Pickford in *The Little Princess*. In 1961, Pitts returned to the local stage at the Wharf Theatre and Opera House in Monterey, starring in the play *The Curious Savage*. (Santa Cruz Seaside Company, Lee Faraola Collection.)

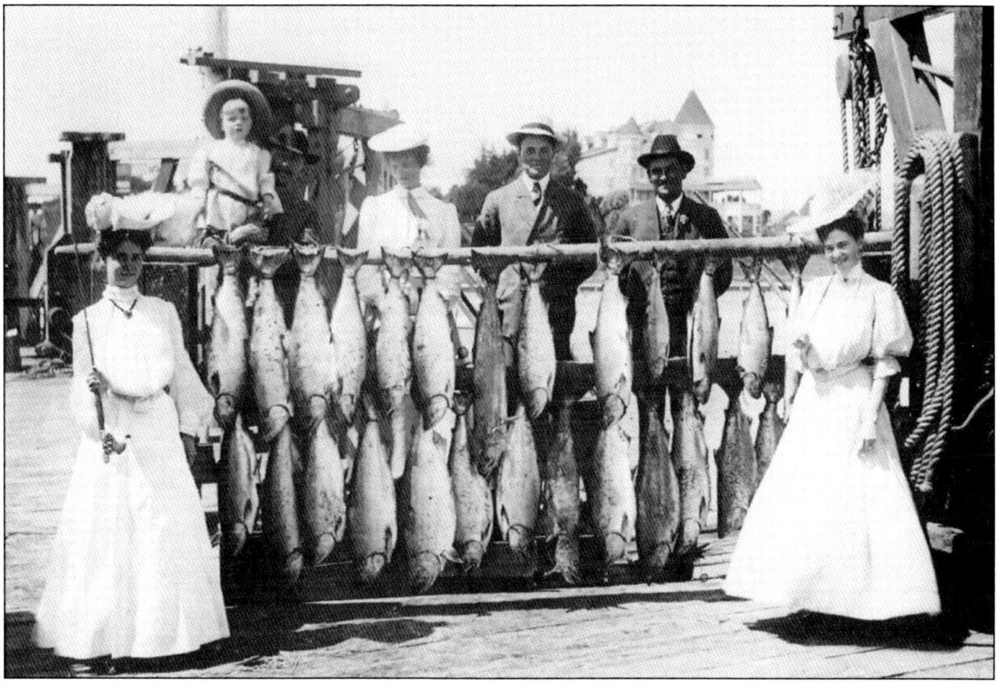

A large salmon catch and one barracuda (top right) were caught by the Faraola fleet in the summer of 1905. John Faraola is in back at right wearing a dark hat. Unidentified family pose with the fish. Visitors to the wharf often had their pictures taken with catches and took the images back to their hometowns as souvenirs. (Santa Cruz Seaside Company, Malio Stagnaro Collection.)

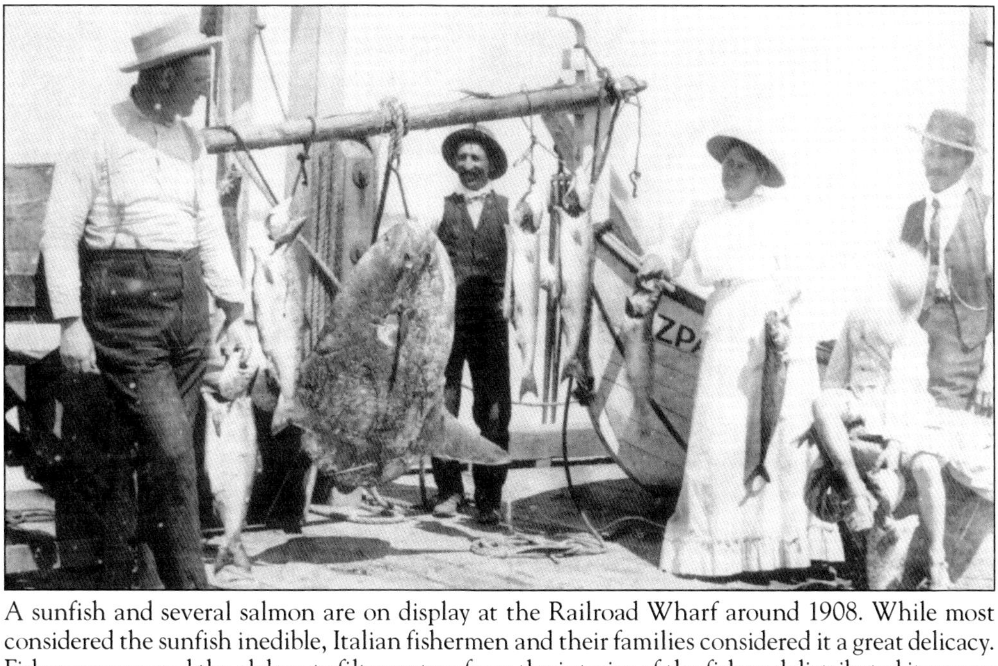

A sunfish and several salmon are on display at the Railroad Wharf around 1908. While most considered the sunfish inedible, Italian fishermen and their families considered it a great delicacy. Fishermen scraped the elaborate filter system from the interior of the fish and distributed it among family and friends, cooking it similar to lobster, with white wine sauces spiced with garlic and parsley. (Santa Cruz Museum of Art & History.)

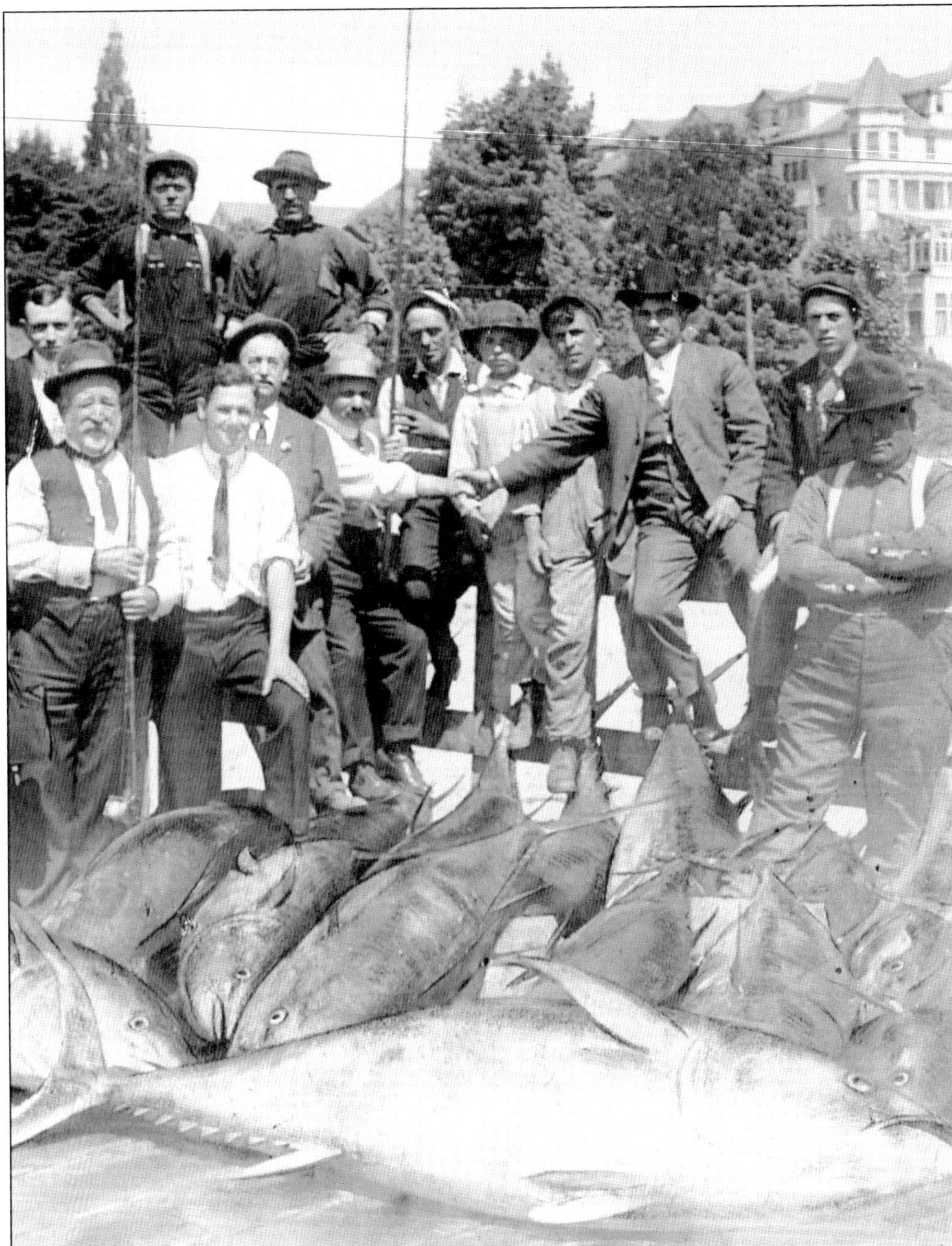

The following sequence of photographs details a record tuna catch in September 1911—and also reveals a great deal about the reliability of photography, oral history, and journalism as historical documents. This image (published for the first time) features 11 bluefin tuna caught off the coast of Capitola by the author's great-grandfather Cottardo Stagnaro I (top right) and great-uncle Joe Loero (top left). An account in the *San Francisco Chronicle* headlines "Tremendous Catch of Tuna Is Made at Santa Cruz" and notes that "over two tons of tuna was stacked on the wharf today. . . . The oldest inhabitants say the catch establishes a record, as these fish are rare here." (Author's collection.)

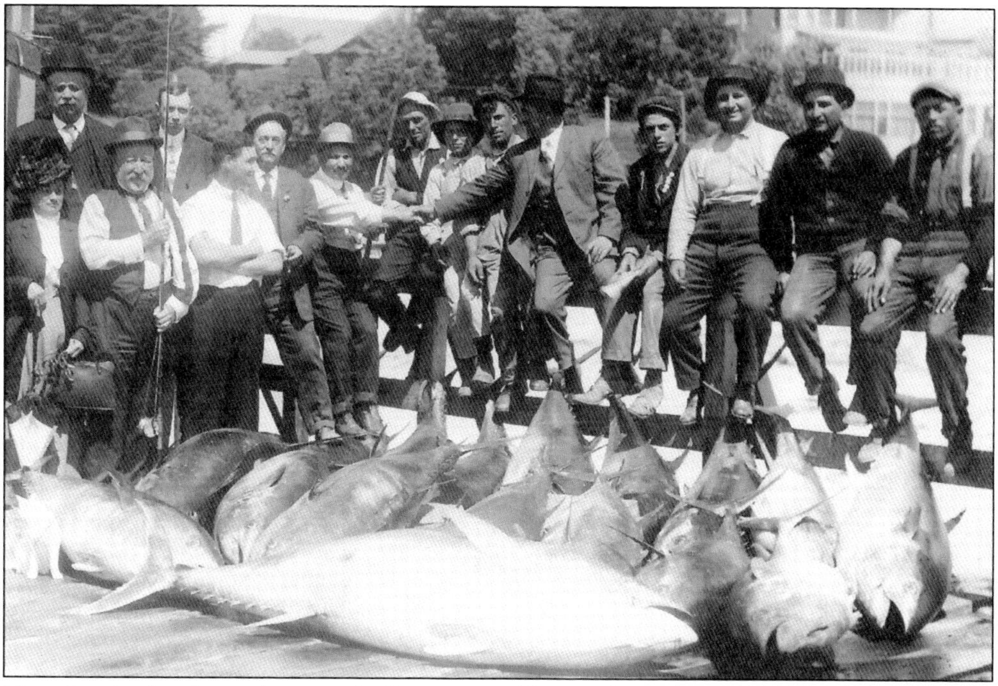

Note that in the above photograph, Stagnaro and Loero, the two men who caught the fish, are gone from the scene. At that time, they were fishing for the Faraola brothers. In the above image, John Faraola (shaking hands, with three-piece suit and hat) and Sunday Faraola (second from left) remain posing with the fish. In the *Santa Cruz Evening News* account of the catch, Stagnaro and Loero are not named, though the people who owned the fishing boats are, including John Faraola. The *San Francisco Chronicle* specifically states that "C. Stagnaro caught eleven fish"—precisely the number in the photograph. In the below version of the famous fish photograph (published in the *San Francisco Call*), John and Sunday Faraola are pictured as though they caught the fish. But even though he only appears in one of the photographs and his name is not mentioned in any of the news articles at the time, the credit for catching the tuna eventually transferred to Loero—and then some. In his obituary, written by Skip Littlefield in 1956, it is proclaimed that Loero "holds the distinction of catching the largest single haul of tuna ever docked by a launch in local waters. The catch contained 27 fish, with the largest hitting the scales at 700 pounds. Receiving $400 for the load, Joe was in the chips." (Both, author's collection.)

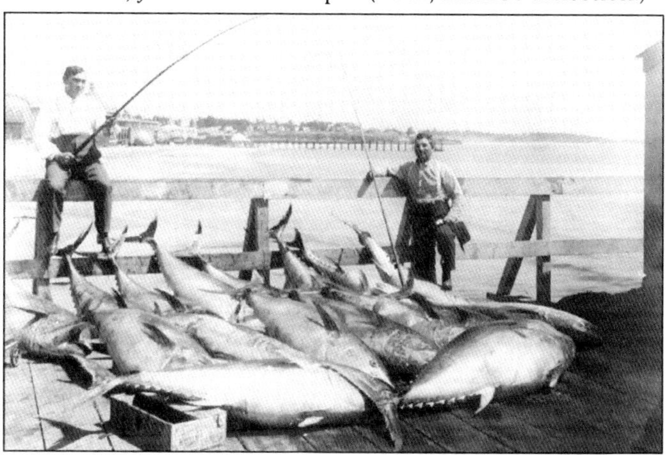

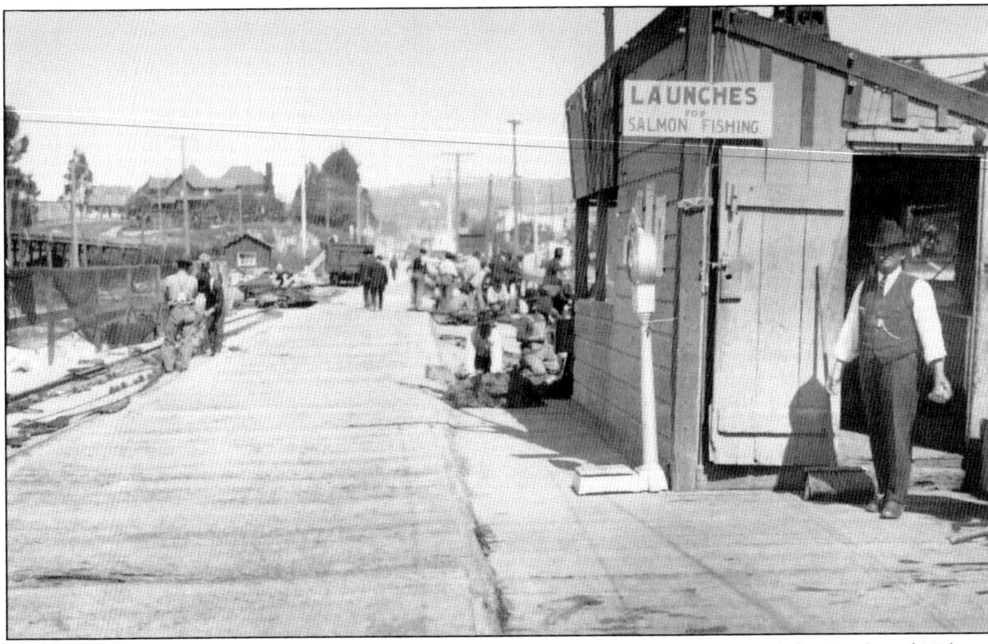

John Faraola is seen leaving his fish shack operations near the beginning of the Railroad Wharf. Fishermen on both sides of the tracks can be seen mending their nets—a daily activity that defined the Santa Cruz waterfront for decades. Overlooking the wharf, the Faraola home can be seen in the background. (Author's collection.)

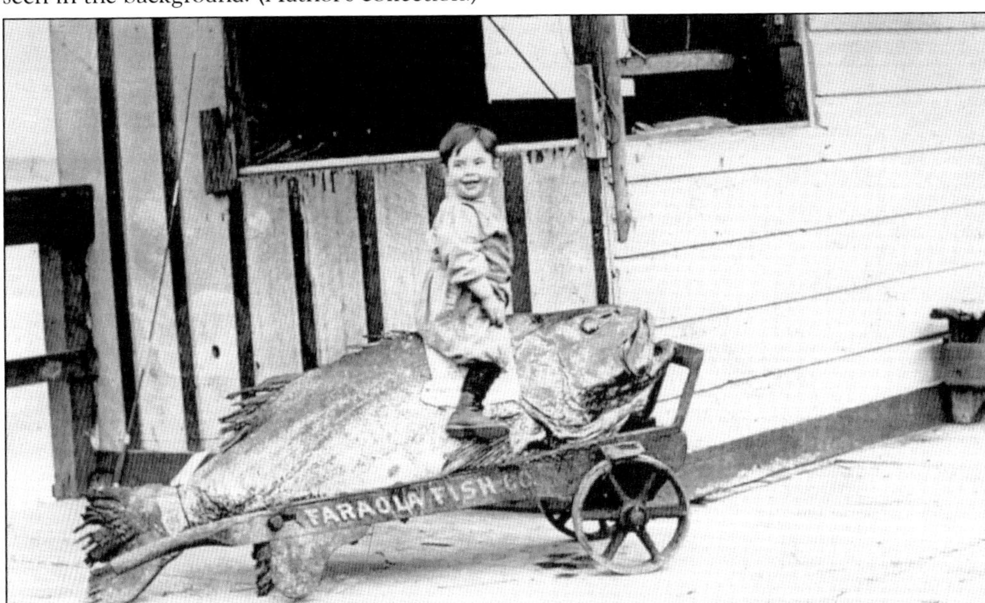

A smiling Jim Moody sits on a giant sea bass resting atop a Faraola hand truck in front of the John Faraola fish shack. Moody was visiting the pier that day with his sister Ella and father, E.V. Moody, who originally came to Santa Cruz as a bondsman for the Southern Pacific Railroad on behalf of two railroad men charged with the shooting of waterfront Greek restaurateur William Tsouvas. Shortly thereafter, Moody purchased the St. James Hotel at the base of the Railroad Wharf. (Moody family.)

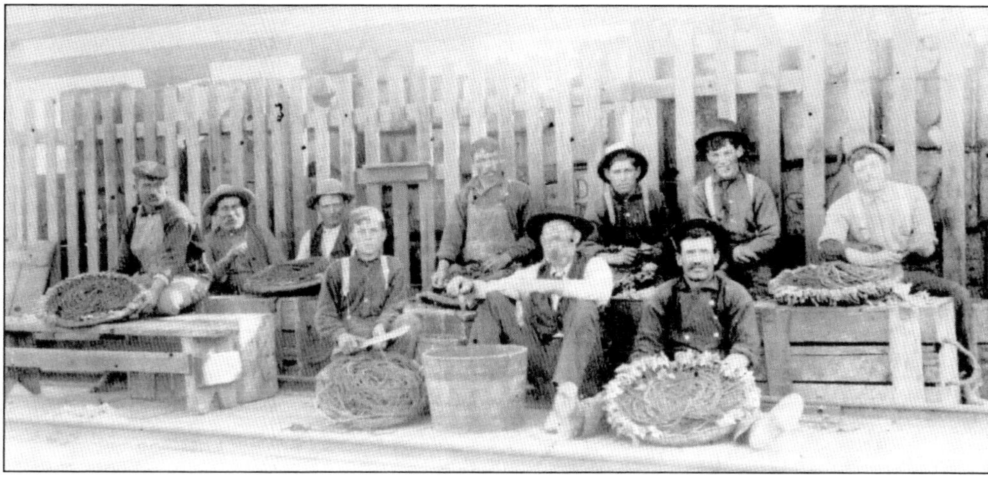

"Faraola Fishermen," the handwritten note on this image, provides important information on the structure of the Santa Cruz commercial fishing industry in 1908. The author's grandfather Cottardo Stagnaro II (back, far right) and great-grandfather Cottardo Stagnaro I (lower right) both fished for the Faraolas until Cottardo II founded the C. Stagnaro Fishing Corporation in the following decade. Others in the photograph include, from left to right, Stefano Ghio, Dario Amaya, Pat Gray, Cottardo "Trub" Ghio (with knife), Achille Castagnola, Ansel Googins, J.D. "Pete" Silvey, and Louis G. Beverino Jr. (Santa Cruz Seaside Company, Lee Faraola Collection.)

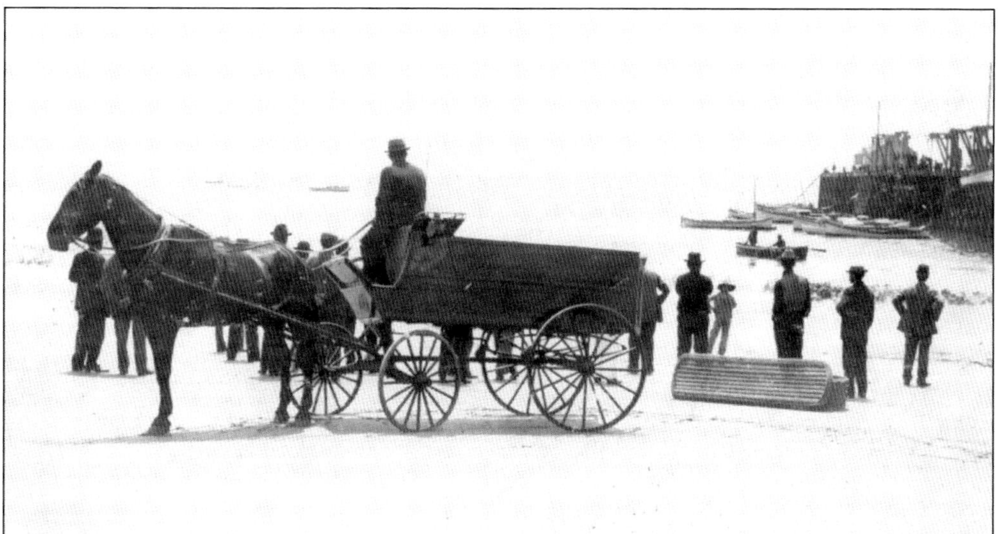

The mystery behind this fascinating photograph was unlocked when the depiction of the suicide of Hertha Page was discovered in the pages of the *Santa Cruz Sentinel* in the fall of 1903. On September 30, of that year, fisherman J.A. Jackson discovered a body in the kelp near Natural Bridges. He is pictured in the rowboat bringing Page's body to shore, where a mortuary coach owned by Wessendorf & Staffler awaits the body's arrival. Page, from a prominent San Jose family, was reportedly despondent over health issues. It was speculated that she also may have been part of a "suicide club" composed of wealthy young women in the Bay Area. (Santa Cruz Museum of Art & History.)

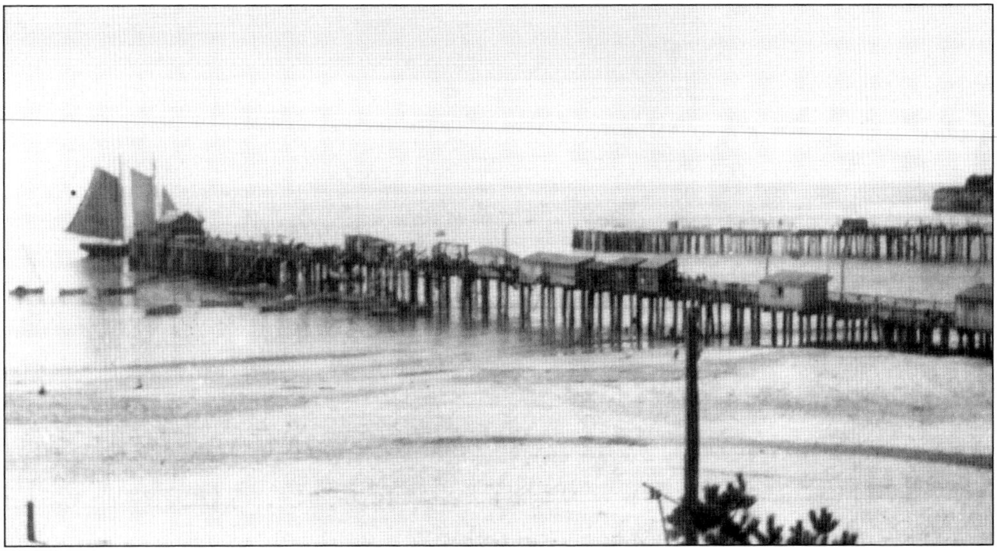

This photograph of the Railroad Wharf (left) and Cowell Wharf (right), taken from the grounds of the Sea Beach Hotel overlooking the Santa Cruz waterfront, shows how short and inadequate both piers were in providing access to large ships seeking portage in Santa Cruz, particularly at low tides. According to newspaper reports, at times the water at the end of the Railroad Wharf was only 14 feet deep. (Author's collection.)

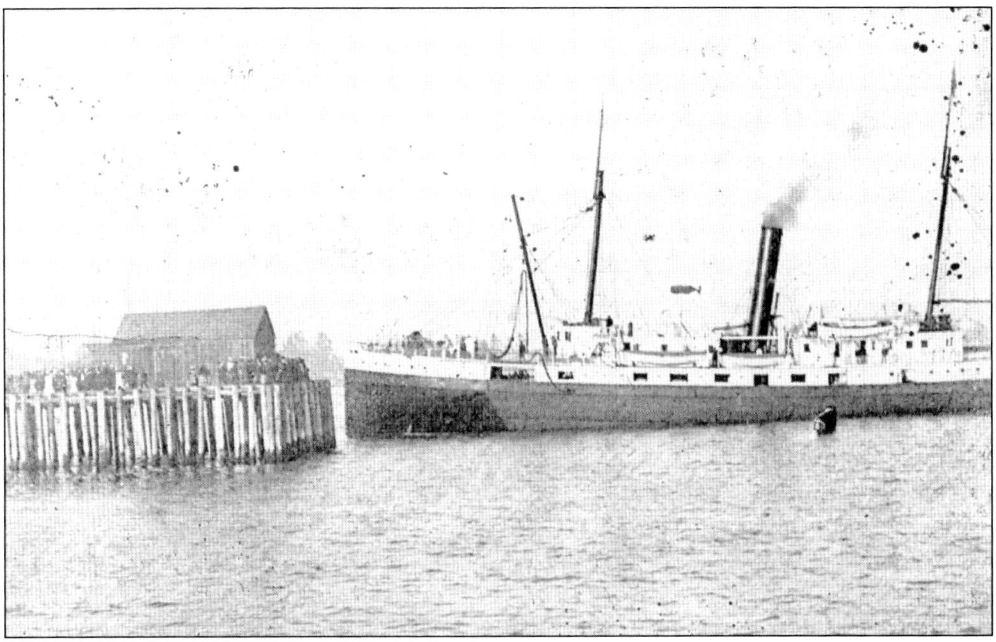

Steamships were forced to tie off on the southeast corner of the Railroad Wharf because of the shallowness of the water, preventing them from docking adjacent to the pier. It was this inability to provide portage for larger steamships that eventually led the City of Santa Cruz to seek a longer wharf structure extending farther into the bay. It began pursuing such a project in 1908. The first proposal included an island serving as a breakwater beyond the pier; the total proposed cost for both the island and the wharf was $79,816. (Author's collection.)

Three

THE PLEASURE PIER

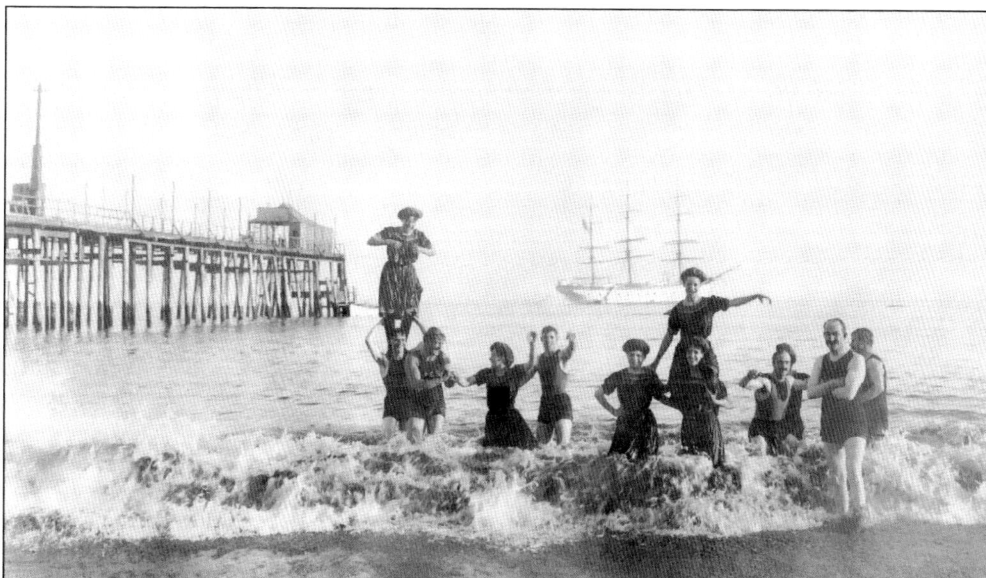

Originally built by the Beach, Cottage & Tent City Corporation (an enterprise later consolidated into the Santa Cruz Seaside Company), the 400-foot Pleasure Pier served as the site for a host of recreational ocean activities, including diving boards, slides, and a trapeze, and also accommodated a loading dock for popular launch and speedboat rides in Monterey Bay. It also provided a structure for piping salt water into the boardwalk's fabled indoor plunge, or "natatorium." Visitors to the Santa Cruz Main Beach (pictured) cool down in the bay, with the Pleasure Pier to the left and the fabled three-masted schooner *Balboa*, rumored to be a "pleasure ship." (Author's collection.)

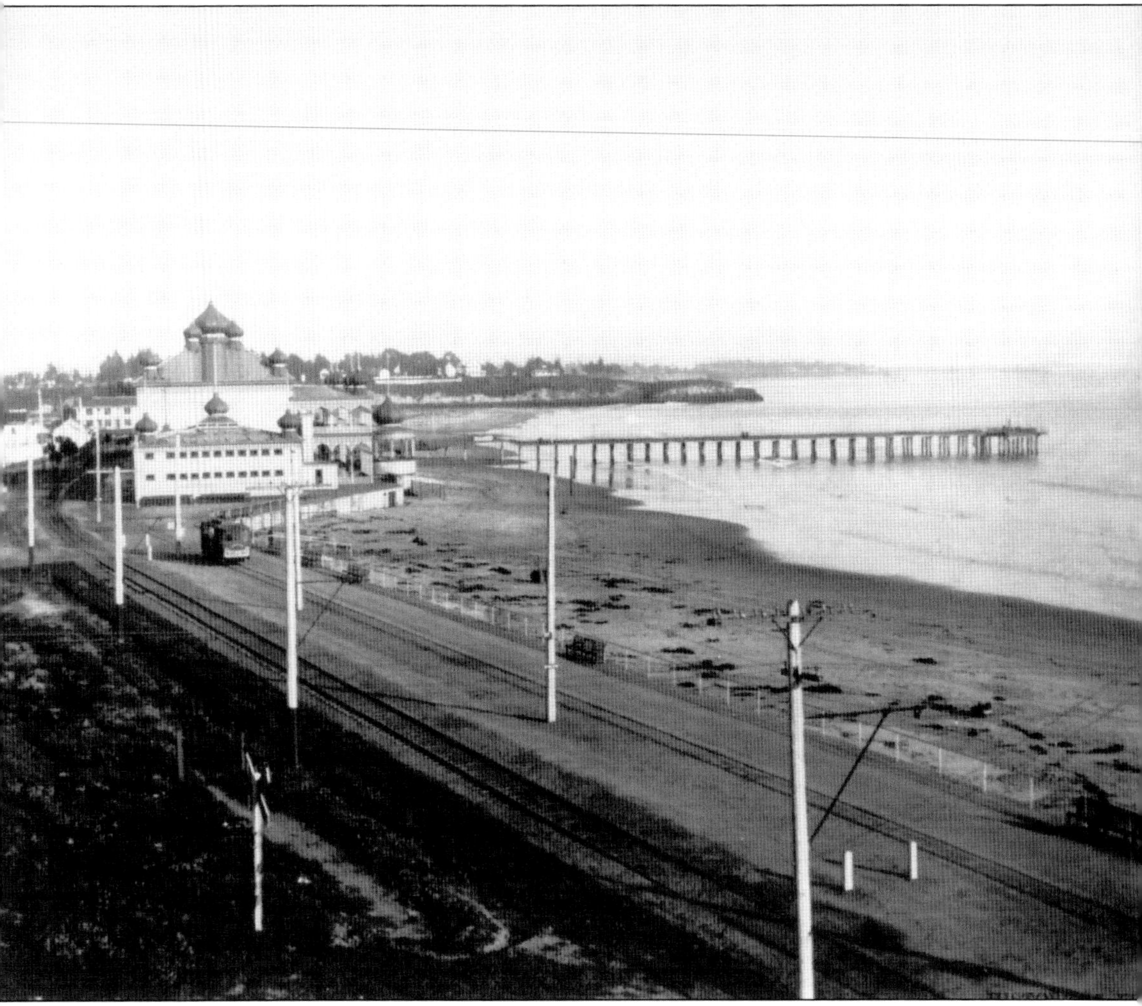

The development of the Pleasure Pier coincided with the construction of the first Neptune Casino, built by legendary Santa Cruz promoter Fred Swanton, a giant in Santa Cruz waterfront history. The building was completed in June 1904, leading Swanton to declare Santa Cruz "the queen of summer resorts." Note the streetcar running along Beach Street, which linked downtown Santa Cruz and the Southern Pacific depot to the waterfront. (Author's collection, from the Warren "Skip" Littlefield collection.)

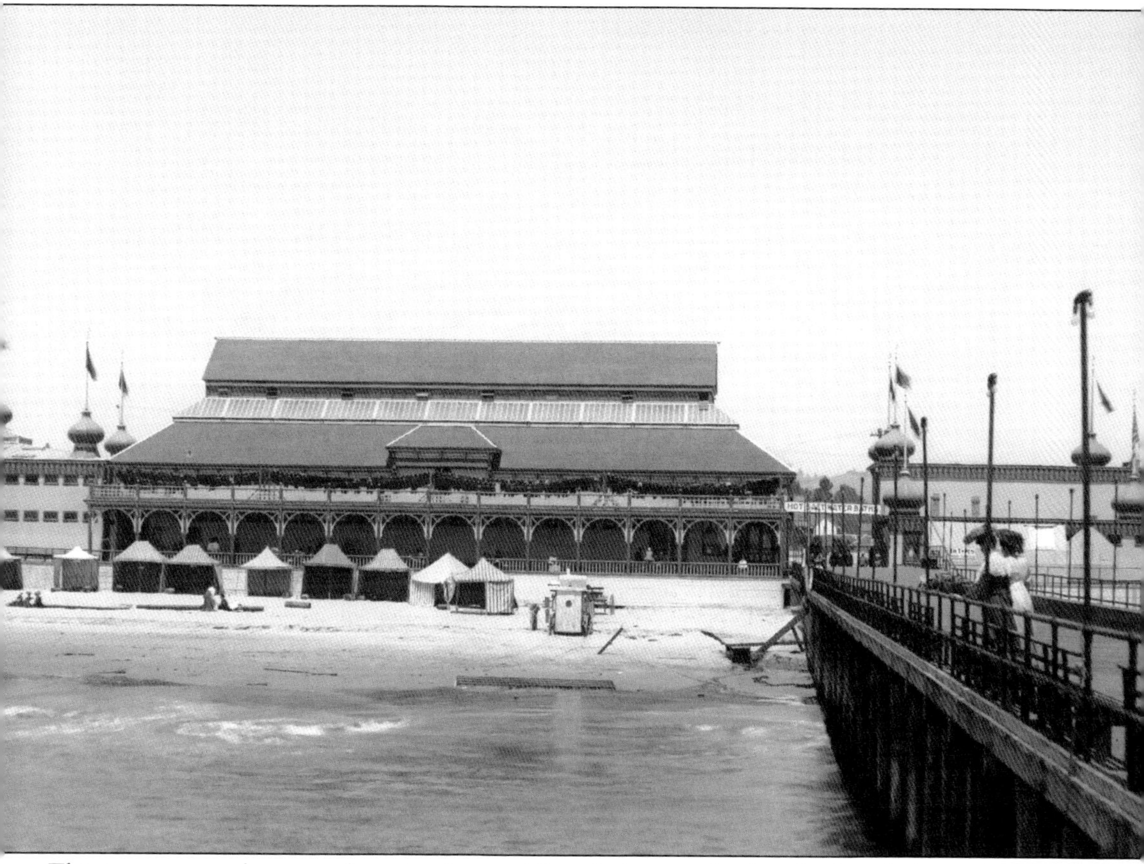

This is an extremely rare and previously unpublished photograph taken by famed Denver-based photographer William Henry Jackson, most likely in the summer of 1905. Part of a triptych taken by Jackson from the Pleasure Pier, this western section features the boardwalk's fabled natatorium, or saltwater plunge. Above the promenade, on the second-story balcony of the plunge, are hundreds of the Santa Cruz Seaside Company's one-piece woolen bathing suits hanging out to dry. (Private collection.)

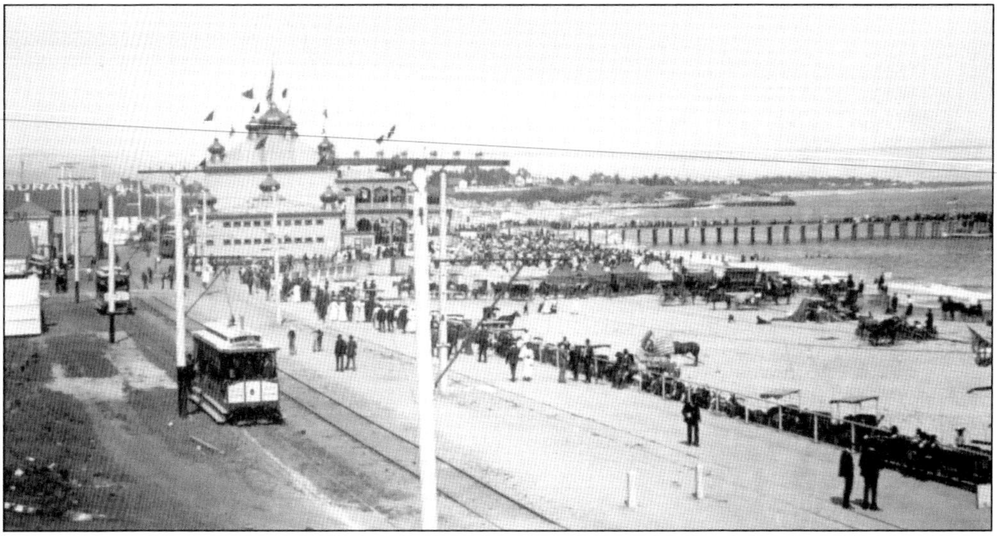

During the hot days of summer in 1905, visitors to Santa Cruz arrived by streetcars and train, while locals often arrived via horse and carriage, which they drove directly onto the beach. (Author's collection.)

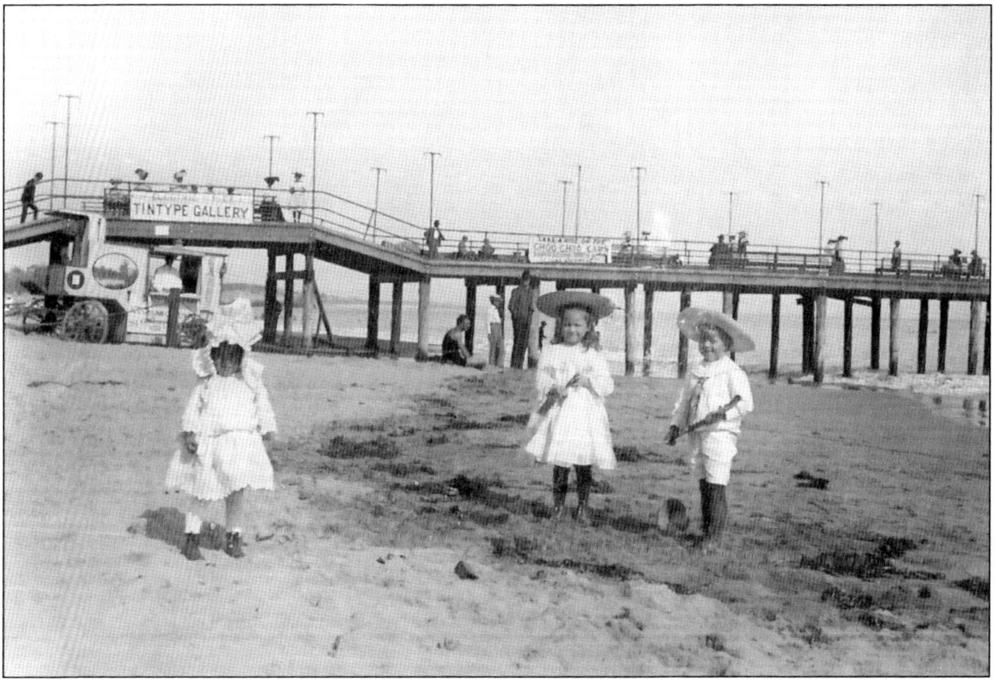

For a short time, the Pleasure Pier was known as the Electric Pier because of lights that were strung along it in the early 1900s. A sign in the background advertises the Electric Pier Tintype Gallery, where visitors could have photographic images taken as souvenirs. The small shack in the sand sold candy and ice cream and featured a painting by William Lemos on its side. (Santa Cruz Museum of Art & History.)

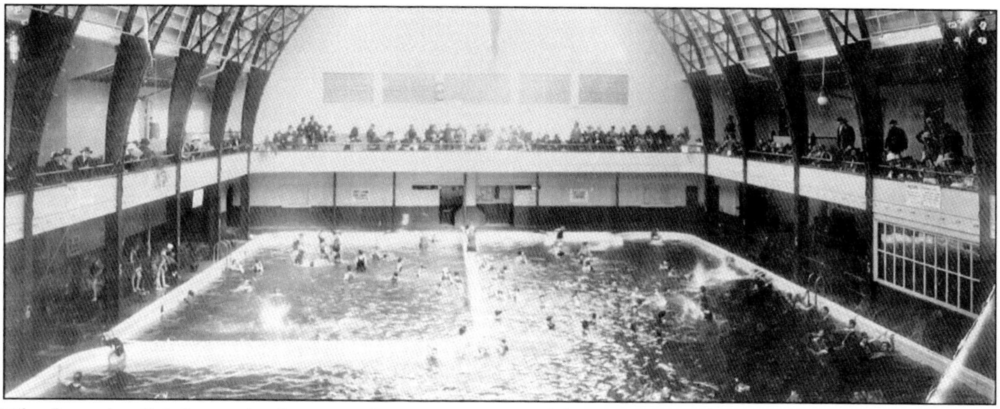

The boardwalk's heated saltwater plunge was one of the most popular swimming venues in the United States. It could host up to 2,500 swimmers and observers at a time. A pumping plant and piping were placed on the Pleasure Pier following its construction to bring salt water from the bay into the plunge. (Author's collection.)

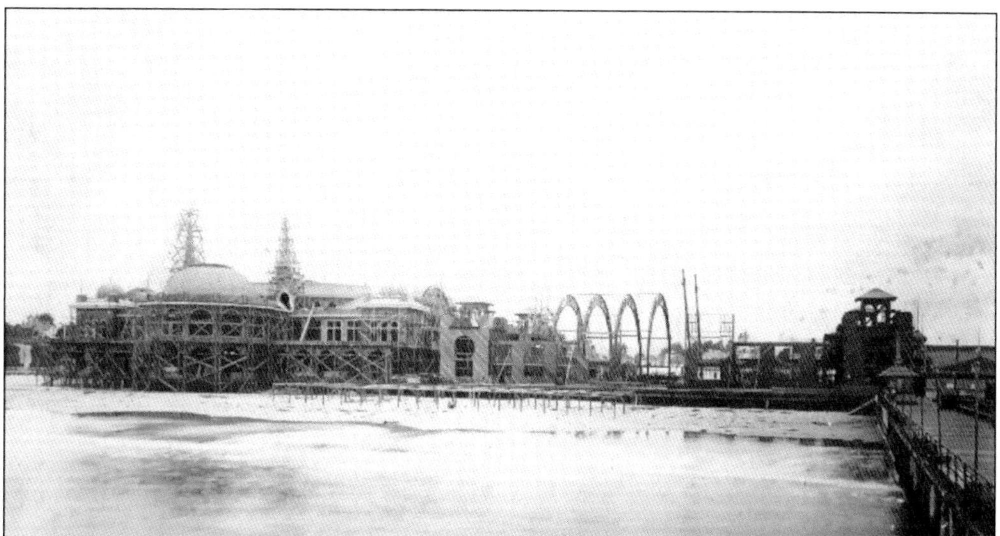

On June 22, 1906, a massive fire destroyed the casino and natatorium. Within days, Fred Swanton had obtained financing to rebuild both structures and assembled a "Five-Hundred-Man Army" to complete the rebuilding, which was completed in less than a year. The Pleasure Pier escaped damage. (Santa Cruz Seaside Company.)

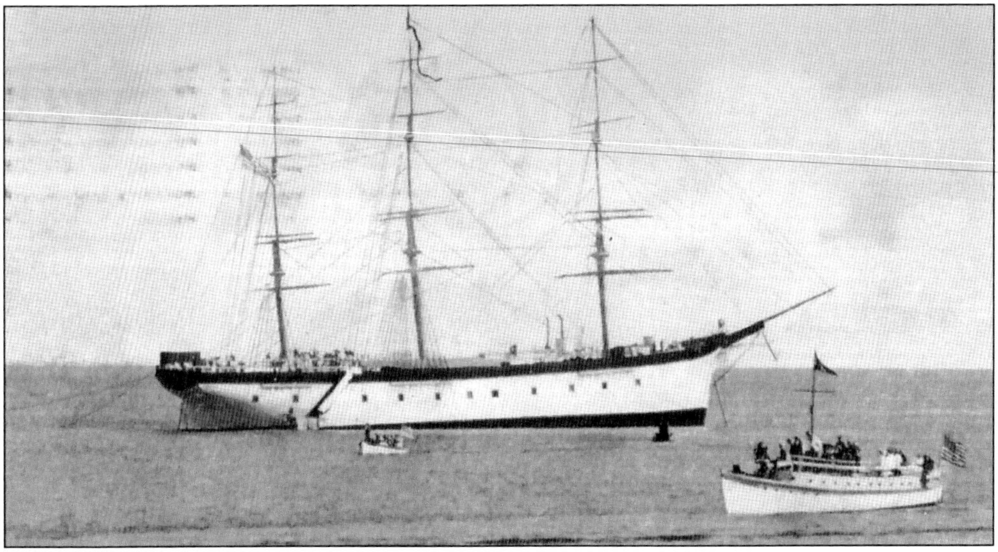

This postcard vista shows the *Balboa* and the smaller launch *Sinaloa*. In the aftermath of the 1906 fire, Swanton announced that Santa Cruz was about to become a "Monte Carlo on the Water." Swanton purchased a massive old clipper ship for the stated purpose of "amusements," all while anchored beyond "the three-mile limit of municipal jurisdiction." Swanton's marketing motto for the *Balboa* left a little wiggle room for the imagination: "Everything to please—nothing to offend." The *Sinaloa* used the Pleasure Pier to tender passengers to and from the larger ship. (Author's collection.)

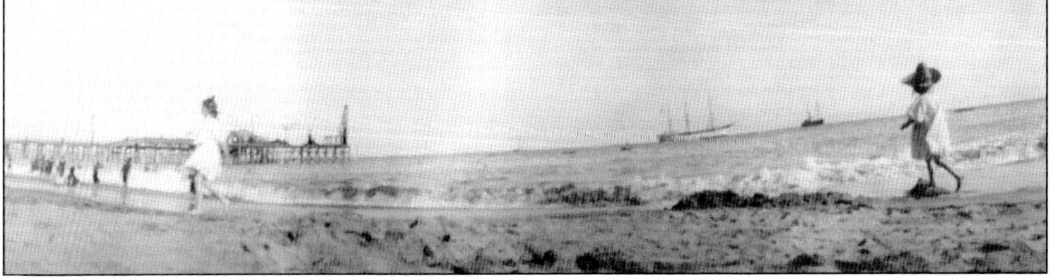

This image is the first in a sequence of rare miniature panoramas taken from the Main Beach upon the arrival of Theodore Roosevelt's "Great White Fleet" in May 1908. The fleet commenced a 16-month global tour in 1907 as a symbol of American naval power and imperial force and arrived in Santa Cruz on May 1, 1908. The *Balboa* went out to greet the fleet, painted white in adherence to the Navy's peacetime color scheme. (Harold Van Gorder collection.)

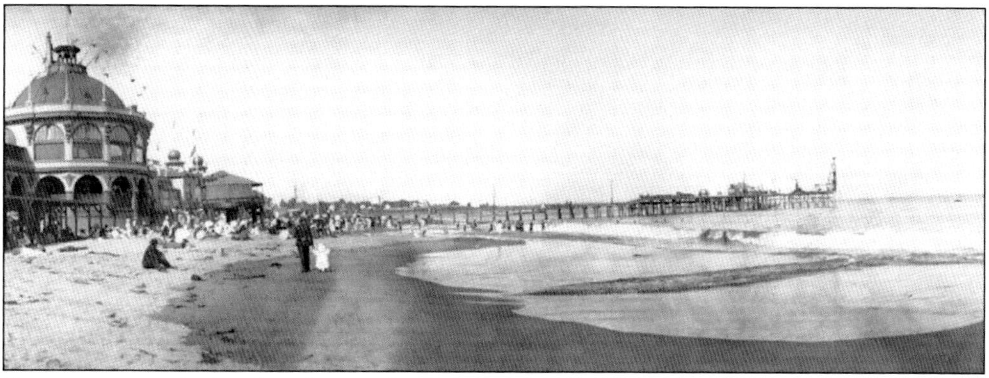

Visitors came to the beach and sat in the sand to watch the fleet's arrival. According to the *Santa Cruz Surf*, "The squadron of battleships leisurely swung its way around the contour of the bay at about an 8-knot speed, coming up abreast, and then maneuvering through a series of changing positions . . . and then standing out in the bay a couple of miles for permanent anchorage." (Author's collection.)

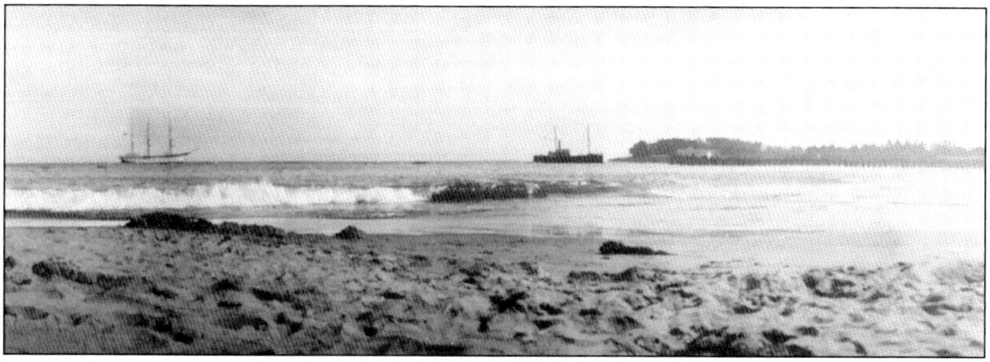

The *Balboa* and a steamship, likely the *Corona*, off the end of the Railroad Wharf, quietly await the arrival of the fleet. The *Santa Cruz Morning Sentinel* reported, "With flags and pennants flying from every building of importance along the beach and animated groups of men, women and children waiting expectantly, the faint smoke of the first squadron was decried on the horizon." (Author's collection.)

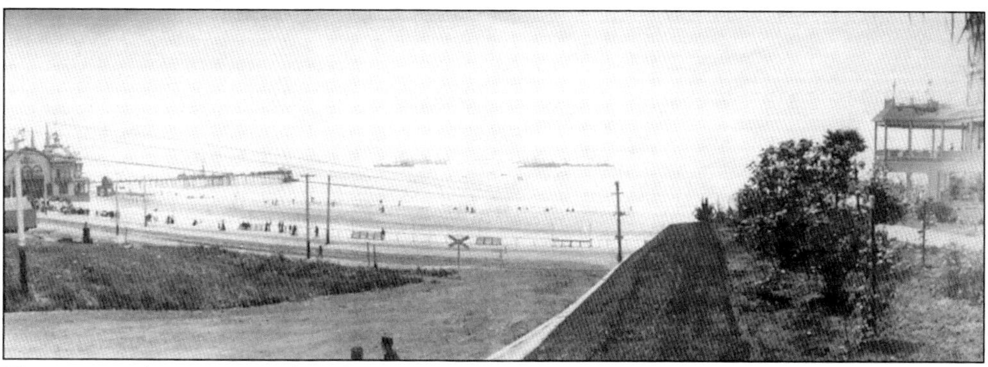

This extremely rare vista taken from the eastern grounds of the Sea Beach Hotel shows some smaller ships of the fleet close to shore. The hotel hosted a reception for admirals and officers on Saturday, May 2. "Now that Santa Cruz has successfully entertained the officers and men of the sixteen warships and their auxiliary ships," the *Morning Sentinel* declared, "we feel able to entertain the Nation." (Author's collection.)

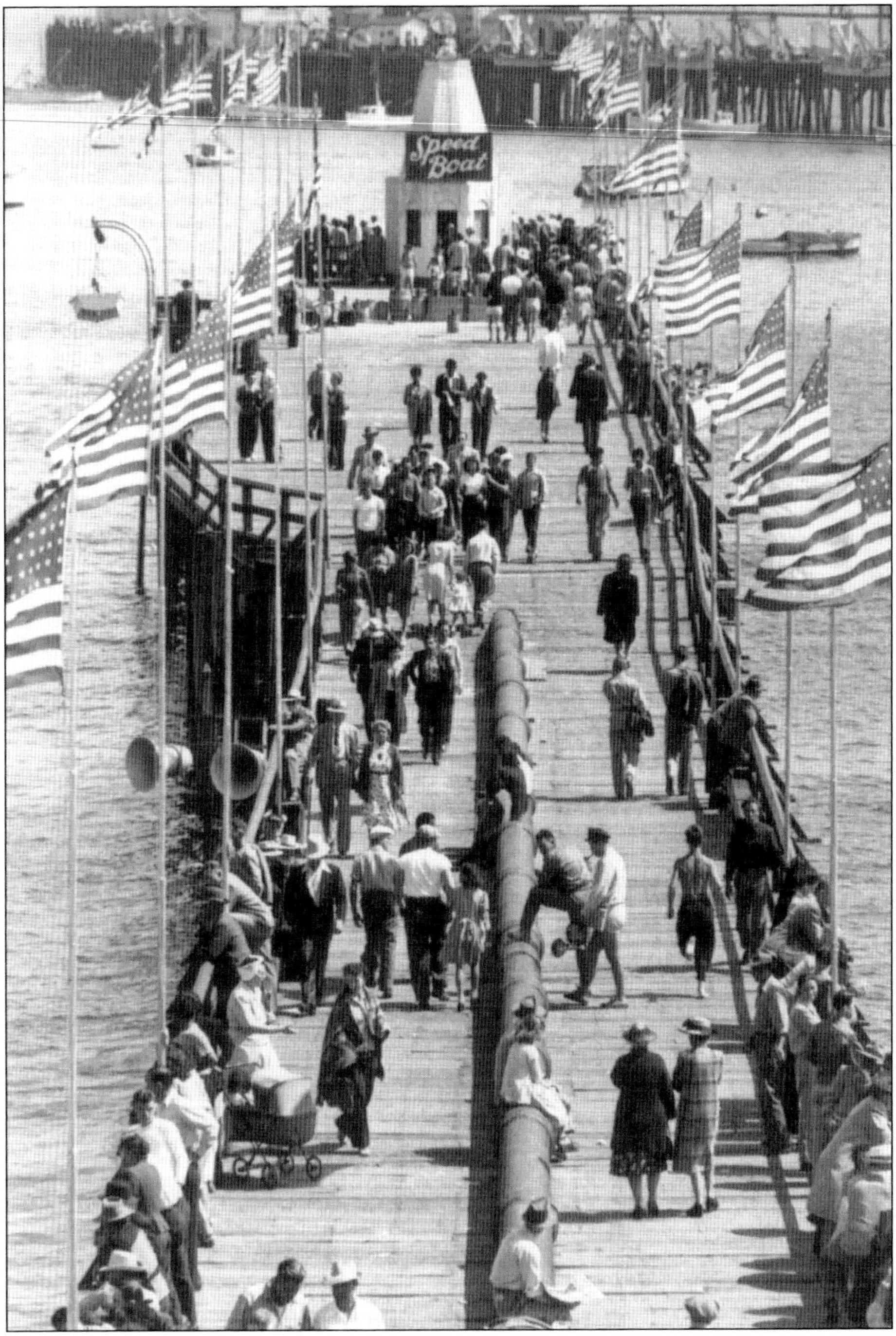

July 4, 1946, is frozen in time with this photograph. From the 1930s through the early 1960s, the Pleasure Pier was a popular destination for strollers and those wishing to ride the C. Stagnaro Company's famed speedboats, docked at the end of the pier. Throngs lined up to get passage fares in the ticket booth. On this particular afternoon, the boardwalk featured the 55-piece San Francisco band at the bandstand. The *Sentinel* estimated that "100,000 vacationists" visited Santa Cruz County for the holiday. (Santa Cruz Seaside Company.)

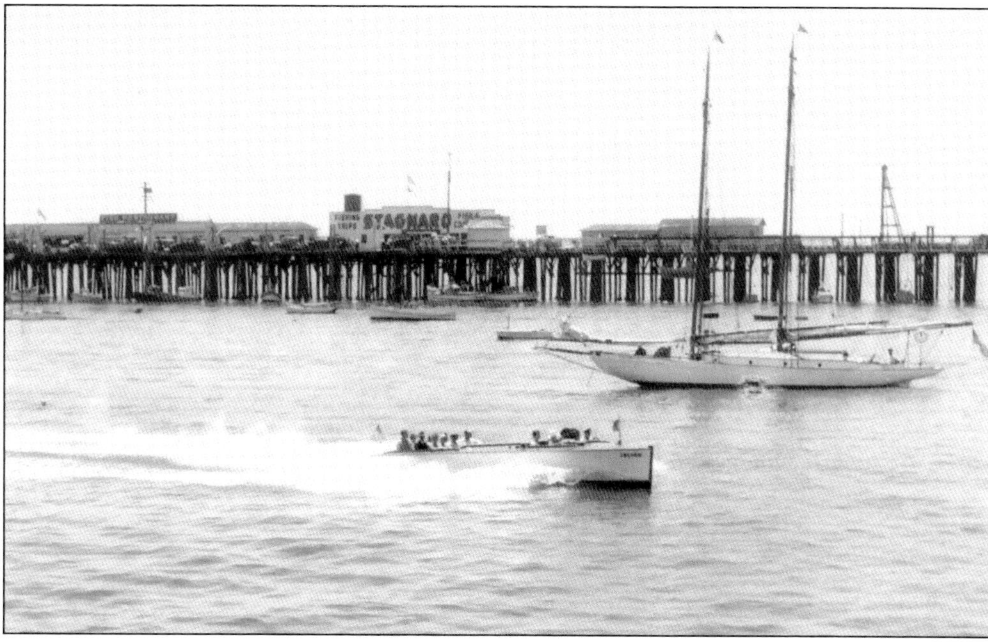

One of the fleet's speedboats, *Miss Stagnaro*, glides through the bay to the dock, with the Santa Cruz Wharf in the background. The fishing family began operating speedboats in 1932, when they had their first boat built by Ernest Philbrook, replete with a 450-horsepower Hall-Scott engine that propelled the vessel to averages of 30 knots. (Author's collection.)

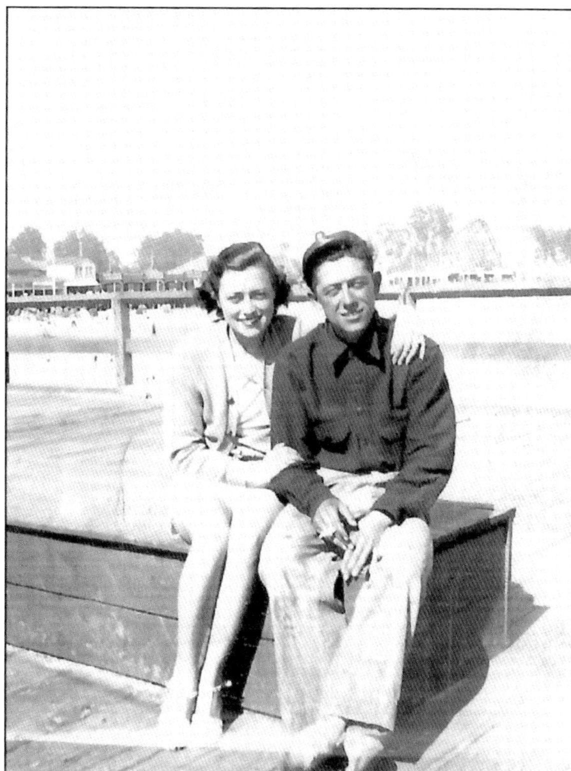

There's nothing like a brief respite on a summer day. The author's mother, Yolanda "Lindy" Stagnaro (Dunn), and her younger brother, Malio H. "Stago" Stagnaro, enjoy a moment of relaxation on the Pleasure Pier in the summer of 1936. Lindy worked as a ticket taker on the Pleasure Pier for many years, while Stago captained one of the family's speedboats. (Author's collection.)

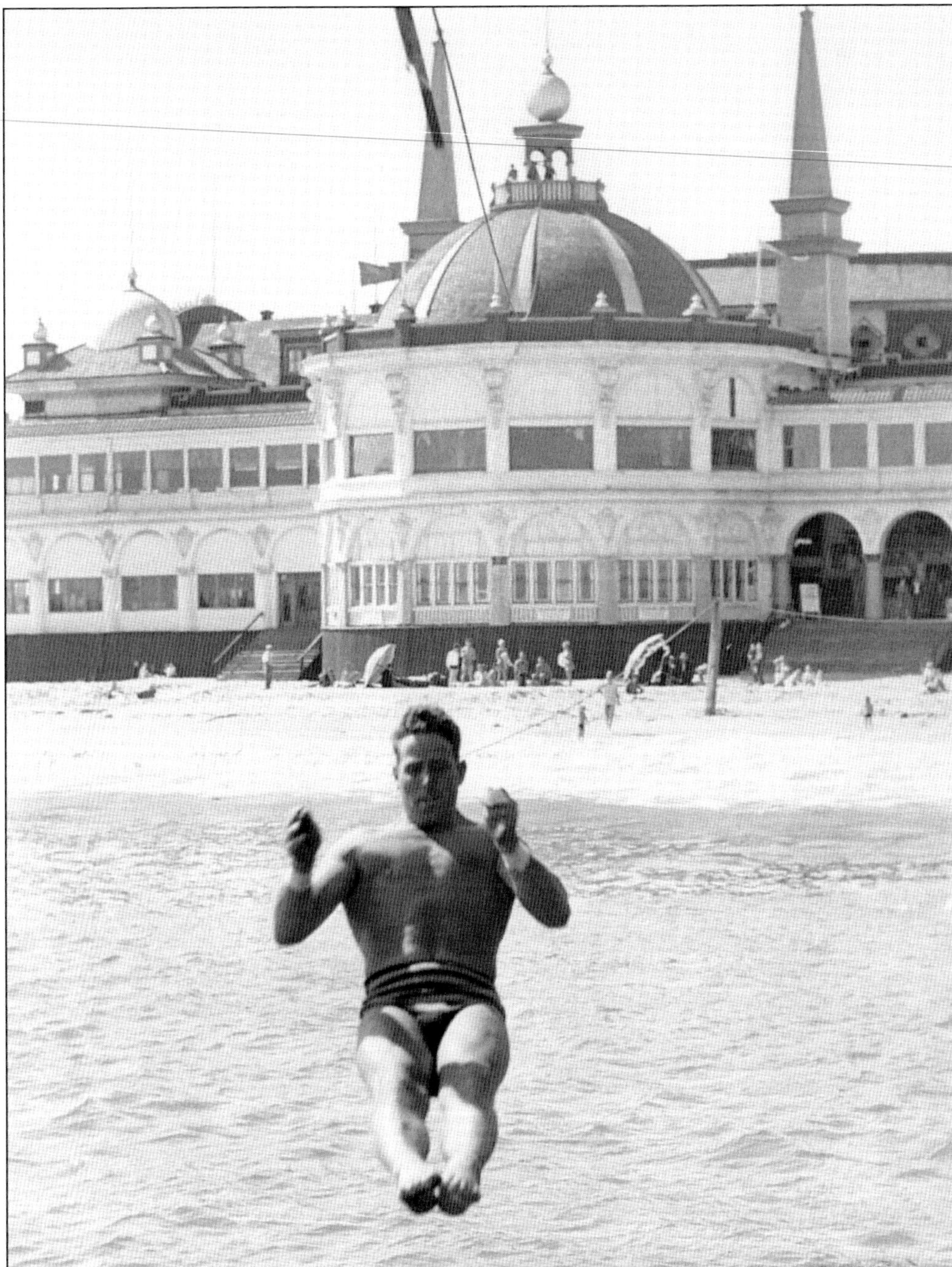

"Mighty Bosco" Patterson was one of the most celebrated watermen in all of California, dating from his youth spent along the Santa Cruz waterfront in the aftermath of World War I. Here, he completes his "Slide for Life," in which he jumped from the top of the boardwalk's casino while holding onto a pulley-and-cable apparatus attached to the end of the Pleasure Pier, 750 feet away, before plunging into the ocean. (Santa Cruz Seaside Company.)

Don "Mighty Bosco" Patterson often turned comedic roles as a strongman in the boardwalk's popular Plunge Carnivals and Waterfront Follies. Here he is flexing his muscles on the Pleasure Pier in the 1930s. Also dubbed "The Man on the Flying Trapeze," Patterson was still performing daredevil feats in the boardwalk's plunge into the 1960s. A superb swimmer, diver, and acrobat, he was also one of Santa Cruz's early board surfers in the 1930s. (Santa Cruz Seaside Company.)

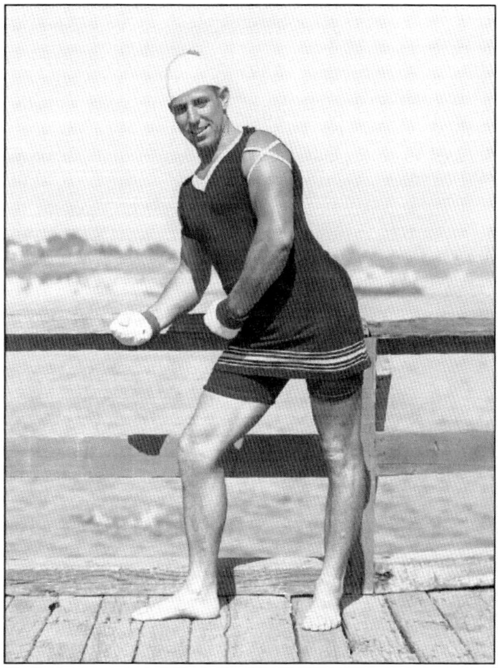

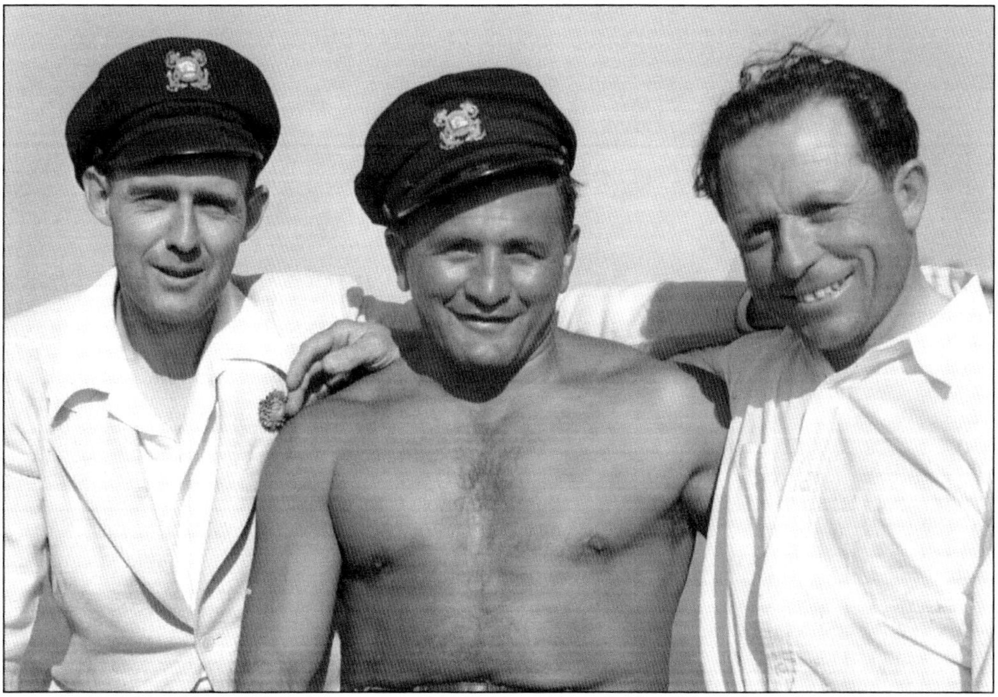

Warren "Skip" Littlefield (left), Ralph "Young Corbett III" Giordano (center), and Malio Stagnaro are pictured on the Pleasure Pier in the 1930s. Giordano was boxing's welterweight champion of the world in 1933 and the middleweight champion in 1938. In September 1938, Littlefield paired Giordano and Stagnaro in a 50-yard benefit race at the plunge. Littlefield wrote in the *Santa Cruz Sentinel* that Stagnaro, "12-pound window weight et al . . . has agreed to take on Corbett III in a spirited aquatic duel." (Author's collection.)

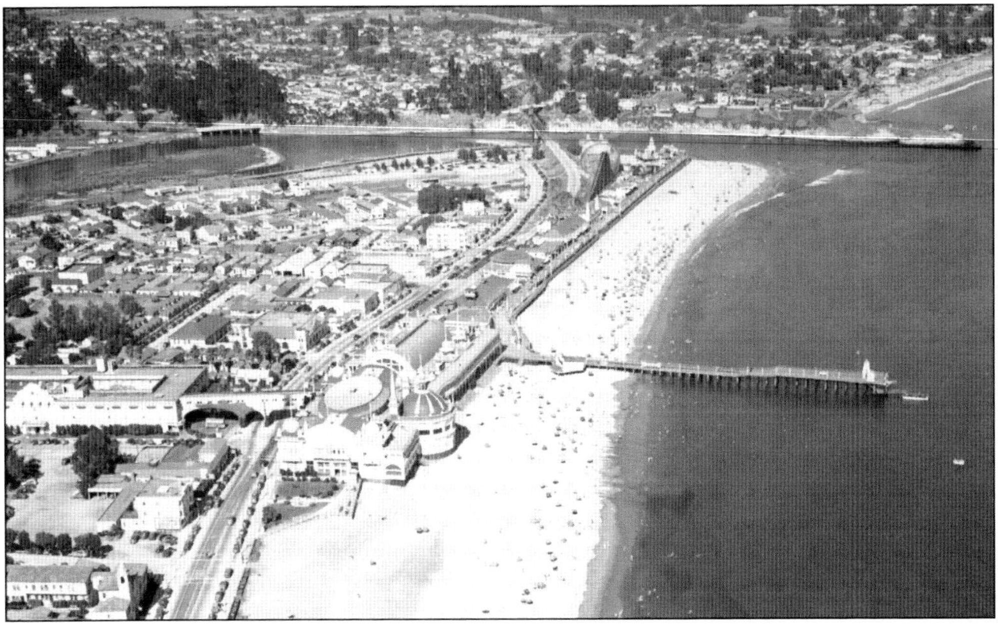

This aerial image of the Santa Cruz waterfront in the 1950s, taken by photographer George Lee, shows the Pleasure Pier extending out to sea and conveys peaceful times. The famed Casa del Rey hotel with its archway over Beach Street can be seen center-left. The boardwalk's bandstand is adjacent to the pier on the beach. (Author's collection.)

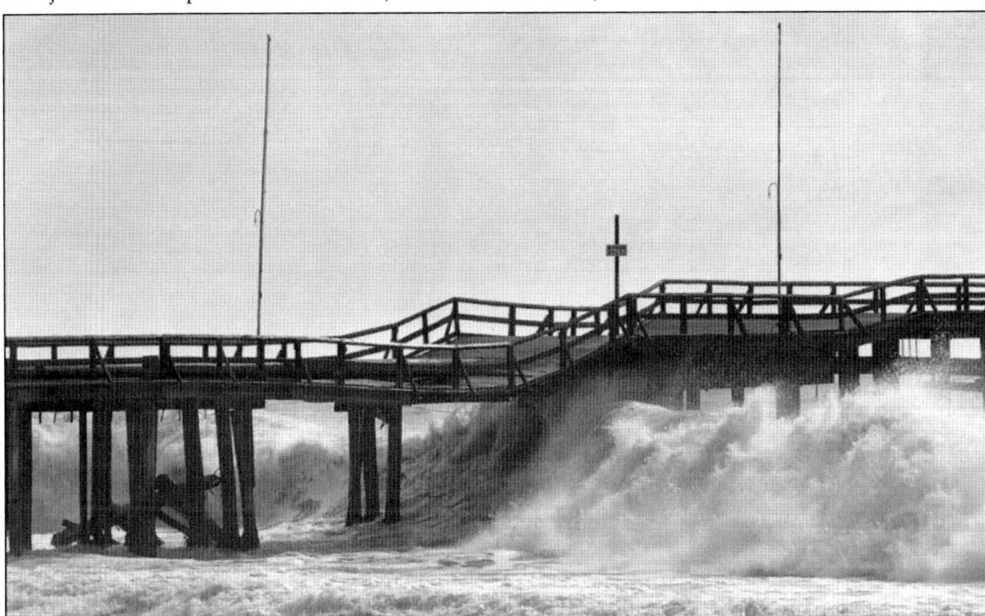

It was the punch that knocked out the Pleasure Pier. Following extensive storm damage in the spring of 1962, the pier was closed to visitors for the summer of that year. In October, it was announced that the pier would be dismantled, as repairs proved too costly. The pilings were removed by bulldozer and cables, with the job completed in November. In the *Santa Cruz Sentinel*, Estrella Stagnaro describes the demolition as "like losing a great love." (Santa Cruz Museum of Art & History.)

Four

A MODERN WHARF COMES TO LIFE

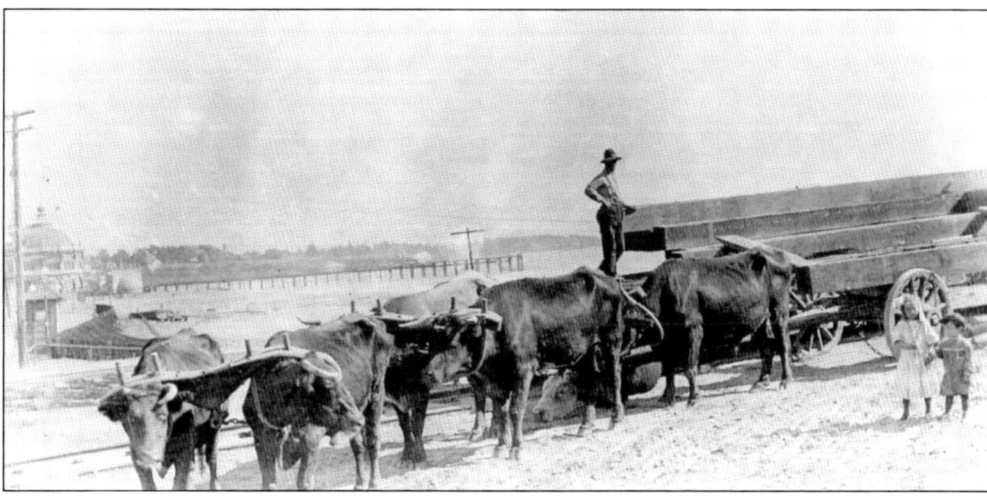

In October 1913, a commission of local citizens, charged with exploring options for a new wharf on the Santa Cruz waterfront, issued a 27-page report in support of a 2,756-foot pier at the foot of present-day Front Street capable of accommodating large steamships with drafts of 30 feet at low tide. The report, addressed to the city council, recommends that a bond measure be placed before the citizens of Santa Cruz to raise the estimated $165,000 needed for construction. Within two months, the council had placed the issue on a special ballot. On December 4 of that year, residents of Santa Cruz registered nearly unanimous support for the new wharf: 3,434 in favor, with only 74 opposed. Construction began shortly thereafter. Here, an oxteam moves crossbeams onto the wharf during construction, with Ella and Jim Moody watching close by. (Moody family.)

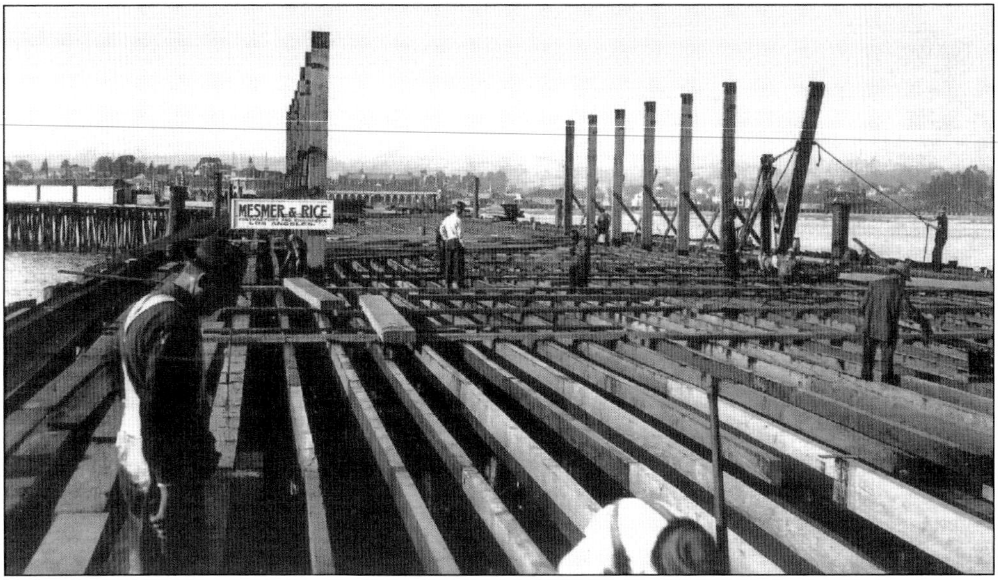

Mesmer & Rice, an engineering firm from Los Angeles, was selected to oversee construction of the new wharf. They were primarily bridge builders in Southern California and had been introduced to Santa Cruz County when bidding on a Soquel Creek bridge in 1912. The vertical beams are part of the large steamship warehouse that was located at the end of the pier. (California Views, Pat Hathaway Collection.)

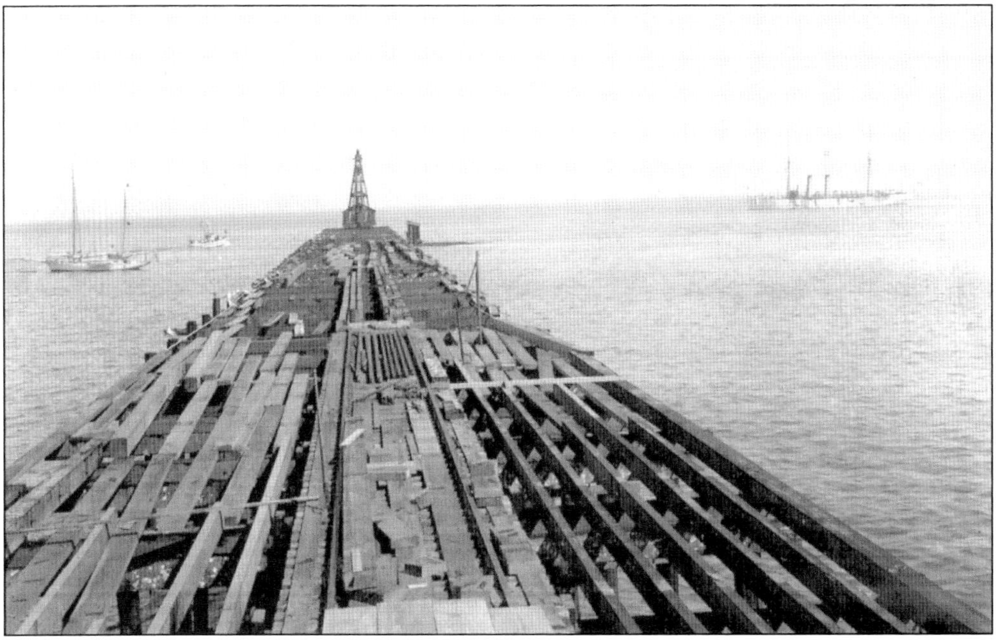

Note the pile driver at end of the pier in this photograph, with a steamship overlooking construction. The construction process was not without its controversies. In October 1914, a member of the Pile Drivers' Union showed up at the wharf, according to the *Santa Cruz Sentinel*, with the intentions of "showing the people of Santa Cruz were being robbed." Mesmer & Rice had him "ordered off the pier." (Moody family.)

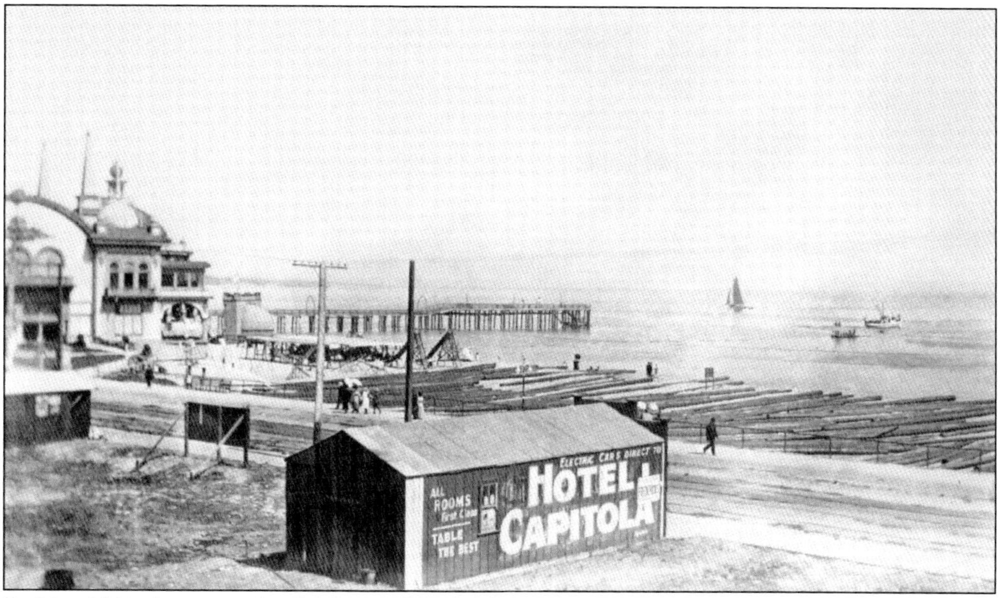

By May 2014, the steamship *Multnomah* had delivered nearly 400,000 feet of creosoted piling for wharf construction. The logs were towed to shore by a cable and launch and then hauled onto the beach by a donkey engine. There were complaints by visitors that their clothes had been ruined by the creosote. The sign on the building in foreground was for the benefit of riders on the streetcar line that went all the way to Capitola—where they could avoid the construction. (Gordon Van Zuiden.)

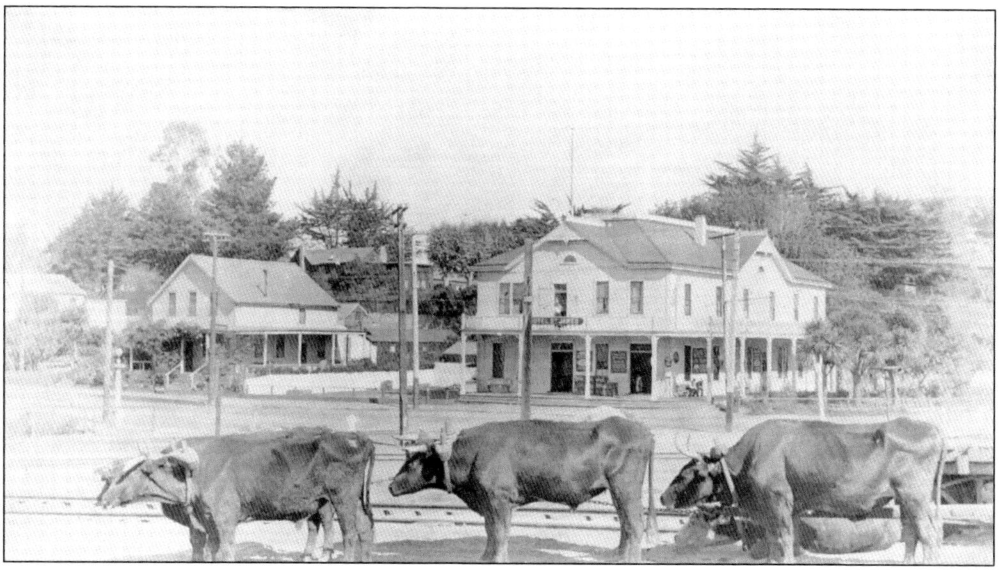
An oxteam at the foot of the wharf hauled construction materials from the Southern Pacific depot to the construction site. Across the street is the famed St. James Hotel, then owned by Edward V. Moody, a former railroad man and a boxing and baseball aficionado who managed a local all-star team. "Despite Prohibition," Skip Littlefield once wrote of the St. James, "the bar never closed. The cocktail hour ran from noon to midnight." Those in charge of building the wharf resided at the St. James. (Moody family.)

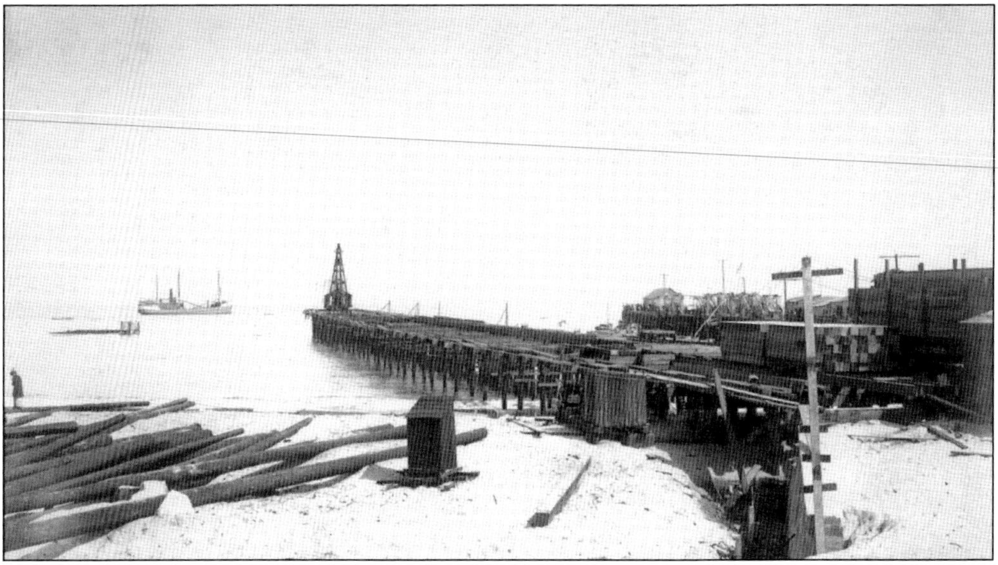

Construction of the wharf took less than a year. Most of the building materials were shipped in from Puget Sound. (Moody family.)

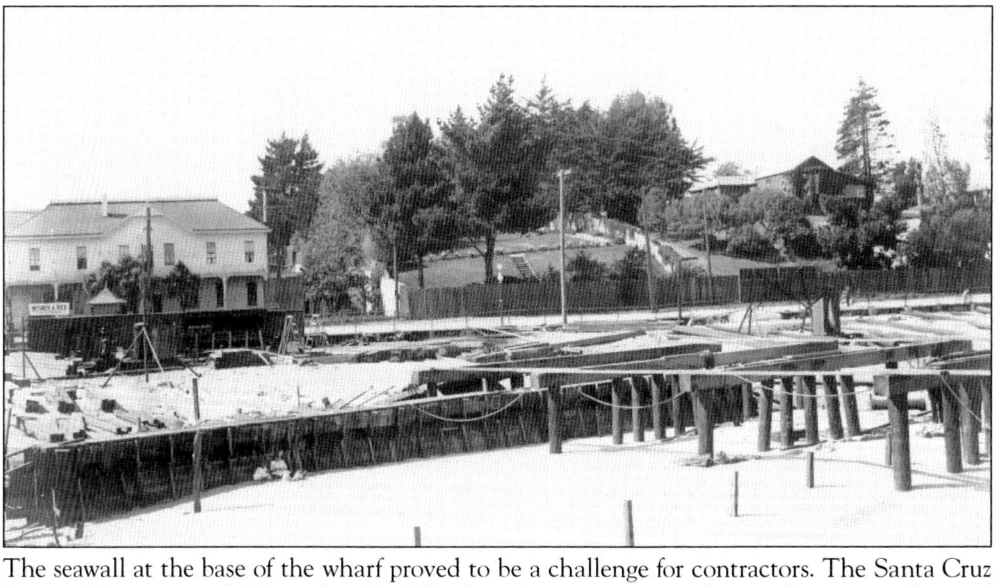

The seawall at the base of the wharf proved to be a challenge for contractors. The Santa Cruz *Evening News* reported: "Considerable difficulty is being experienced . . . in digging out the sand for the seawall of the new municipal wharf. The water is so plentiful that it fills up the excavation, carrying with it the sands from the sides. A box-like form has been constructed, and the men are digging from the inside, at the same time sinking the box into the sand." (Moody family.)

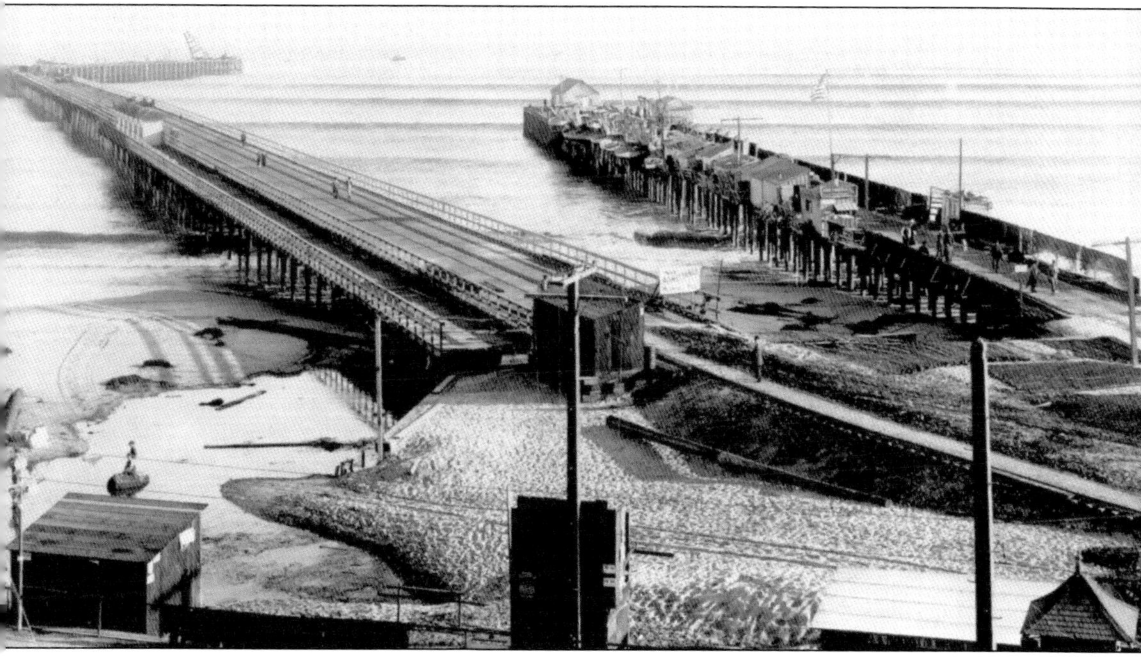

The construction of the wharf continued with steady progress into the summer and autumn of 1914. By May, the *Evening News* began running a column entitled Municipal Wharf Chips, which contains regular reports about progress. By May, the paper noted proudly, the new wharf was more than "100 feet longer" than the Railroad Wharf, and it would eventually grow more than three times as long. No activity seemed too small to record. The June 4 issue of the paper notes that "Joe Silva dove to the bottom" to retrieve a lost crowbar. (Author's collection.)

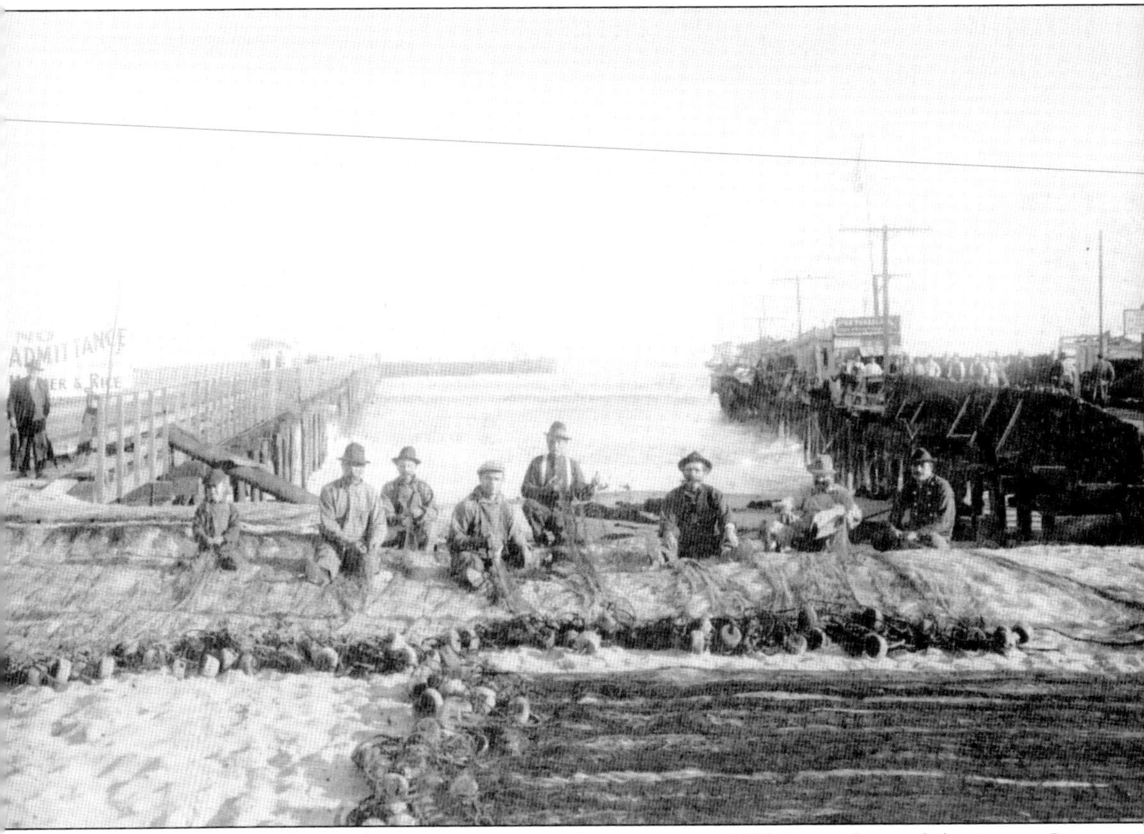

As the new wharf neared completion in the late autumn of 1914, members of the Santa Cruz Italian fishing colony were posed with their nets between what would become the past and the future. From left to right are Cottardo "Monk" Loero, Achille Castagnola, Tomaso Ghio, Lapanino Ghio, Giacomo Stagnaro, Cottardo Stagnaro I, Stefano "Taraloto" Stagnaro (who died at sea in 1921), and Dante Canepa. When the new wharf opened, they remained with the old for the first few years. They were not included in the opening day festivities. (Author's collection, photograph by Ole Ravnos.)

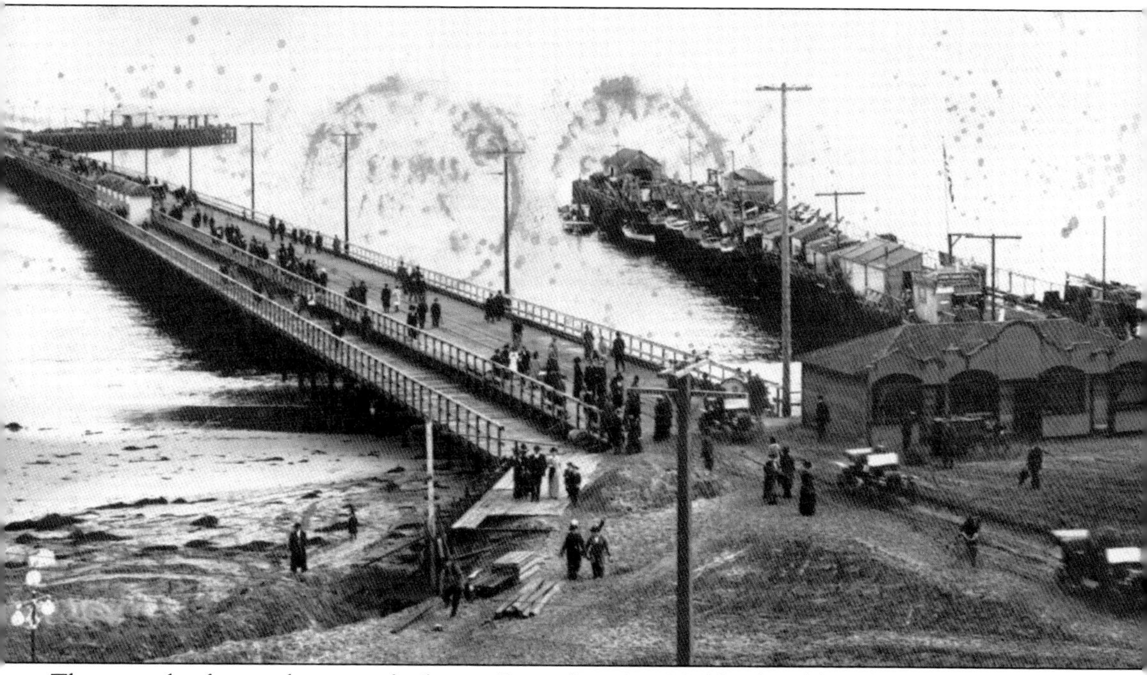

The new wharf opened to great fanfare in December 1914. Unlike the old Railroad Wharf, the new wharf was user-friendly. It had railings and a smooth walkway so that strolls out to the end, nearly a half mile from shore, were safe for visitors. At the entrance is a structure that was added near the end of construction for steamship ticket sales. (Author's collection.)

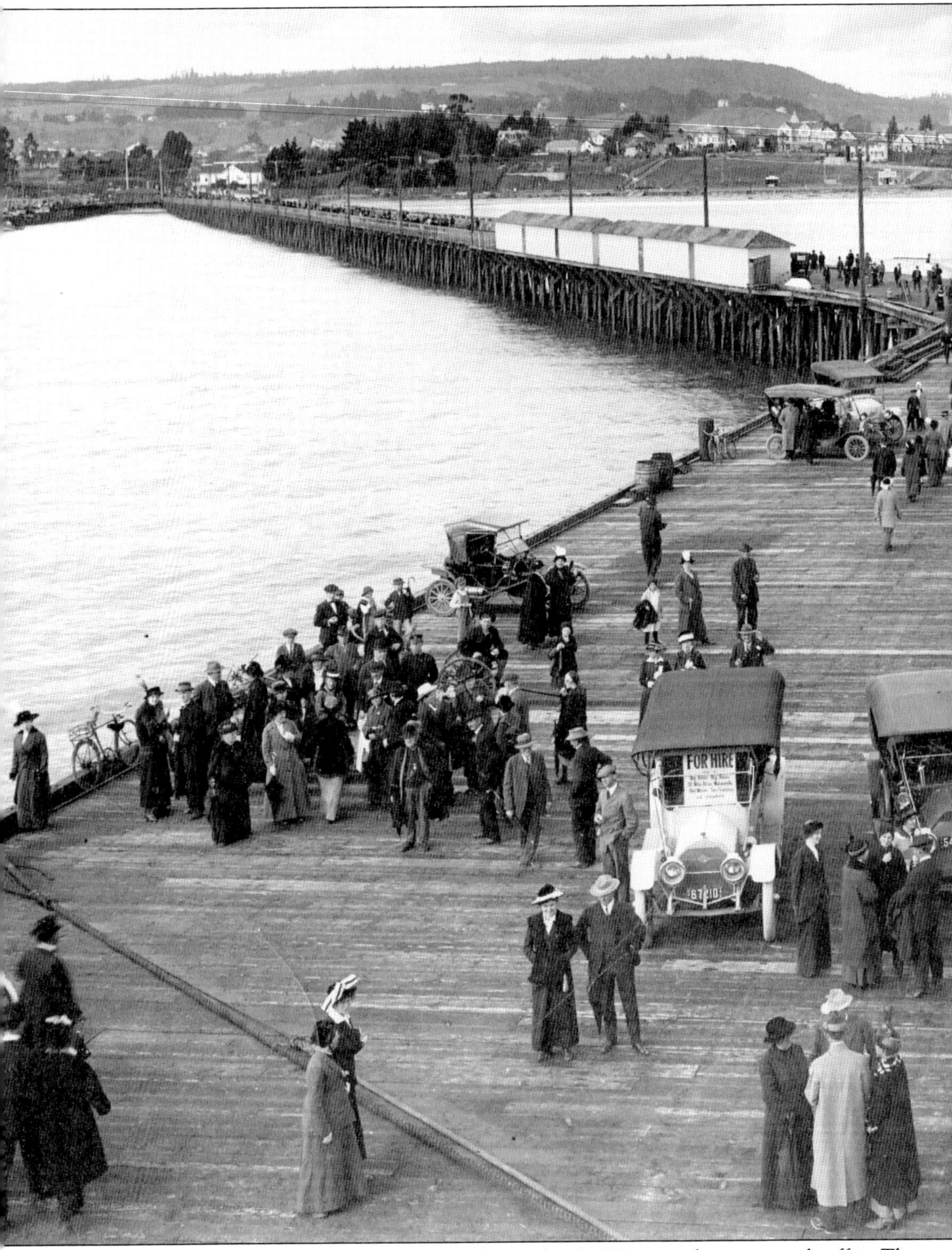

The grand opening of the wharf on Saturday, December 5, 1914, was a boisterous gala affair. The day was observed as a formal holiday in Santa Cruz. A "Fish Bake Barbecue and Basket Picnic"

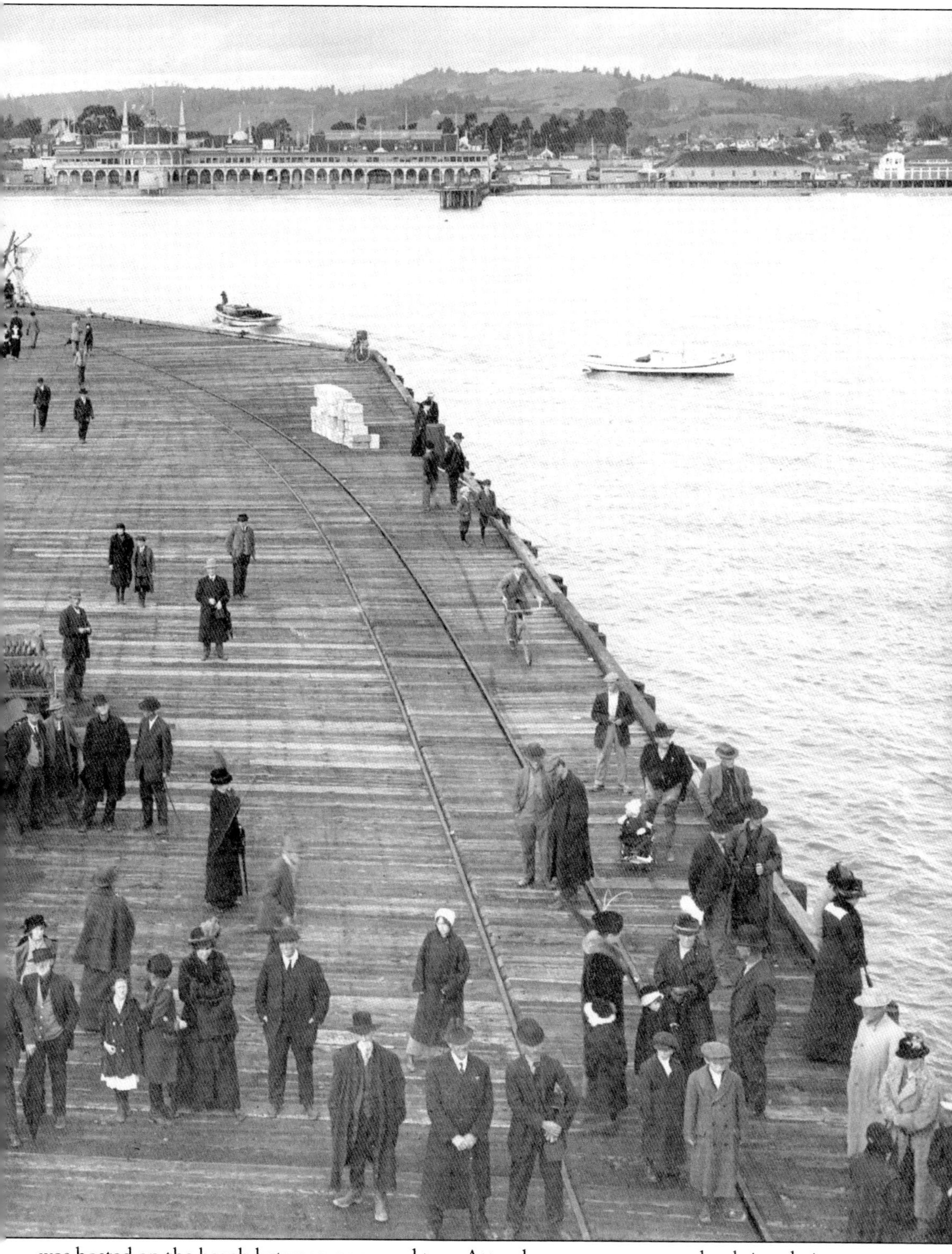

was hosted on the beach between noon and two. Attendees were encouraged to bring their own "knife, fork and cup." (Author's collection.)

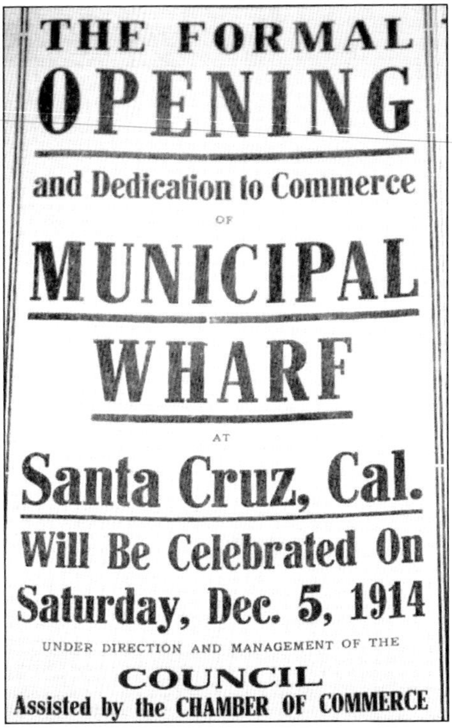

THE FORMAL
OPENING
and Dedication to Commerce
OF
MUNICIPAL
WHARF
AT
Santa Cruz, Cal.
Will Be Celebrated On
Saturday, Dec. 5, 1914
UNDER DIRECTION AND MANAGEMENT OF THE
COUNCIL
Assisted by the CHAMBER OF COMMERCE

This advertisement appeared in the *Santa Cruz Sentinel* for the wharf's opening. Note the reference to "dedication to commerce." The business of the wharf was, ultimately, business. What that commerce would ultimately become was uncertain. One local proprietor proposed a large fruit stand on the wharf; it never happened. Santa Cruz was being hailed as the new "Coney Island of the Pacific." (Dan Coyro collection.)

The SS *Roanoke*, a prominent vessel in the fleet of the North Pacific Steamship Company, which sailed the Pacific coast from Seattle down to Los Angeles and as far south as San Diego, was scheduled to reach its new port at noon that day for the people of Santa Cruz to absorb its grandeur. When it arrived, throngs rushed to the end of the pier to get on board. This image, taken by Ole Ravnos, was a gift to the author from the late Harold Van Gorder, who was born in 1902 and lived to be 107 years old. A note on the back reads: "I was there." (Author's collection.)

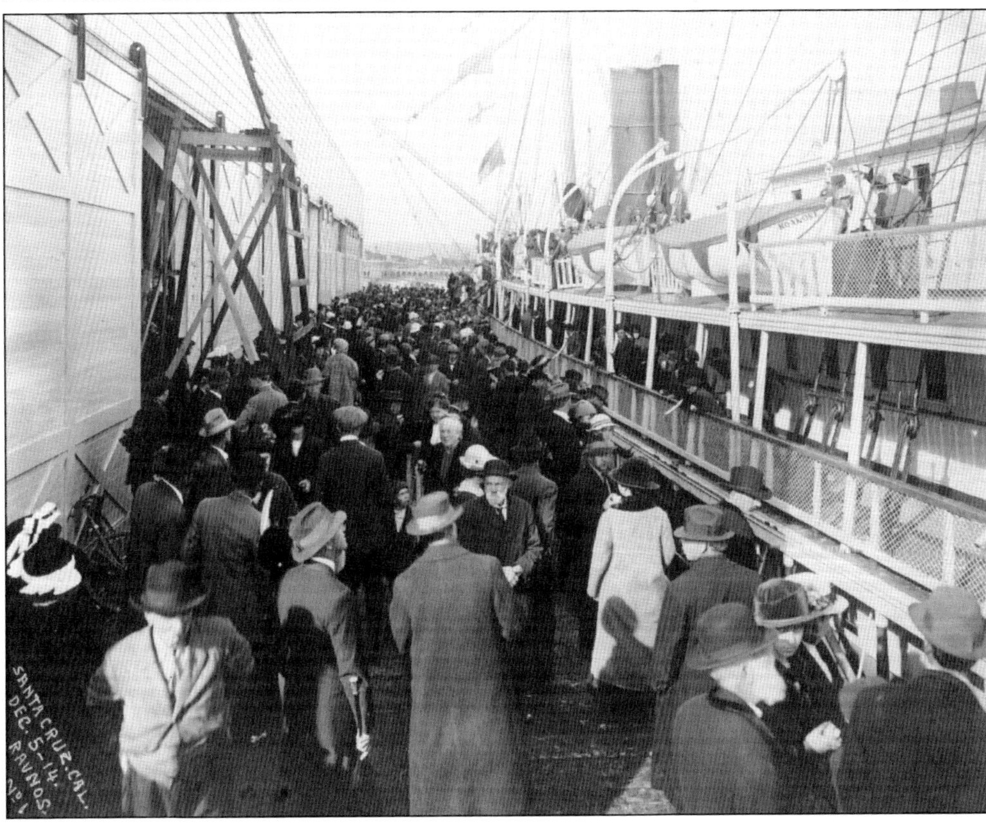

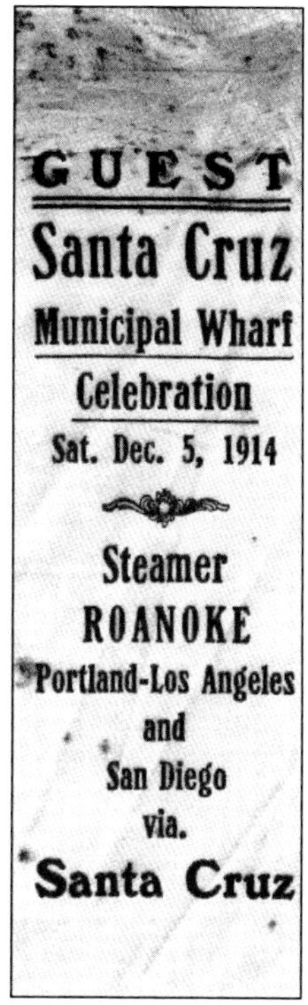

A rare souvenir ribbon was issued to those who made it aboard the steamship. With the addition of the wharf, Santa Cruz had made it on the map (literally) in terms of steamship runs. The *Roanoke* had been built in 1882 in Chesterfield, Pennsylvania, and was 257 feet long and 40 feet wide with gross tonnage of more than 2,300 tons. (Santa Cruz Seaside Company.)

This photograph captures another view of the *Roanoke* loading passengers. On the very first day of operation, the *Roanoke* unloaded pianos, automobiles, and linoleum. Two years after its initial docking in Santa Cruz, in May 1916, rough weather split the *Roanoke* in two off Point Buchon, between Morro Bay and Avila Beach. The ship was bound for South America with an overloaded cargo of explosives, wheat, oil, and gasoline. Capt. Richard Dickson, his wife, and 45 crew members were lost at sea. There were only three survivors. (Author's collection.)

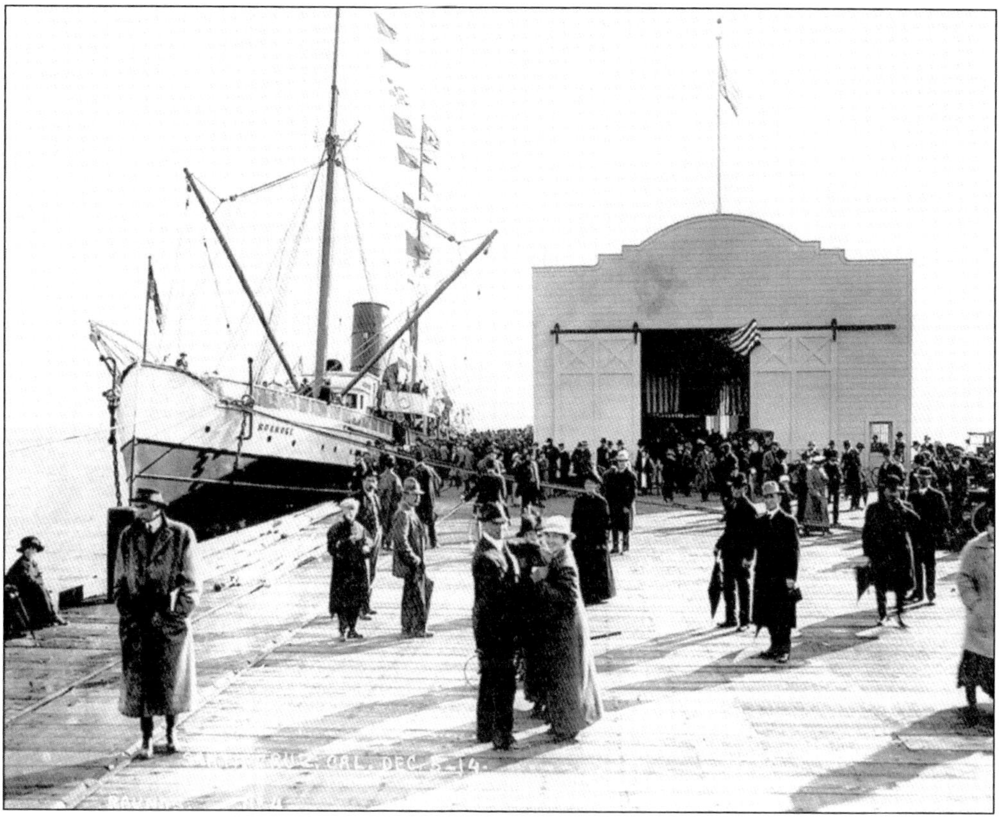

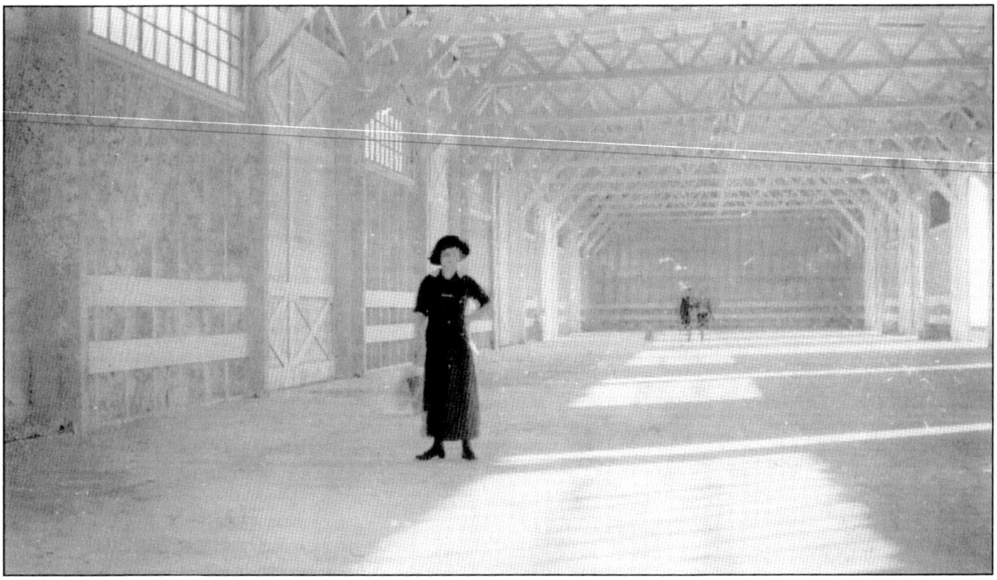

This rare interior image of the warehouse at the end of the wharf was also taken on opening day. The woman and couple are unidentified. The warehouse was intended for storage of items intended for export and for goods and supplies being delivered to Santa Cruz. Openings on both sides of the warehouse facilitated easy access from the ships. (City of Santa Cruz.)

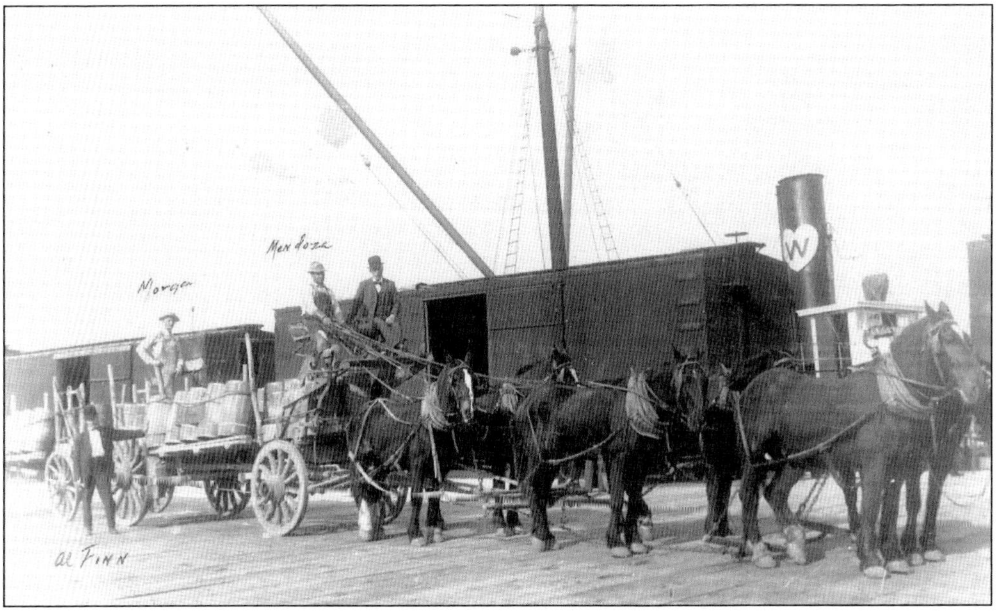

Three modes of transportation on the wharf are seen here up close and personal. Horse-drawn wagon, railroad boxcars, and steamship all blend together in this c. 1915 photograph. The wagon is carrying limekiln barrels from for the Cowell limestone operation at what is now the University of California, Santa Cruz. Identified, from left to right, are Aloysius G. "Al" Finn, then working for the San Francisco and Monterey Bay Steamship Co.; "Morgan"; and teamster Frank Mendoza. (Harold Van Gorder.)

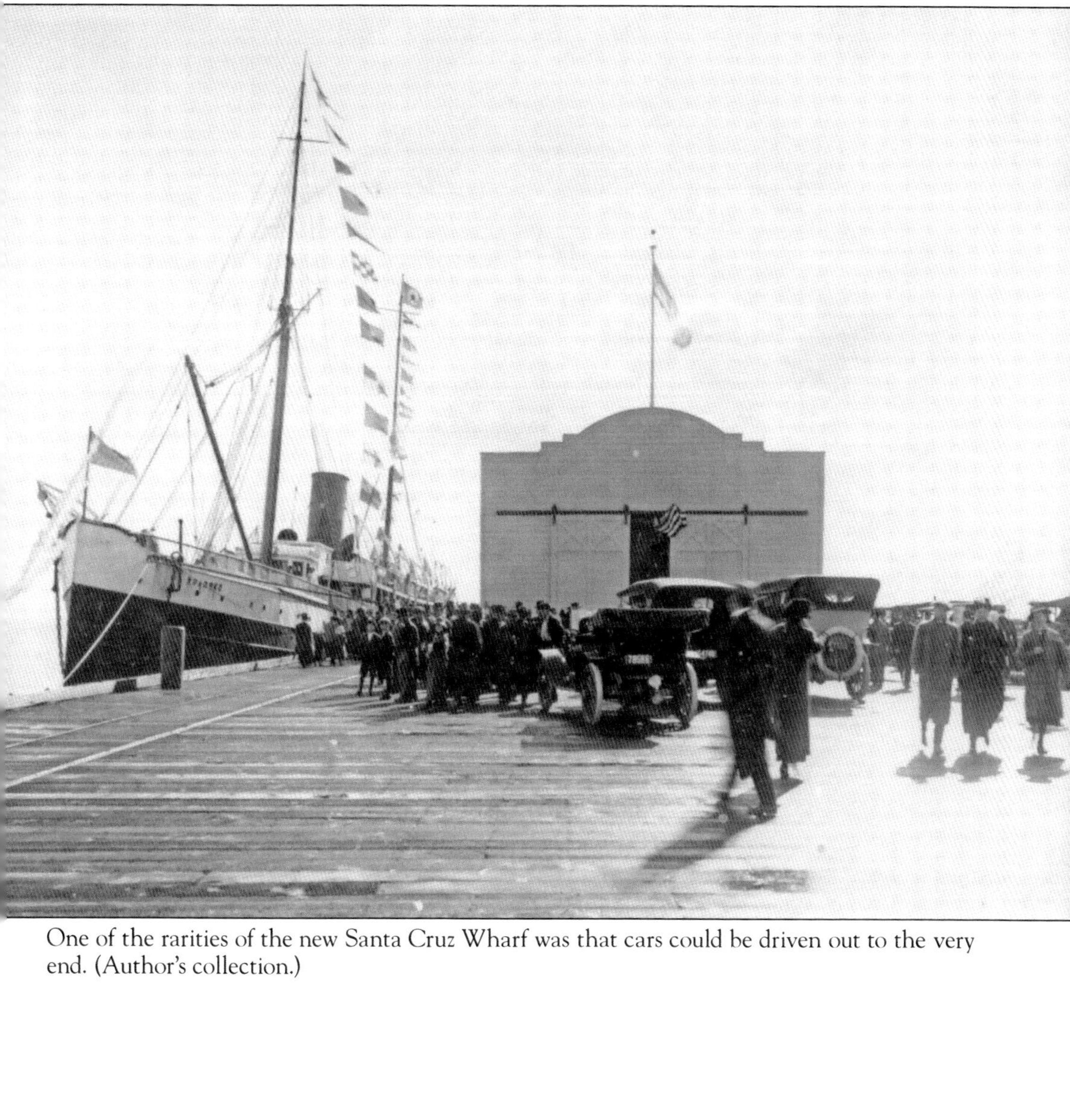

One of the rarities of the new Santa Cruz Wharf was that cars could be driven out to the very end. (Author's collection.)

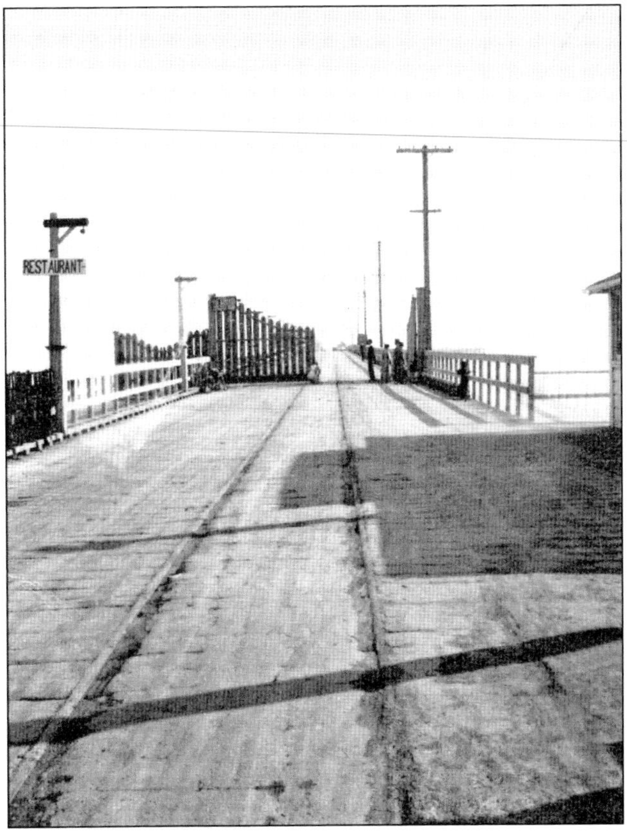

For many years, a gate marked the entrance to the wharf. It closed to business between 10:00 p.m. and 5:00 a.m. Santa Cruz waterfront promoter and legendary booster Fred Swanton actually had a vision of what the wharf could become as early as 1909. He advocated for a double-decker structure, with the top tier containing seats, a pavilion, and a bandstand and the bottom for the actual work of a wharf. He suggested charging 10¢ for entrance to the top tier, where a city band would be hired for the summer season. (Author's collection.)

In its early years, the wharf was bustling with enterprise. Here, three ships are docked at the wharf at the same time, railroad cargo cars await loading, and fishermen's nets are drying on the deck. (Author's collection.)

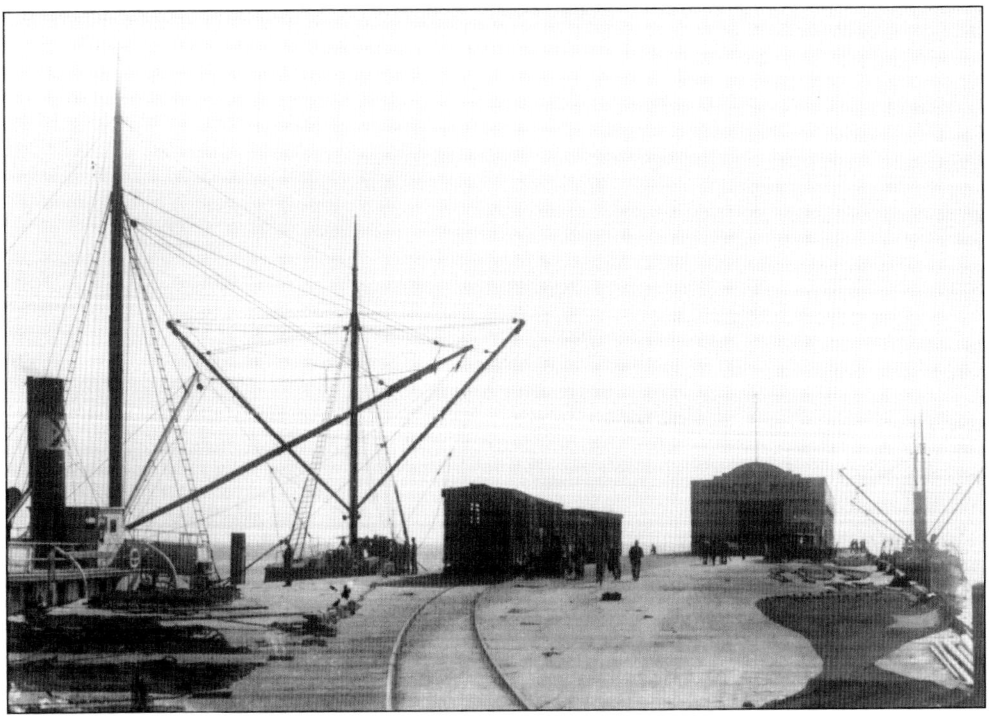

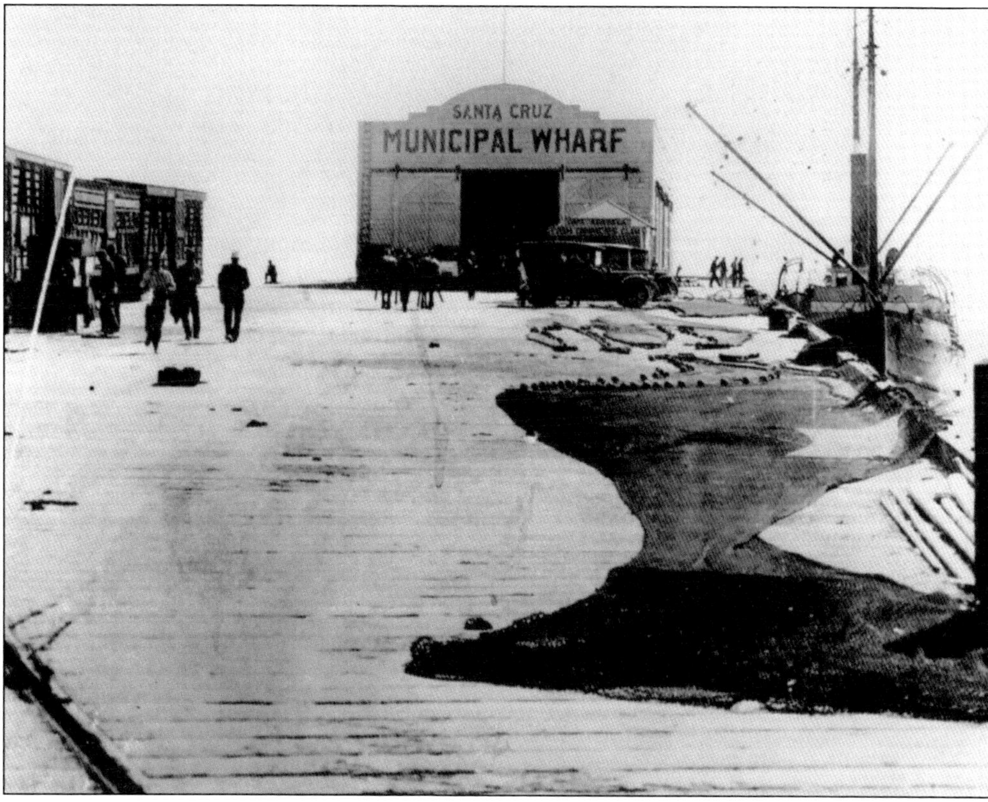

During the Alaskan gold rush of the 1890s, the *Corona* (above right and below) carried gold-seekers to and from the Klondike. In February 1896, the *Sentinel* reported: "The steamer *Corona* arrived today from Eureka with one more passenger than when she started. Off Point Arena, Mrs. A. C. Seidel gave birth to a baby girl." (Both, author's collection.)

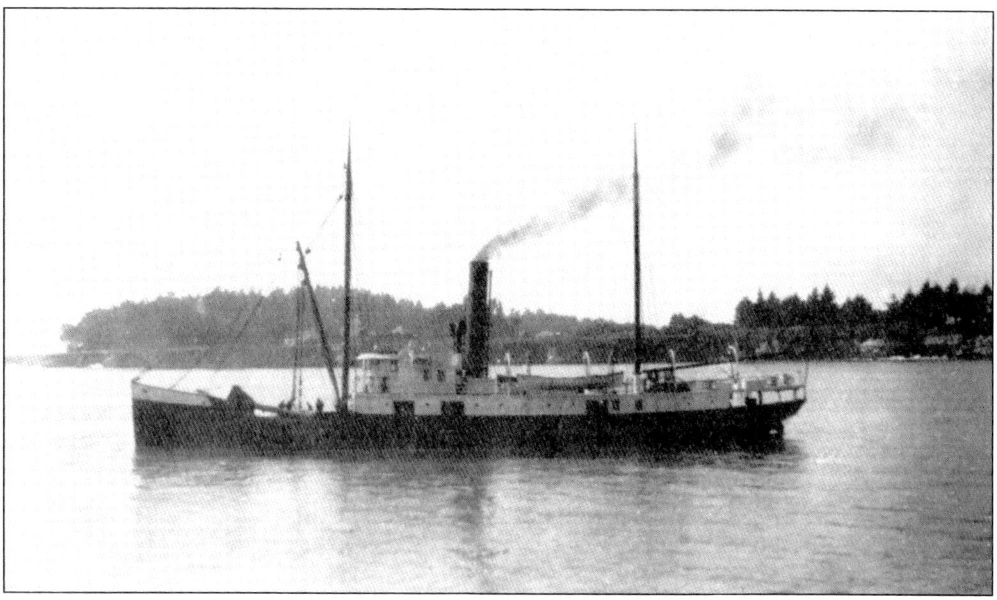

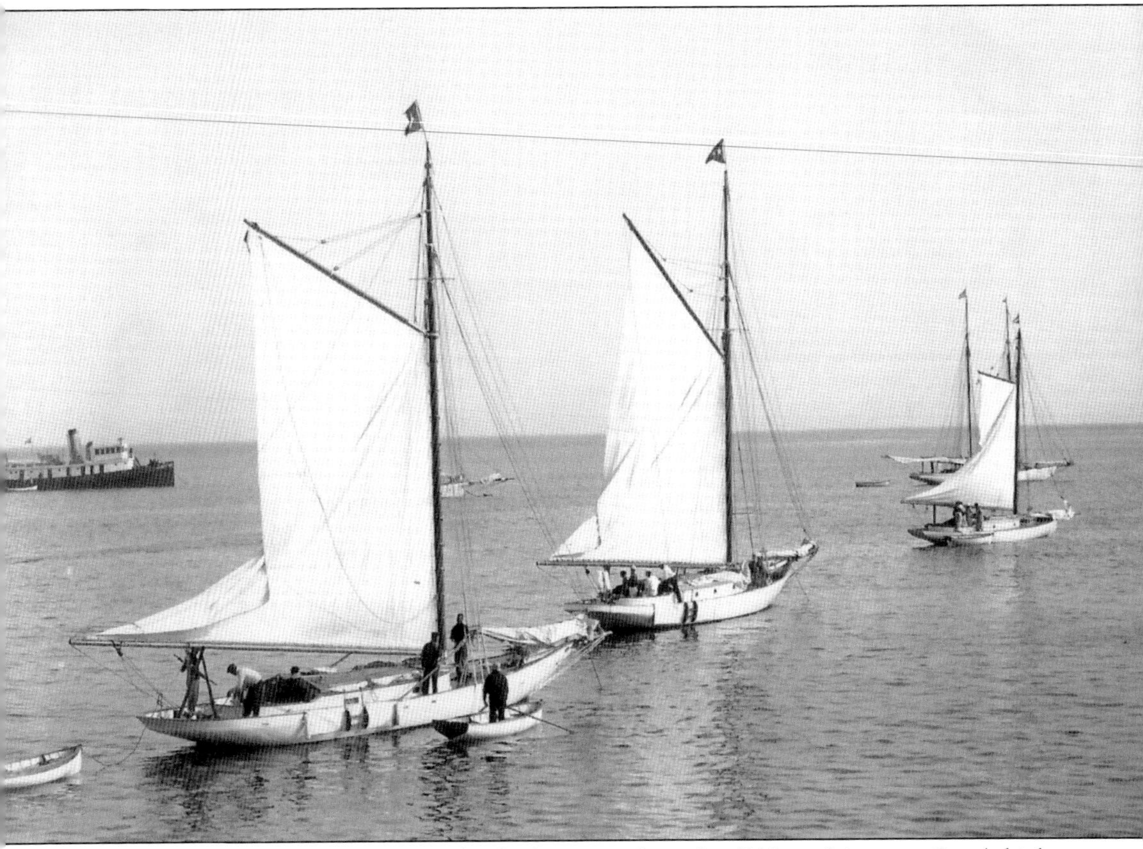

Yacht racing began in Santa Cruz for the haut monde in the 1910s on Monterey Bay (which was often referred to by locals as "Santa Cruz Bay"), primarily during the summer months, as Santa Cruz did not have a permanent harbor until 1964. The Santa Cruz Yacht Club was organized in 1928 and held its offices on the wharf until the 1960s. (Author's collection.)

Edward Flanders Ricketts was Nobel laureate John Steinbeck's best friend, sounding board, mentor, drinking companion, and perhaps most importantly, his collaborator, who provided the colorful and complex persona for Steinbeck's bittersweet portrayal of "Doc" in both *Cannery Row* and its sequel *Sweet Thursday*. He was also one of the most respected marine biologists on the Pacific coast. A recently discovered ledger book in the Santa Cruz Museum of Art & History revealed that Ricketts rented space on the Santa Cruz Wharf during the late 1920s. (California Views, Pat Hathaway Collection.)

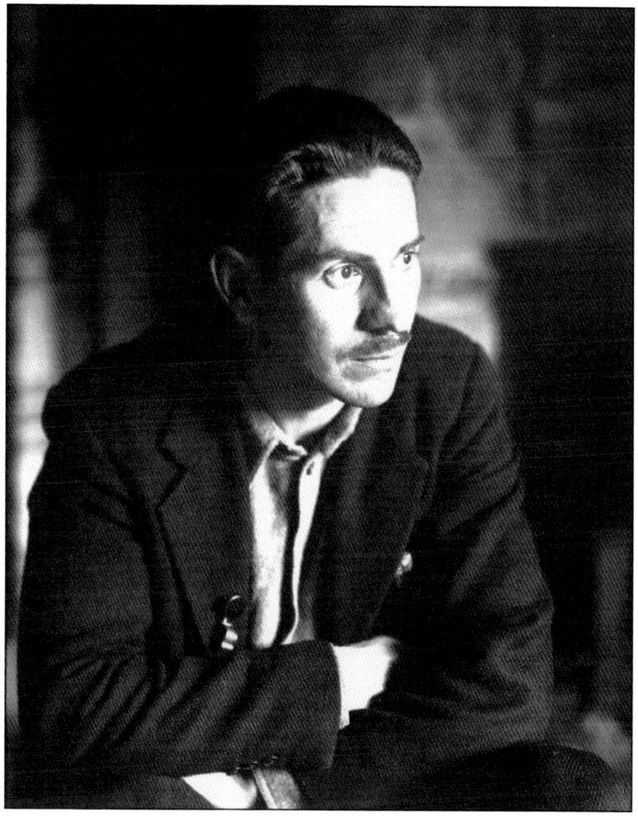

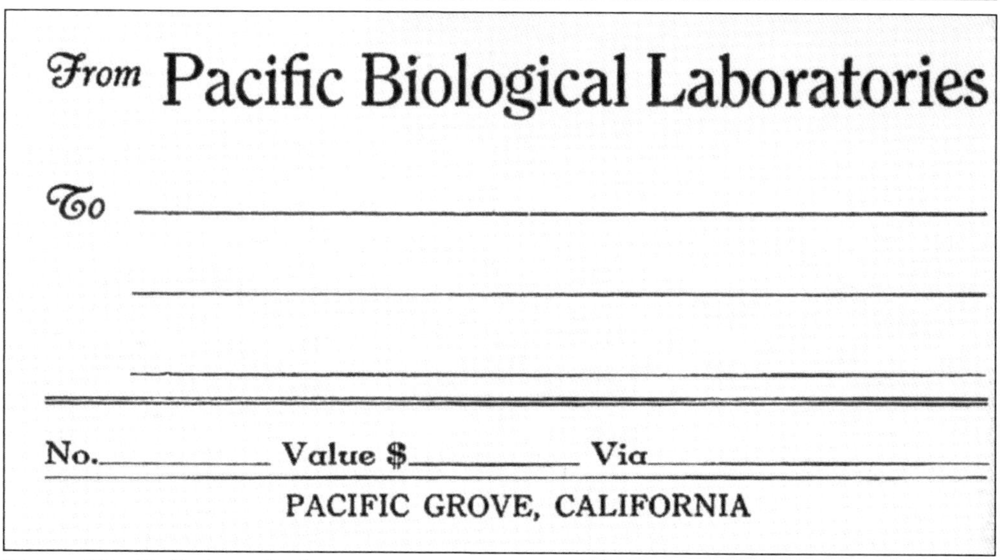

From **Pacific Biological Laboratories**

To ______________________________

____

____

No.__________ **Value $**__________ **Via**______________

PACIFIC GROVE, CALIFORNIA

Ricketts' Pacific Biological Laboratories, a specimen supply business, was initially located in Pacific Grove. His original partner, Albert E. Galigher, left the business in 1925. That May, Ricketts opened the Santa Cruz operation with an associate named William Martin. It lasted until January 1928, six months before Ricketts left his laboratory in Pacific Grove and purchased waterfront property at 740 Ocean View Avenue in New Monterey—later to be renumbered 800 Cannery Row. This image was a gift from Carolyn Swift. (Author's collection.)

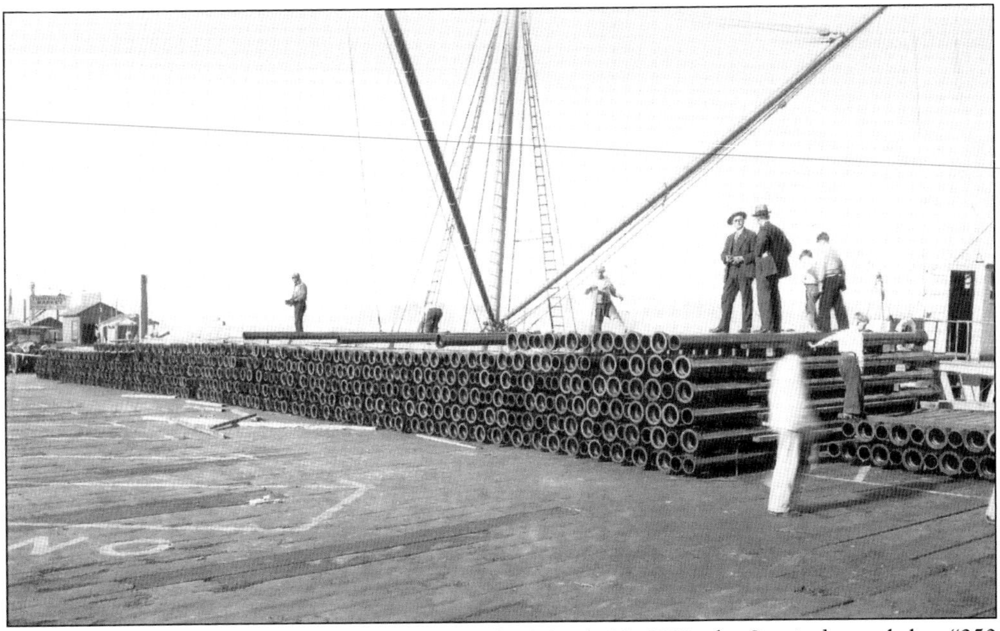

A schooner unloads sewage pipe in the 1930s. On March 23, 1932, the *Sentinel* noted that "250 tons of pipe for the Public Utilities system in the mountains" and "118 tons of gas pipe mains" had been delivered to the wharf in the same week. (Santa Cruz Museum of Art & History.)

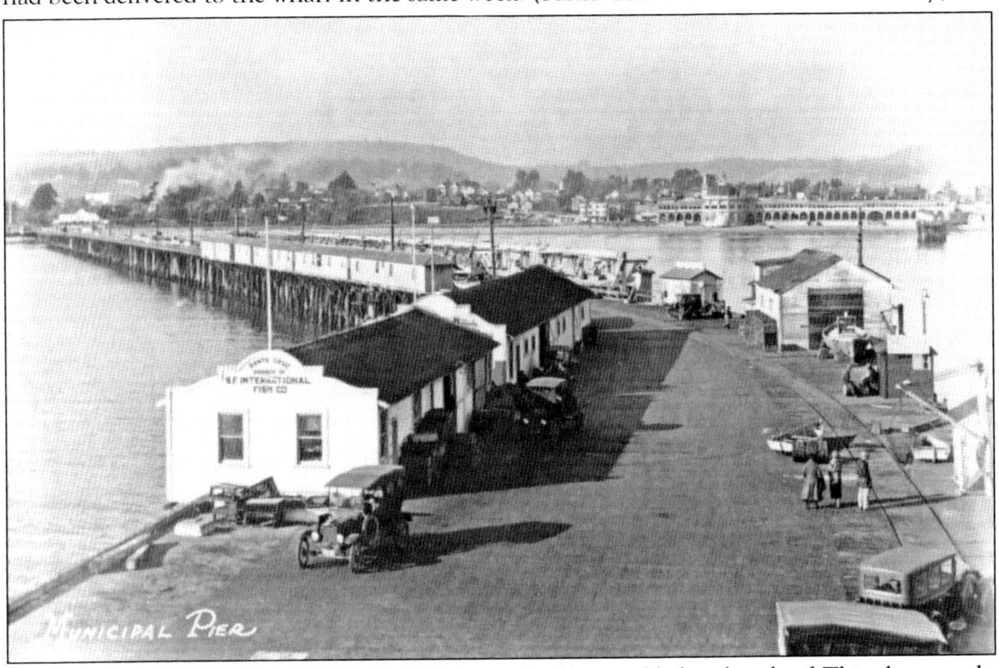

By the 1920s, a considerable amount of construction had been added to the wharf. This photograph, taken from atop the steamship warehouse, shows the San Francisco International Fish Company (foreground, left). The next row of buildings is believed to have housed Ricketts' Pacific Biological Laboratories. By then, the Italian fishing fleet had moved to the new wharf. A long row of davits lines the eastern side of the wharf (right, middle); across the street is a long line of storage sheds or mini-warehouses for the fishermen to store their nets and other fishing gear. (Author's collection.)

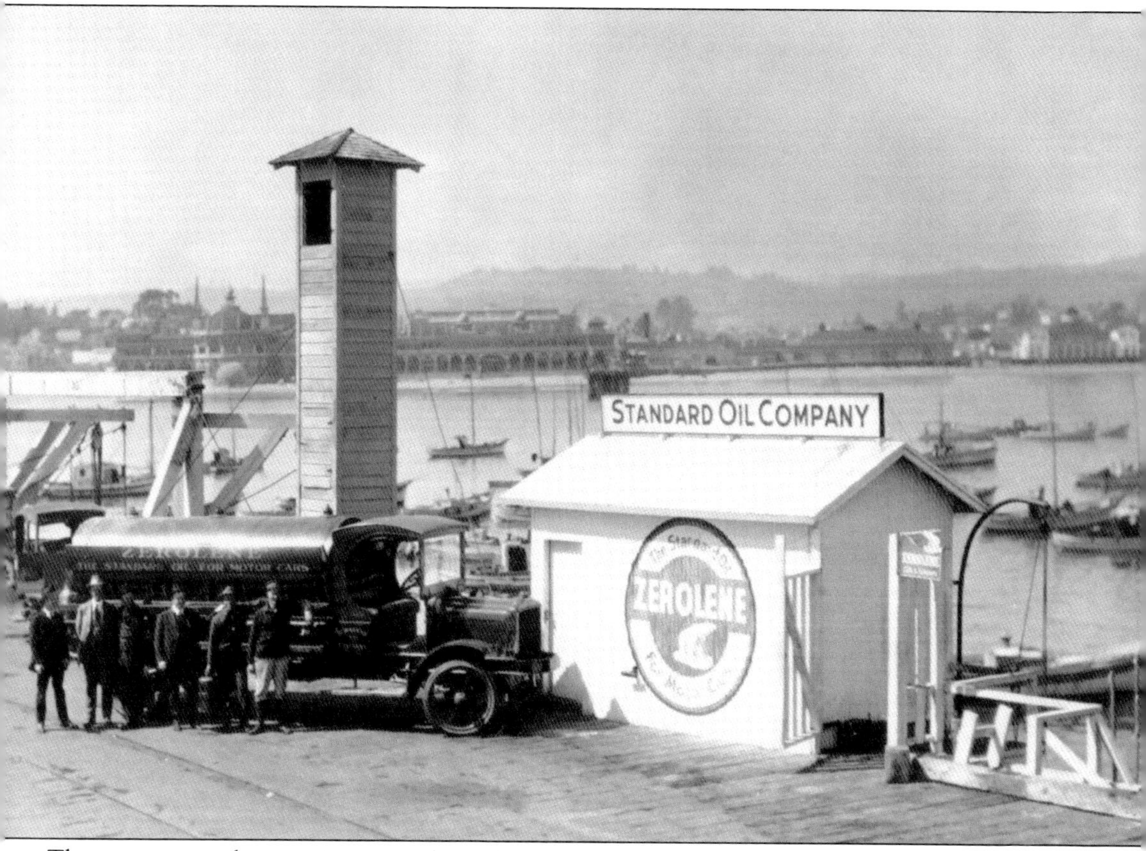

There were several gas stations near the end of the wharf that were used for fueling fishing boats and other vessels throughout the year. Malio Stagnaro took over the operation in the spring of 1921, when he was just 20 years old. Stagnaro once joked that during Prohibition, the rumrunners fueled up on one side of the pier and federal revenue agents fueled up on the other. Standard Oil produced Zerolene, an oil for both auto and marine engines subject to severe weather changes. (Author's collection.)

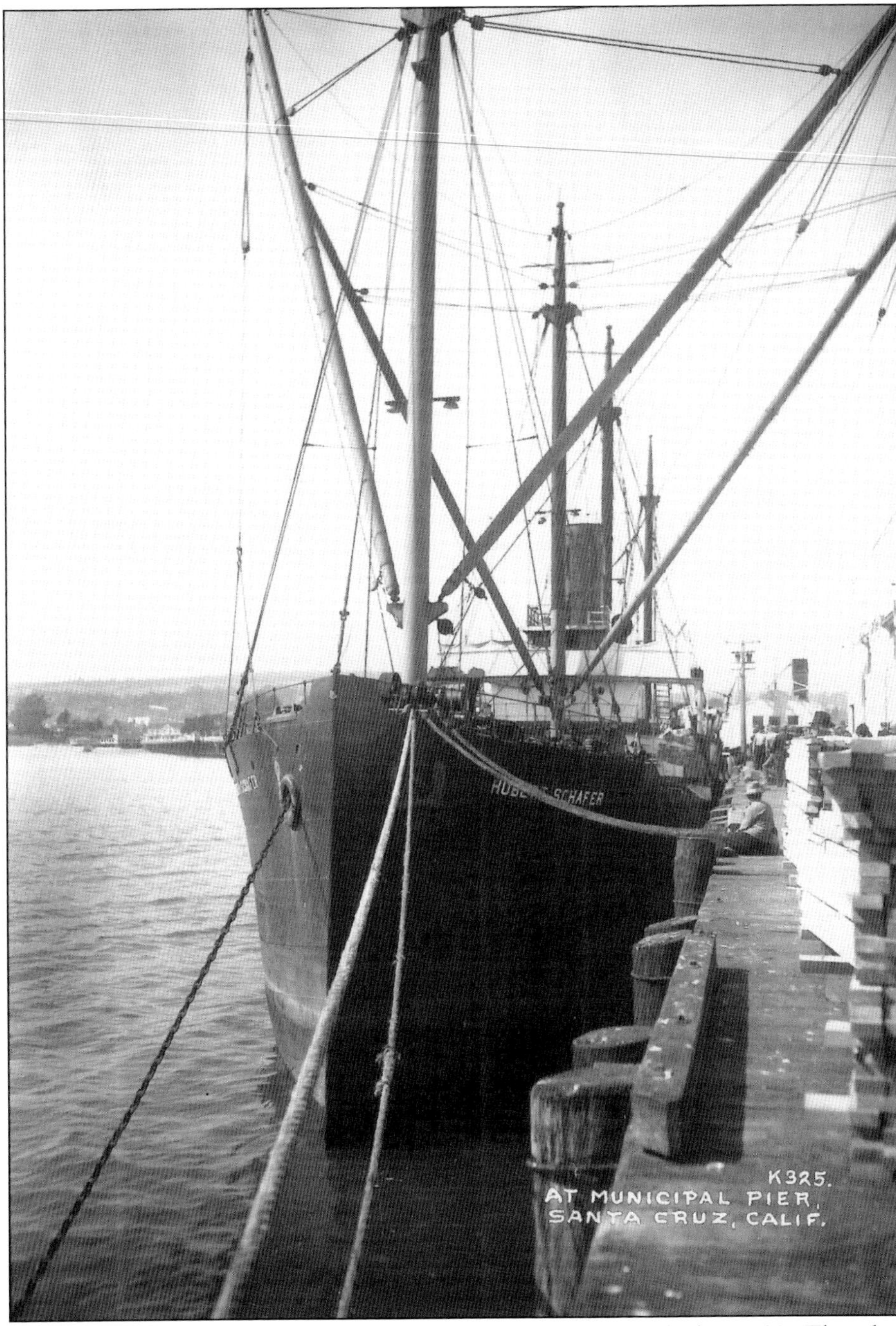

The schooner *Hubert Schafer* still unloaded freight on the wharf into the late 1930s. The schooner was part of a fleet owned and operated by the Schafer Brothers Logging Company out of Gray Harbor, Washington. It was one of the largest family-owned logging operations in the Pacific Northwest. Hubert Schaefer, the eldest brother and founder of the company, died unexpectedly in 1931. The ship was christened in his honor in 1932. That same year, more than 3 million linear feet of lumber were unloaded from 15 different schooners on the wharf. (Santa Cruz Museum of Art & History.)

Five

The Italian Fishing Colony

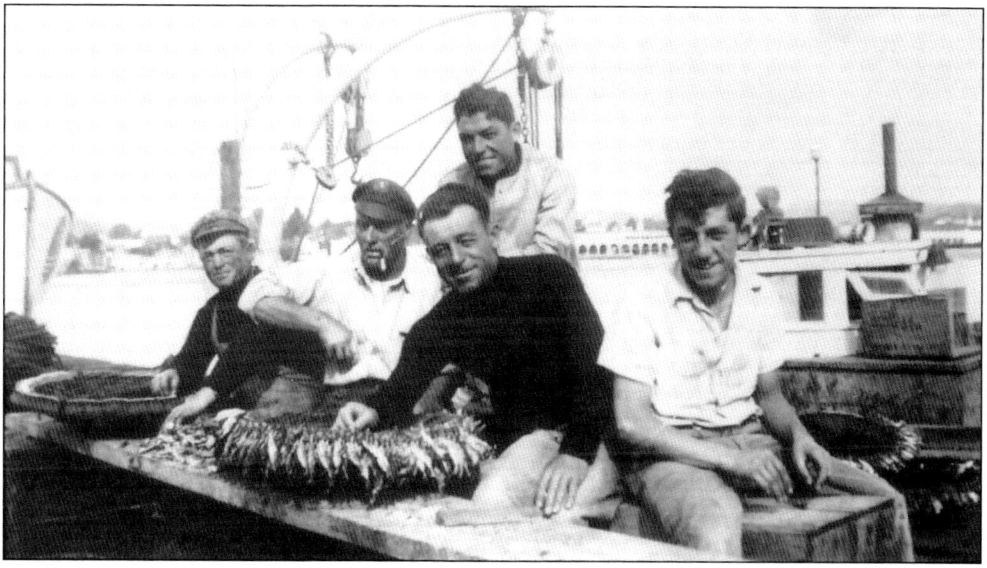

Within a few years following the completion of the municipal wharf, the Santa Cruz commercial fishing fleet, along with several wholesale and retail fish operations, began migrating to the newer venue. Between the late 1890s and 1920s, more than 60 families immigrated to Santa Cruz from a small fishing village on the Italian Riviera called Riva Trigoso. Employing traditional *lampara* nets from the Mediterranean and Portuguese "long lines" from the Azores, the *Rivani*—a complex network of families with last names that included Bassano, Bregante, Canepa, Carniglia, Cecchini, Dentone, Ghio, Loero, Olivieri, Stagnaro and Zolezzi—fished the waters of Monterey Bay for the better part of a century. Many of these founding fishing families from Riva Trigoso still have holdings on the Santa Cruz Municipal Wharf today. Here, from left to right, Joe Loero, Lawrence Zolezzi, Risho Ghio, Joe Stagnaro and Robert "Big Boy" Stagnaro prepare Portuguese long lines during World War II. (Author's collection.)

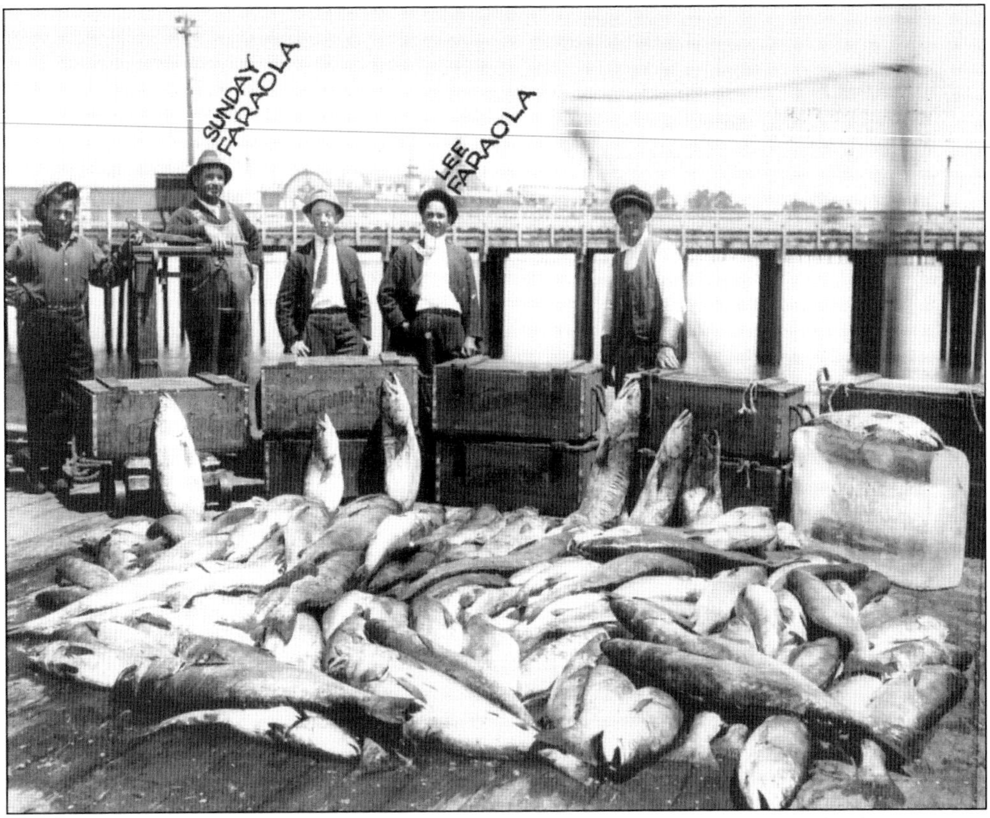

Italian fishermen arrived in the region as early as the 1860s, with small colonies in both Santa Cruz and Capitola. One early account in the *Santa Cruz Weekly Sentinel* noted that Italian fishermen off Soquel Landing (Capitola) were "endeavoring to make a haul in the kelp." In 1866, the paper reported that "Messrs. Antone & Co., the Italian Fishermen," had hauled a dead whale "into camp, near the Powder Company's Wharf." The Faraola family's roots on the waterfront stretched back to that era; John and Sunday Farcola's stepfather was Charles Garboni, a native of Italy and an early Santa Cruz fisherman. (Santa Cruz Seaside Company, Lee Faraola Collection.)

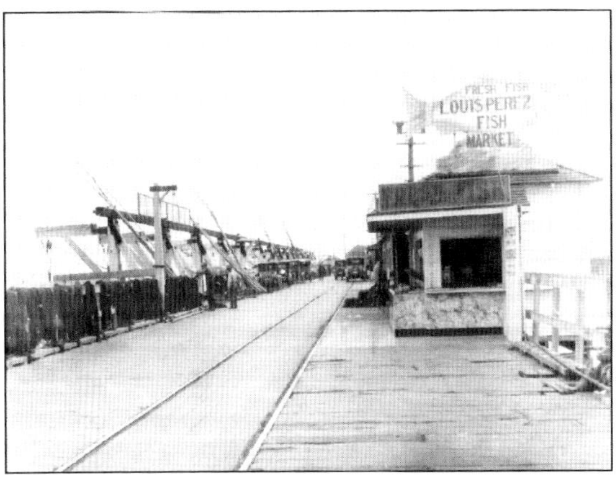

Louis "Big Jim" Perez eventually moved his operations from the Railroad Wharf to the new wharf. In 1926, according to waterfront reporter Ernest Otto, Perez executed an upgrade that included "enclosed glass display windows and refrigerator improvements" intended "to meet every sanitary convenience." The railroad line still ran out to the end of the wharf in the 1920s, and the row of davits (left), small crane devices used to pull fishing boats to the safety of the wharf, was in use throughout the year. (Author's collection.)

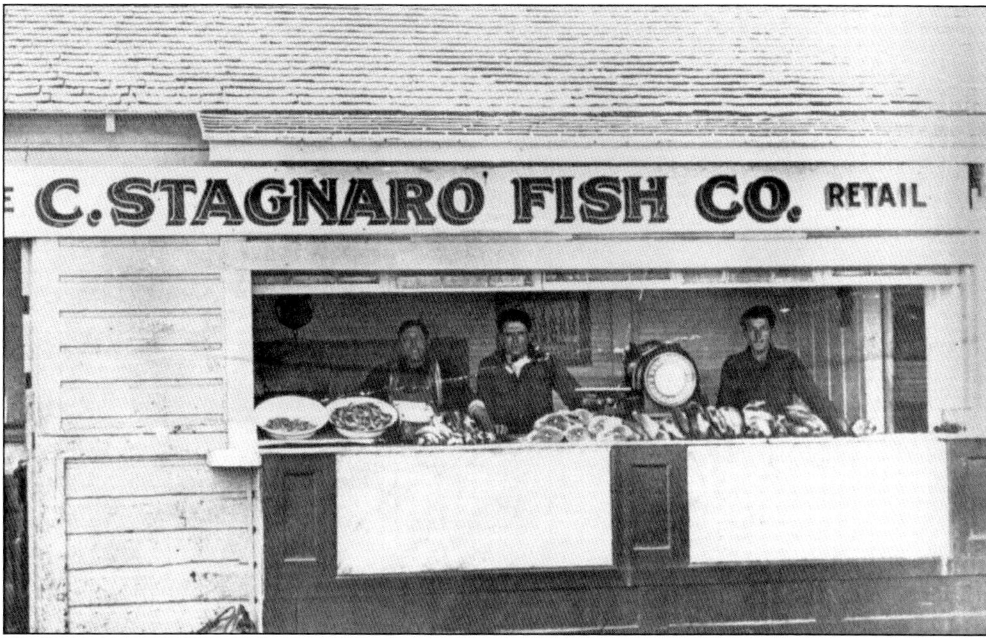

The C. Stagnaro Fish Company's retail fish market opened on the new wharf in 1916. The company's president and founder was Cottardo Stagnaro II (left), born in Riva Trigoso, Italy, who immigrated with his father and mother to the United States in 1898. At center are his younger brother, Malio J. Stagnaro, born in 1900, and his eldest son, Cottardo III "Babe," born in 1907. (Author's collection.)

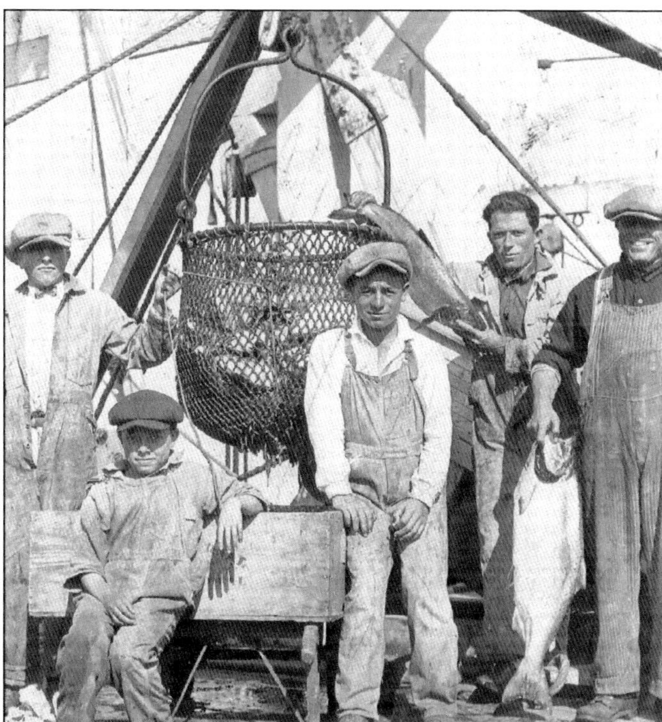

The C. Stagnaro Fish Company grew to employ many extended family members. Pausing from hauling in a load of rockfish and salmon in 1924 are, from left to right, John "Tisto" Loero, Batista "Dodie" Stagnaro, Cottardo "Risho" Ghio, Malio Stagnaro, and Cottardo Stagnaro II, directly across the street from the family's retail fish market. (Author's collection.)

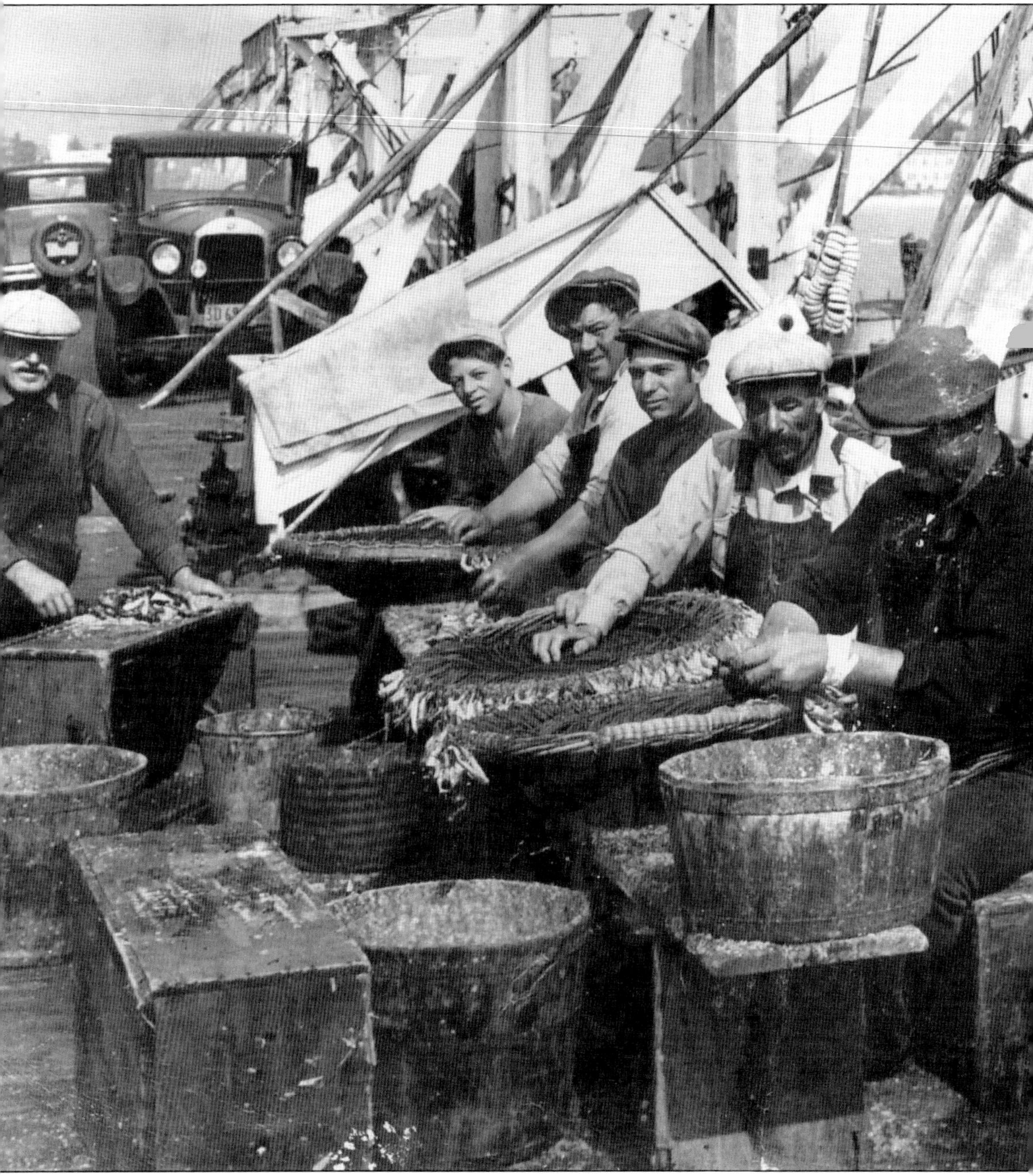

Italian fishermen provided a colorful daily presence on the burgeoning wharf. Here, Italian fishermen including, from left to right, Serafino Canepa, John Carniglia, unidentified, Johnnie Cecchini, Achille Castagnola, and Marco Carniglia bait Portuguese long-line baskets. (Author's collection.)

Prior to World War II, it was rare for women from the Italian fishing colony to actually work on the wharf, but they provided critical stability at home in what was called the "Barranca," the name given to the large Italian neighborhood west of Bay Street and north of Lighthouse Avenue on Santa Cruz's west side. Here, from left to right, Mary Bregante (Carniglia), "Marinin" Stagnaro Bregante, Clara Loero (Ghio), and Josephine "Josie" Loero are busy repairing nets. (Author's collection.)

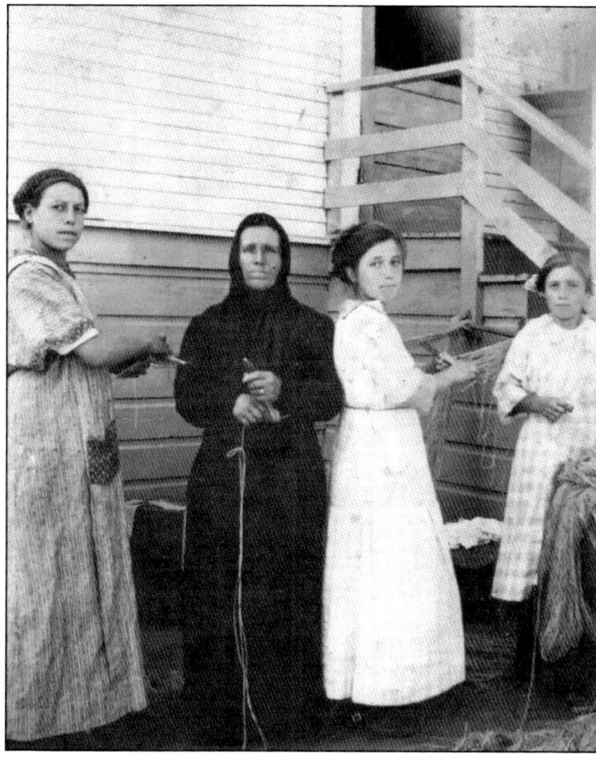

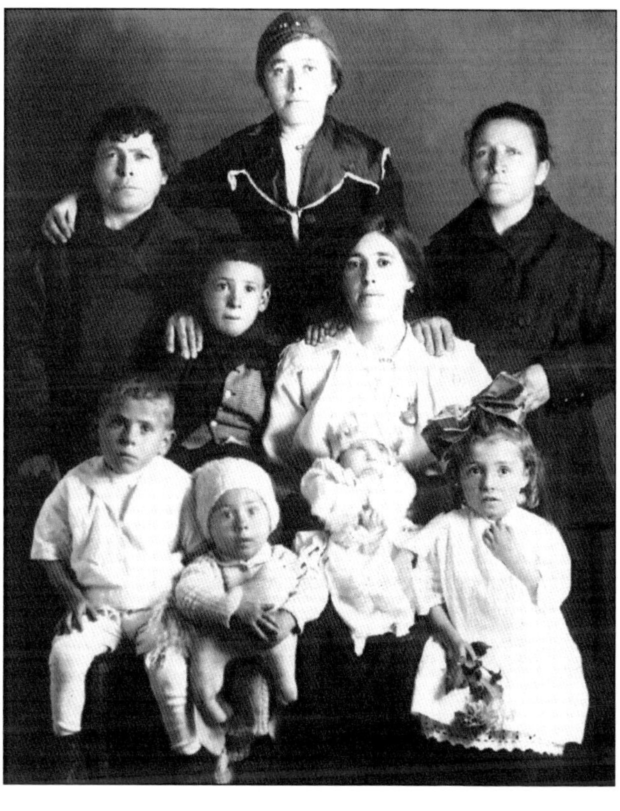

If the men dominated the waterfront, the women anchored the home life. Here are three generations of Santa Cruz Italian matriarchs and their children around 1920. Pictured, from left to right, are (front row) Batista "Lily" Ghio; Victor Cottardo Ghio; Vittorina "Sista" Ghio (Gemignani); and Yolanda "Lindy" Stagnaro (Dunn); (middle row) Steve "Ghigi" Ghio and his mother, Caterina; (back row) Vittorina Stagnaro Ghio; Clara Loero Ghio; and Celestina Stagnaro Loero. (Author's collection.)

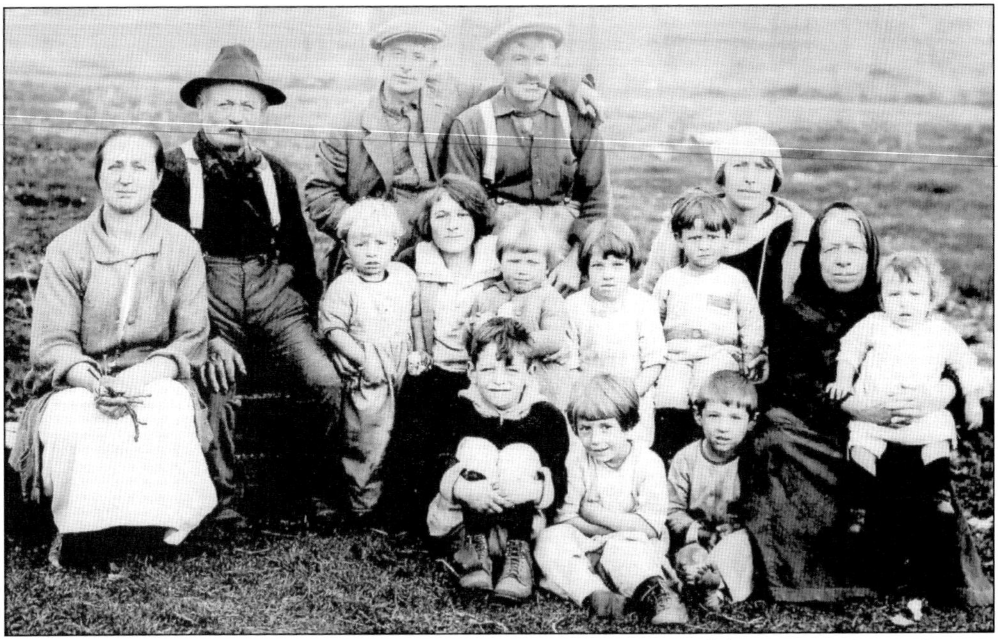

Another image shows the tight kinship patterns of the Genovese fishermen in Santa Cruz in the mid-1920s. Included in the photograph are members of the Carniglia, Giudice, Bregante, and Ghio families. (Author's collection.)

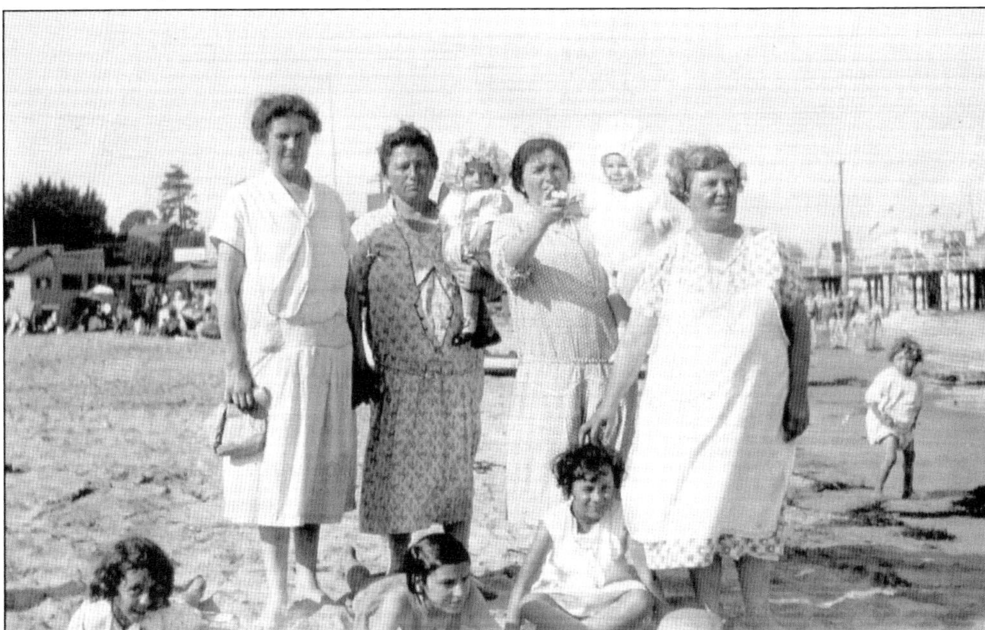

By the 1920s, Italian families were enjoying days at the beach. At the center of this photograph from the summer of 1929 are Batistina Loero Stagnaro (holding son Robert "Big Boy") and Jenny Zolezzi (holding daughter Lillian). At lower left is five-year-old Gilda Stagnaro, who would later become a mainstay on the wharf, and next to her is her cousin and namesake Gilda Zolezzi (Firenze). At the water's edge is Bettina "Betty" Stagnaro (Lamb). (Lillian Zappelli.)

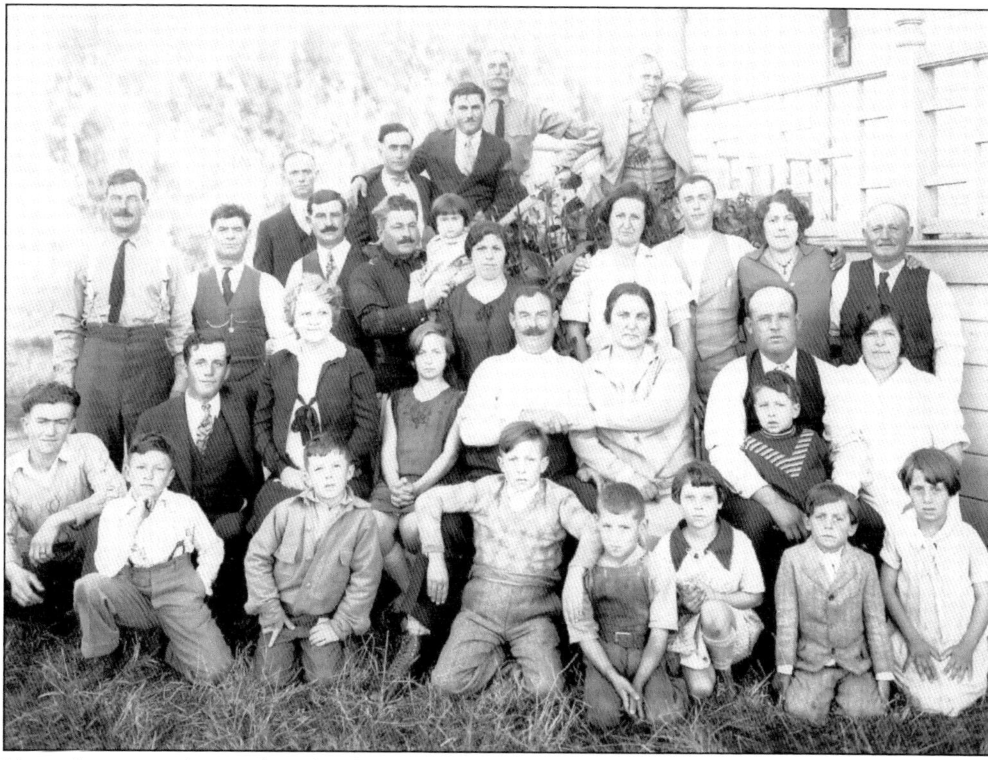

Visits from out-of-town friends often resulted in huge family gatherings and sit-down dinners in the Barranca on Sundays. This congregation around 1928 includes members of the Giudice, Stagnaro, Bregante, and Carniglia families. At lower left in the first row are John and Ernie Stagnaro; at far right in the second row are Mary and Marco Carniglia. Behind them are Steve and Alma Giudice and Giovanni Bregante. Giudice and Carniglia kids are scattered through the front row. (Author's collection.)

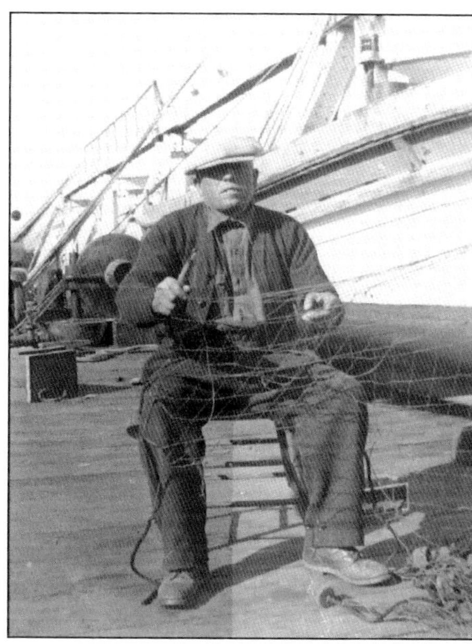

Cottardo Stagnaro II is seen here mending nets. Contrary to popular conception, he (not his father) was the founder of the C. Stagnaro Fishing Company. Born in Riva Trigoso in 1885, Stagnaro immigrated with his parents, Cottardo I and Maria Zolezzi Stagnaro, to Santa Cruz in 1898. He attended Bay View School for two years and then began fishing for the Perez and Faraola families locally, as well as in San Francisco, before forming a fishing partnership with Domenico Castagnola in his early 20s. He married his first cousin, Batistina Loero, in 1906. Five generations of the family have worked on the wharf. Note the circular water engine in the background. (Rex Walker.)

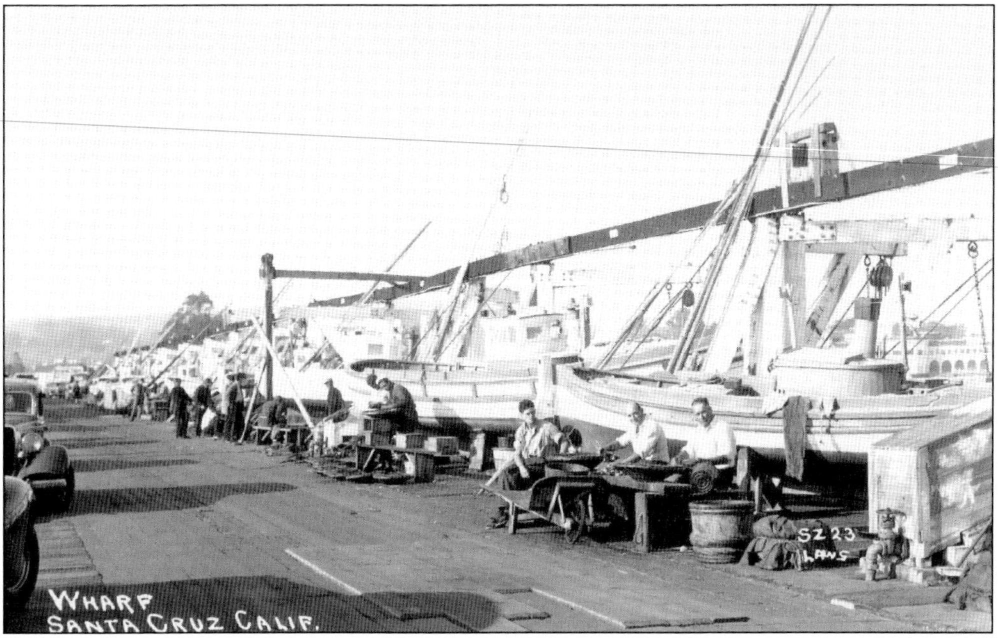

The wharf was literally covered with fishermen and fishing boats from the 1920s into the mid-1960s. *Sentinel* reporter Ernest Otto recorded catches on a near-daily basis in his reporting for the *Santa Cruz Sentinel.* (Author's collection.)

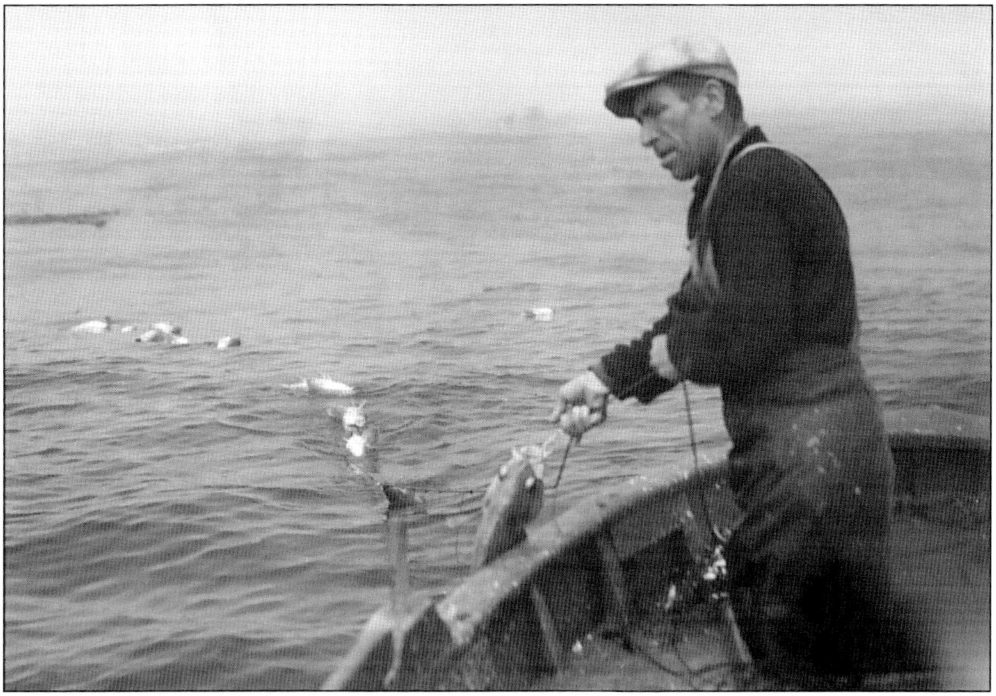

A very rare photograph shows a solitary fisherman, Steve Ghio, out at sea, pulling in rockfish from his long-line operation, in 1936. The fishermen would pull in the lines by hand, taking off the fish one by one as they re-coiled the line in their baskets. Their arms were like steel and their hands like sinew. (Santa Cruz Seaside Company.)

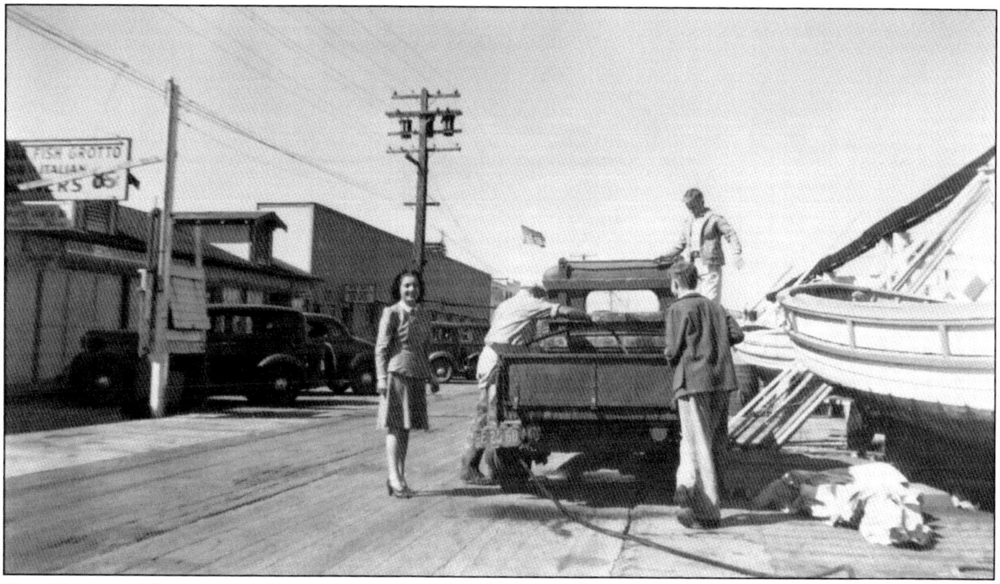

Families would occasionally come to the wharf to drop by supplies (or lunches) and visit. By the 1930s, most families owned trucks to haul nets, fishing baskets, and bait and would deliver fish to markets off the wharf. (Santa Cruz Museum of Art & History.)

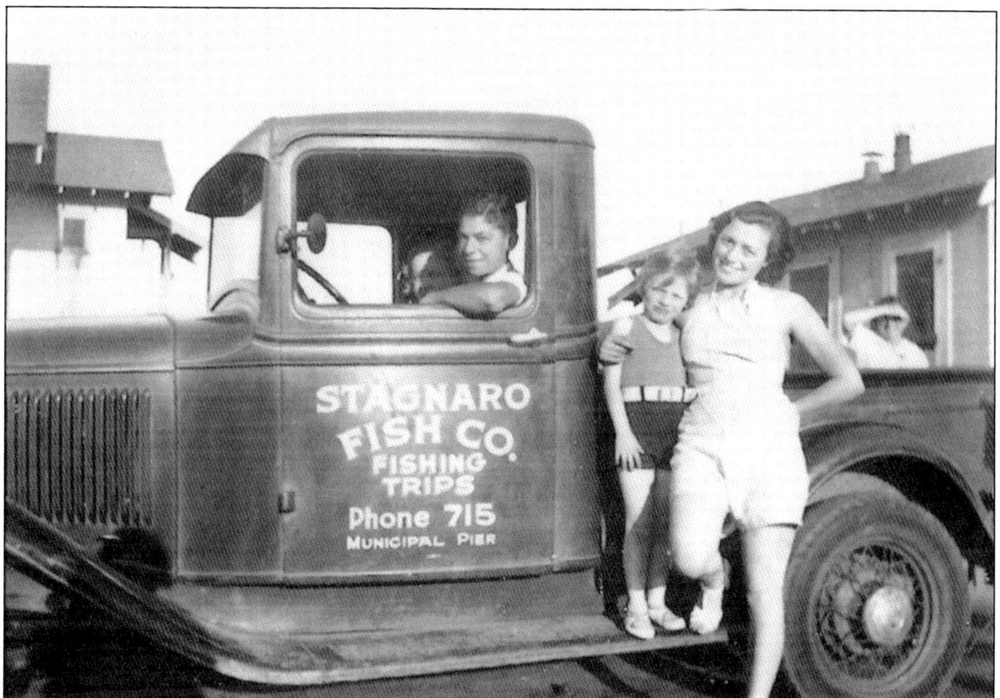

The C. Stagnaro Fish Company expanded its operations to include both commercial and sportfishing boats in the 1930s. Here, Joe Stagnaro drives the family fish truck with an unidentified passenger, his sister Lindy with her arm around an unidentified young woman, and his mother, Batastina Stagnaro, in the background. (Author's collection.)

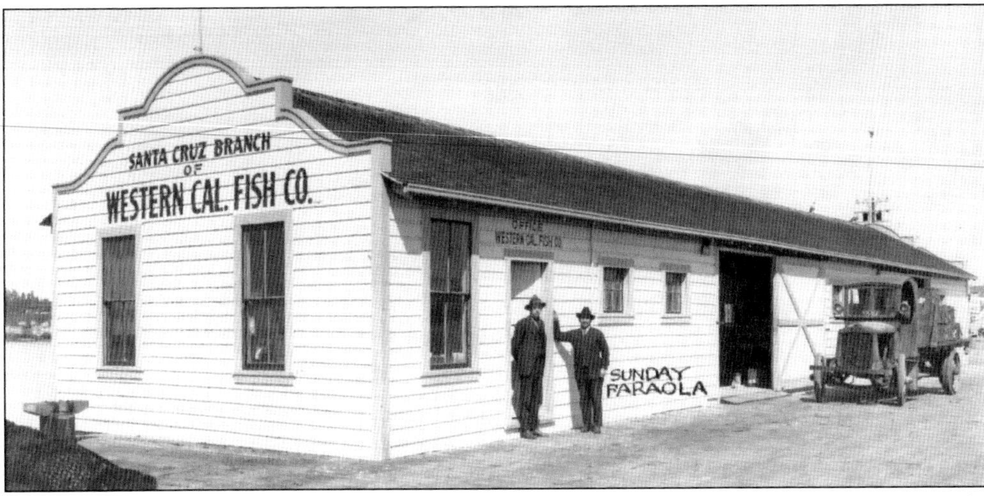

The Western California Fish Company (WCFC) of San Francisco purchased the holdings of the Faraola family in 1915 and relocated to the new wharf. Sunday Faraola is pictured here with WCFC partner Theodore Weissick in 1921. Both John and Sunday Faraola continued working for the company into the 1920s. In 1926, Sunday Faraola went to work for the Paladini Fish Company. (Santa Cruz Seaside Company, Lee Faraola Collection.)

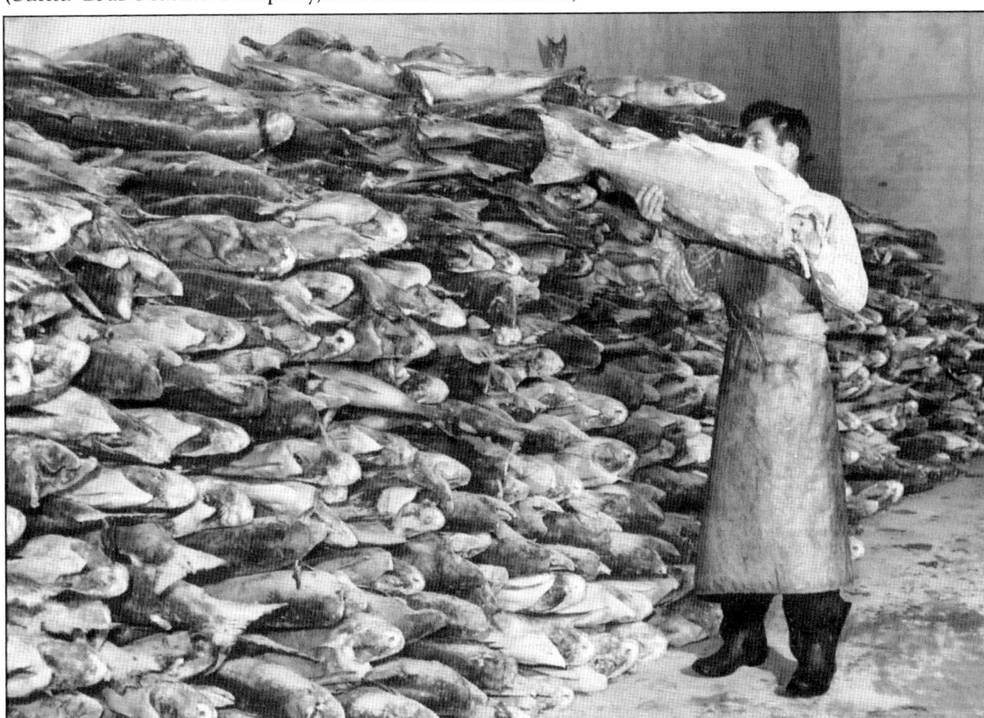
Glazed salmon are being stacked by Tisto Loero in the walk-in freezer of the General Fish warehouse at the end of the wharf. Immediately after being cleaned, whole salmon were dipped into briny ice water (with sugar added) to form layers of ice on the fish. The process was repeated several times until there was a quarter-inch coat of ice sealing the fish and keeping it "fresh" for up to six months. Italian fish merchants on the wharf developed the practice and called glazed salmon "logs." (Santa Cruz Seaside Company.)

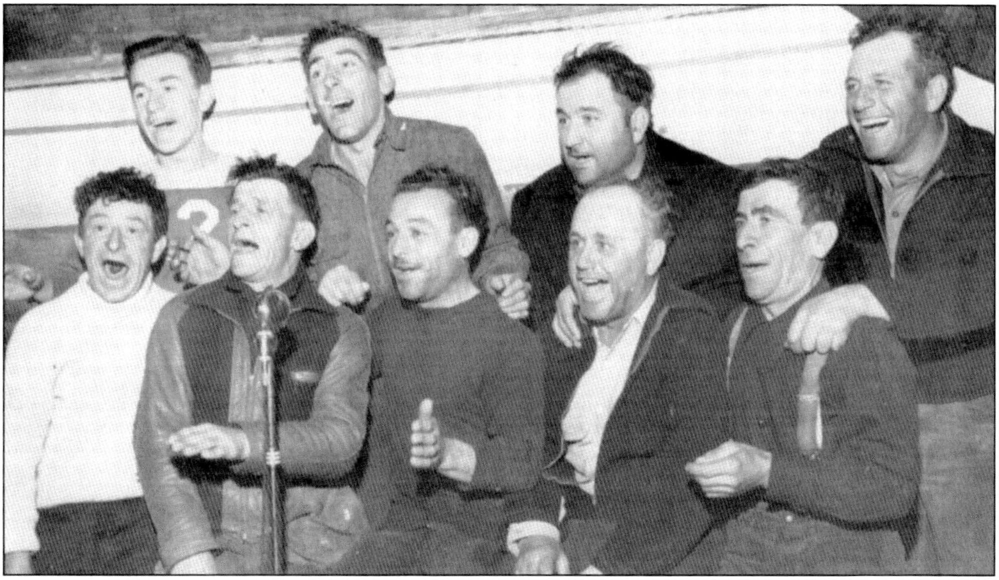

Members of the Ghio fishing family rehearse for the annual "Day on the Bay" celebrations held annually in the early 1940s to promote Santa Cruz as a tourist and fishing mecca for more than 200 visiting journalists. The trick to getting the fishermen to perform, according to Skip Littlefield, was to have enough red wine available to loosen up their pipes—but not too much. Pictured, from left to right, are (front row) Manuel, Cottardo "Trub," Battista "Risho," Tom "Bodega," and Steve Ghio; (back row) Johnnie, Batista "Lily," Tony, and John "Lefty" Ghio. (Santa Cruz Seaside Company.)

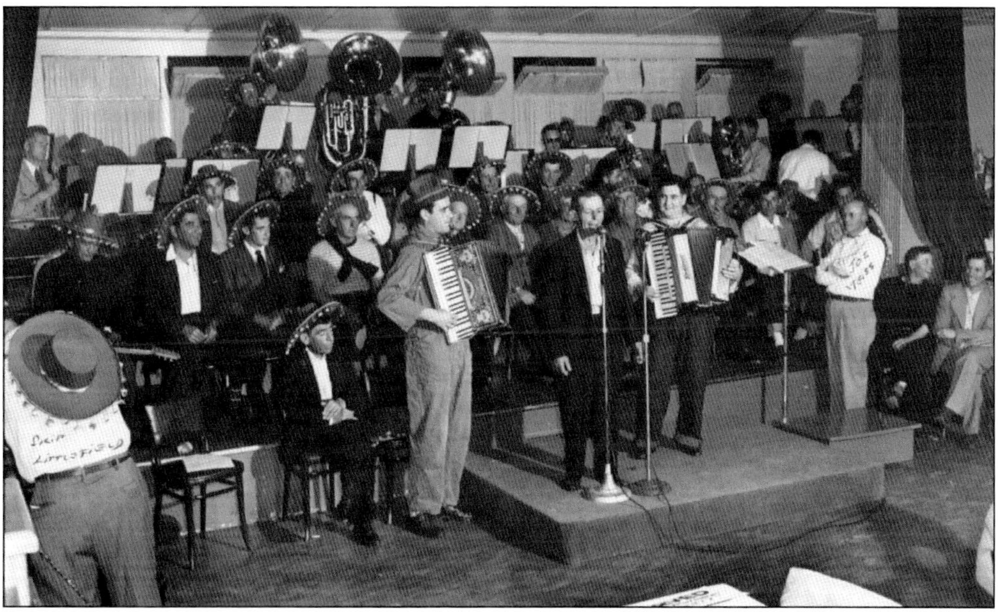

An actual performance of the Fishermen's Chorus, as it was dubbed, features legendary Dave Ferrari on accordion (left), Joe Bogero on accordion (right), promoter Skip Littlefield (with his back to the left), and musical director Joe Weiss, who, according to Littlefield, was placed in charge "knocking off the rougher barnacles" of the performance. Maurice Kealoha Krauser is at far left playing the Hawaiian steel guitar. (Santa Cruz Seaside Company.)

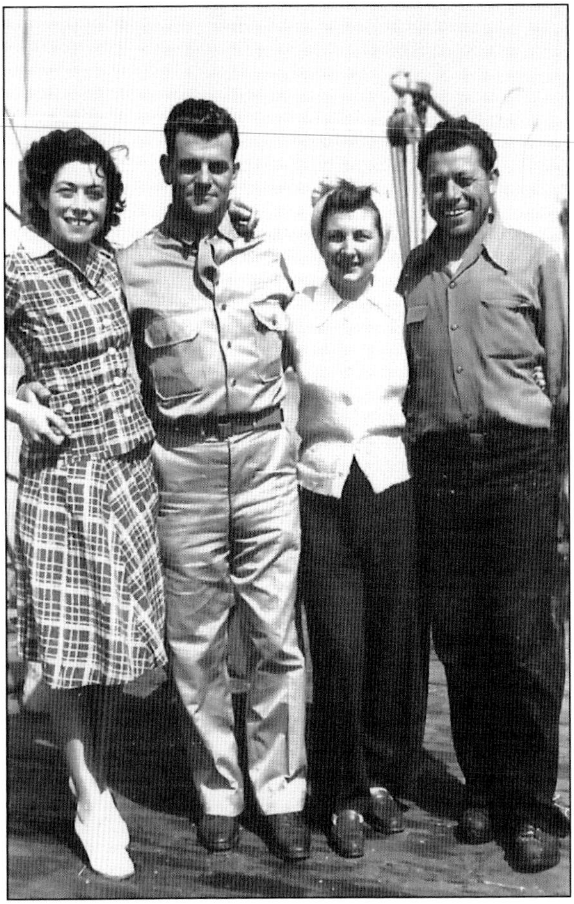

During World War II, the wharf provided a warm welcome for returning and visiting servicemen and women. Siblings Estrella (left) and Dodie Stagnaro (right) bookend close family friends Paul and Josephine Pappas. Paul was discharged from the Army as a sergeant in October 1945. (Author's collection.)

At the beginning of World War II, so-called enemy aliens of Italian, Japanese, and German descent were targeted by the Western Defense Command of the US Army for a variety of restrictions. Many members of the Santa Cruz Italian fishing colony had never received their citizenship. Veteran Santa Cruz fisherman Steve Ghio—who had several sons serving in the armed forces—was one of a dozen Italian fishermen who were barred from the wharf. In a front-page article with banner headlines, the *Santa Cruz Sentinel* declared: "Fishermen with 23 Sons in Army and Navy Are Bound to Wharf While Boats Lie Idle and Sea Food Is Needed." (Author's collection.)

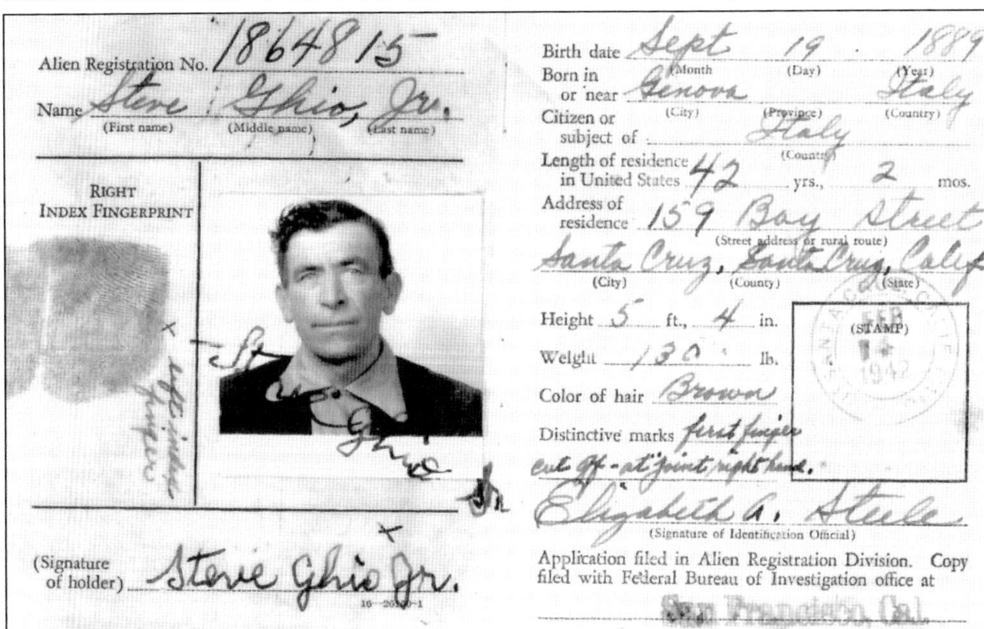

Alien Registration No. 1864815
Name Steve Ghio, Jr.
(First name) (Middle name) (Last name)

RIGHT INDEX FINGERPRINT

left index finger

(Signature of holder) Steve Ghio Jr.

16—26150-1

Birth date Sept 19 1889
(Month) (Day) (Year)
Born in or near Genova Italy
(City) (Province) (Country)
Citizen or subject of Italy
(Country)
Length of residence in United States 42 yrs., 2 mos.
Address of residence 159 Bay Street
(Street address or rural route)
Santa Cruz, Santa Cruz, Calif
(City) (County) (State)

Height 5 ft., 4 in.
Weight 130 lb.
Color of hair Brown
Distinctive marks first finger cut off - at joint right hand.

(STAMP)

Elizabeth A. Steele
(Signature of Identification Official)

Application filed in Alien Registration Division. Copy filed with Federal Bureau of Investigation office at San Francisco, Cal.

16—26150-1

In February 1942, Celestina Stagnaro Loero, the author's great-grandmother, was designated an "enemy alien" by the Western Defense Command. Although she had lived in Santa Cruz for four decades and was 74 years old, she was informed by federal agents that she had 48 hours to move herself and her belongings inland of Highway 1 (Mission Street, in Santa Cruz) or she would be subject to immediate arrest. Two of her grandsons were serving in the US Navy at the time. (Author's collection.)

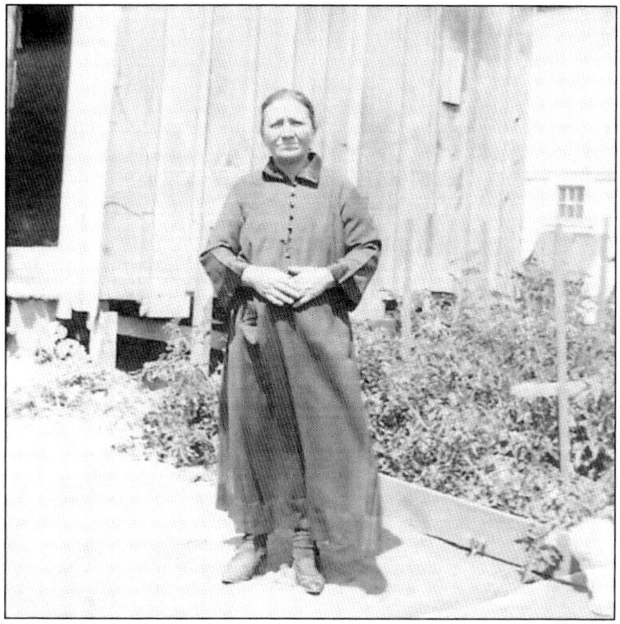

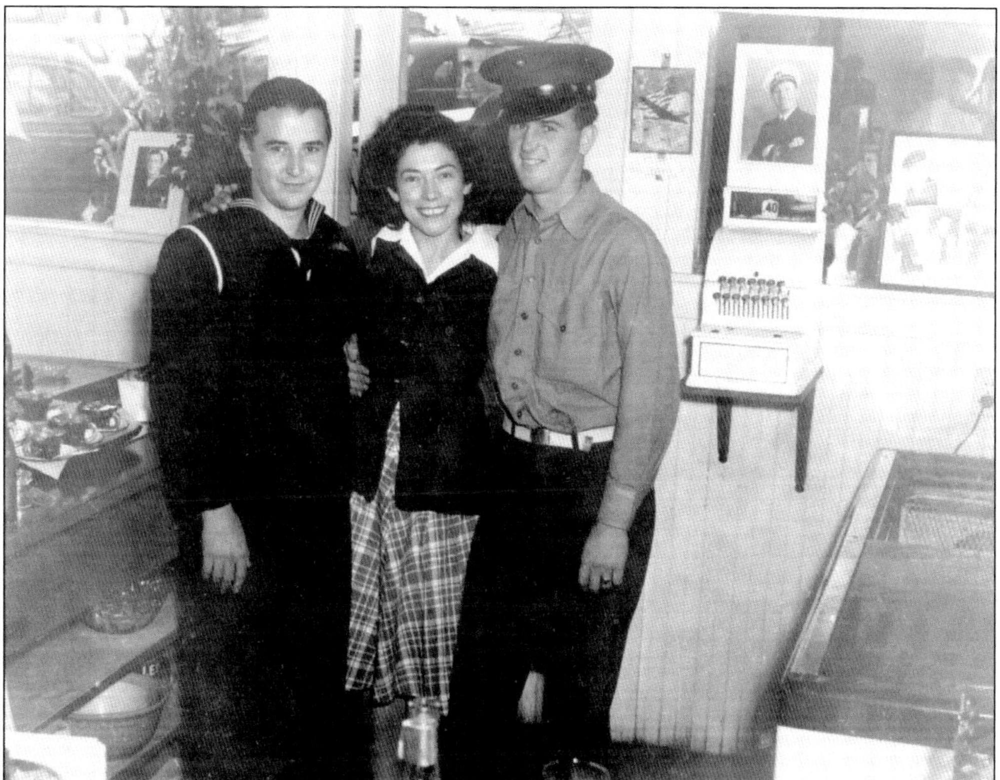

Members of Italian fishing families proudly displayed pictures of their family members in uniform at wharf businesses. Estrella Stagnaro poses with two unidentified servicemen with photographs of her brother Stago and uncle Malio, both in their Navy uniforms, in the background. (Author's collection.)

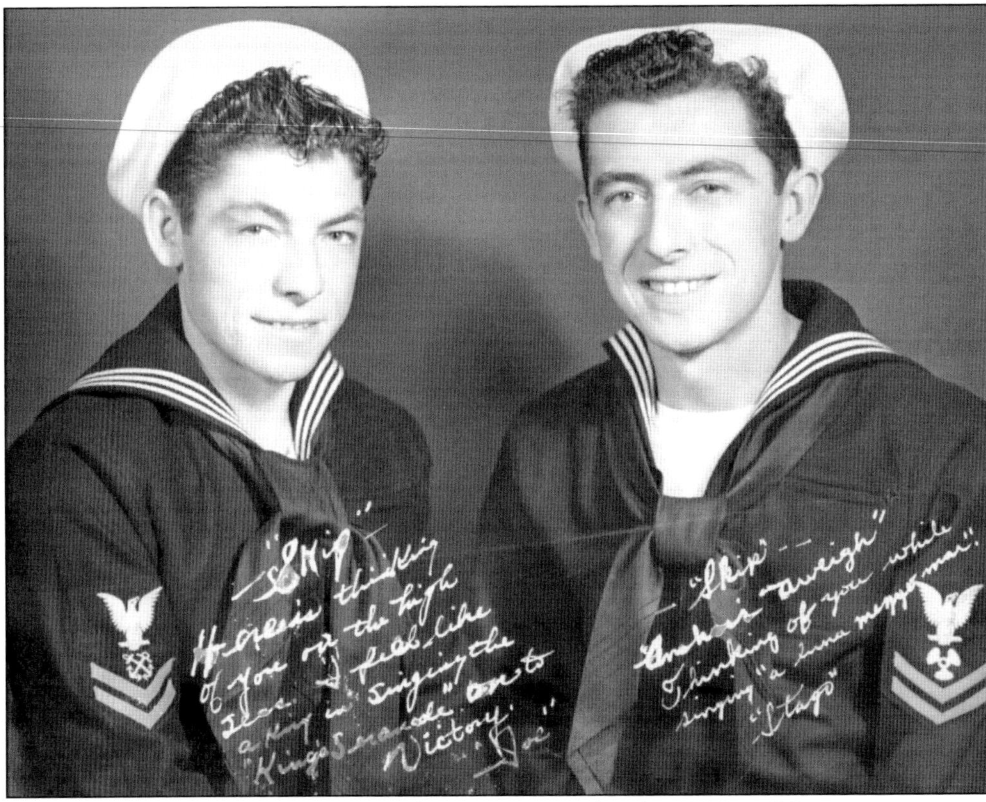

This portrait of the author's uncles Joseph E. Stagnaro and Malio H. "Stago" Stagnaro was signed to Skip Littlefield. Joe writes: "Here's thinking of you on the high seas. I feel like a king in singing 'The King's Seranade' on to victory." Stago writes: " 'Anchors Aweigh.' Thinking of you while singing 'A Luna Mezzo Mare.' " Both sang for Littlefield in the Day on the Bay celebrations. (Santa Cruz Seaside Company.)

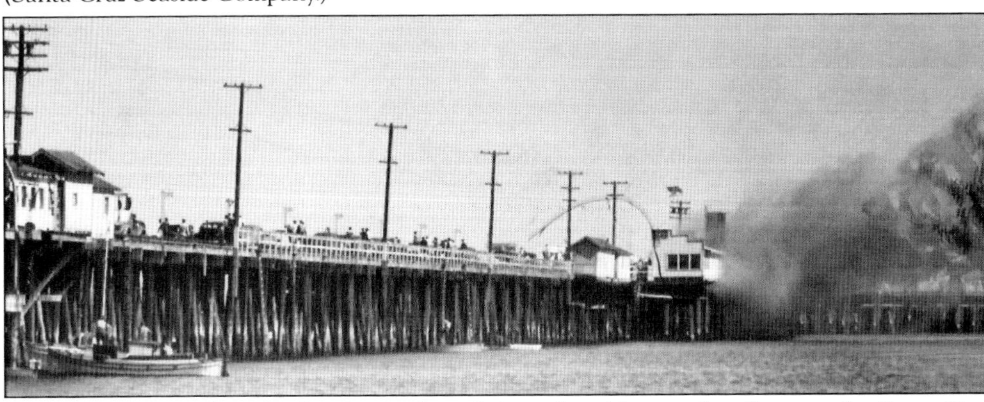

A series of fires on the wharf in September 1941 produced banner headlines in the *Santa Cruz Sentinel* proclaiming: "Suspect Sabotage in Wharf Fires." The main blaze, depicted here, threatened to consume the entire wharf. Italian-owned businesses were thought to be the subject of the arson. All of the fires were put out by Italian fishermen, who stationed their boats under the wharf with fire hoses dousing the flames. There was one injury: 10-year-old Johnny Ghio was overcome with exhaust fumes while assisting his father on his boat. He survived. Carelessly tossed cigarette butts were eventually determined to be the cause of the fires. (Author's collection.)

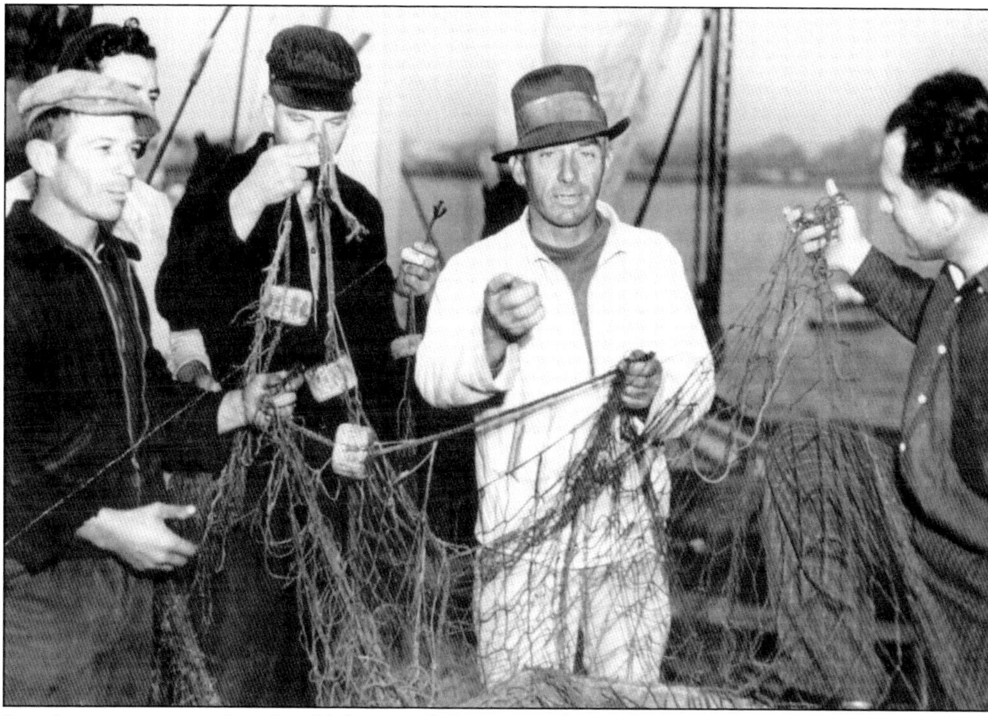

In calmer times, popular wharf fishermen Johnnie Cechinni (left), Lawrence Zolezzi (center), and Malio Stagnaro (right) pose for photographers while mending nets. The Italian fishermen were popular subjects for photographers visiting Santa Cruz looking for local color. This image was sent out nationwide. (Author's collection.)

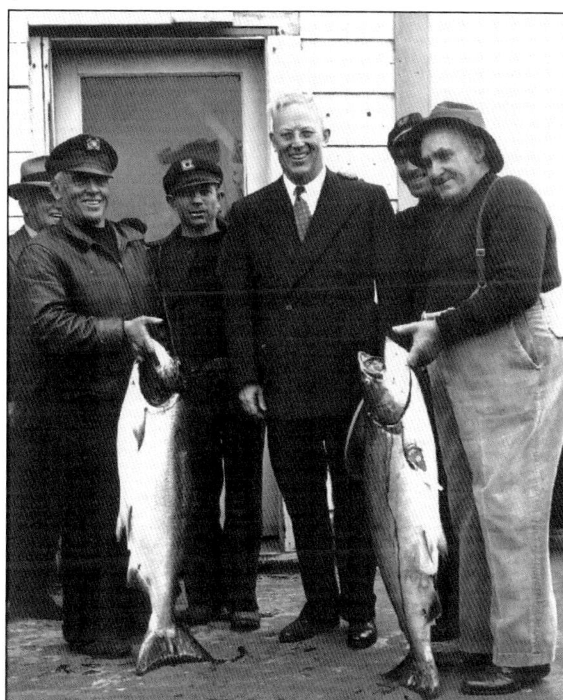

The wharf was always a popular setting for politicians to get their photographs taken with fishermen—even for a future chief justice of the Supreme Court. As a popular district attorney in Alameda County, Earl Warren was a frequent visitor to the wharf. He was elected attorney general of California in 1938 and governor in 1942. In 1946, he was running for reelection and gave a speech to 300 invited guests on the wharf in an event chaired by Malio Stagnaro. Warren (center, with tie) is pictured here with, from left to right, Lawrence Zolezzi, John Cechinni, Lily Ghio, and Floyd Uhden. "Undaunted by a sharp, cold wind," the *Sentinel* reported, "the governor made a plea for four more years." (Santa Cruz Seaside Company.)

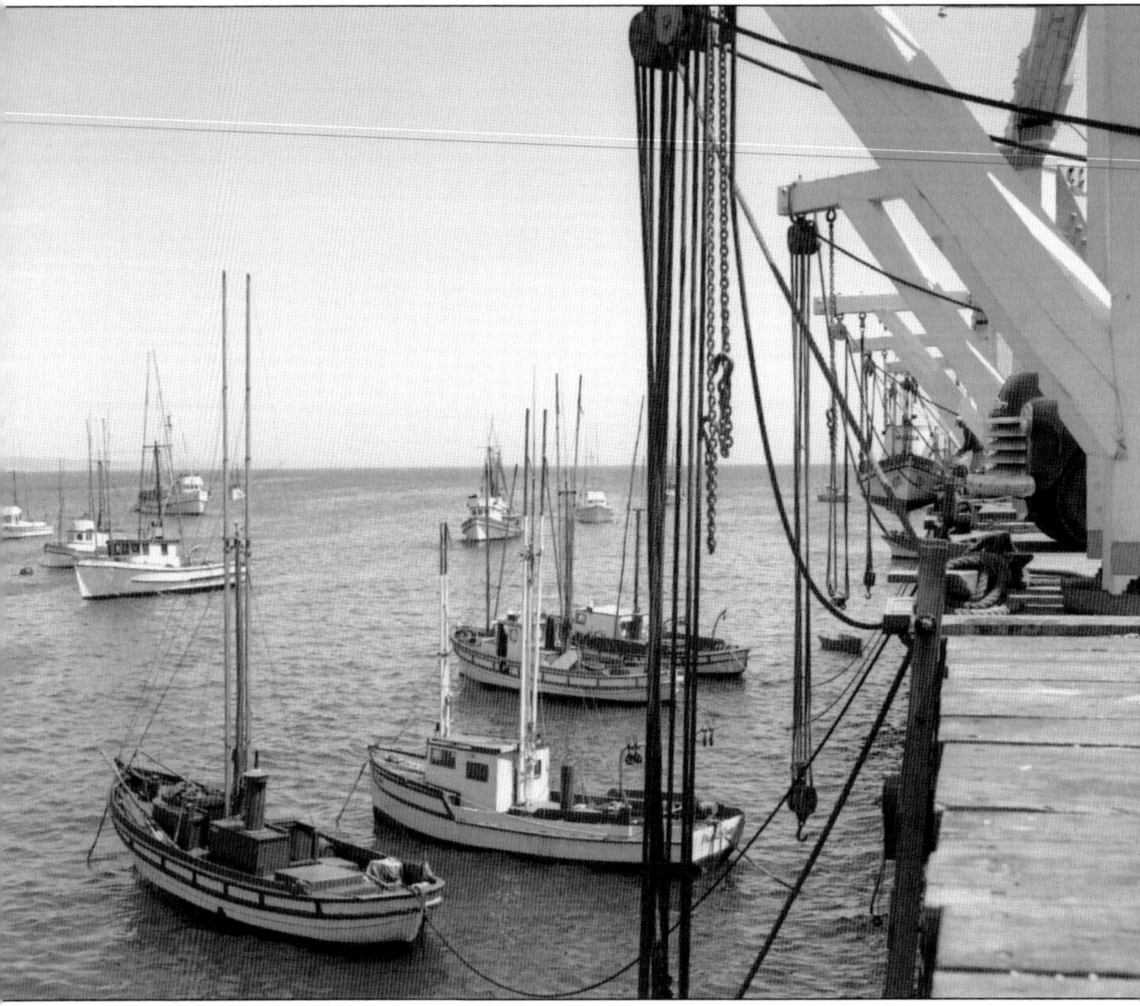

In this everyday view from the eastern edge of the wharf in the 1950s, boats are linked to the wharf with stern lines and anchored off the bow. Currents, groundswell, and traditional wave patterns kept the boats drifting in a direction away from the piling. Other fishing vessels are anchored farther away. Their crews approached the wharf by skiff. The eastern side of the wharf was covered with ladders that allowed fishermen to climb up to the wharf's deck. Block-and-tackle lines from the davits swayed in the wind. (Author's collection.)

Six

Welcoming Visitors

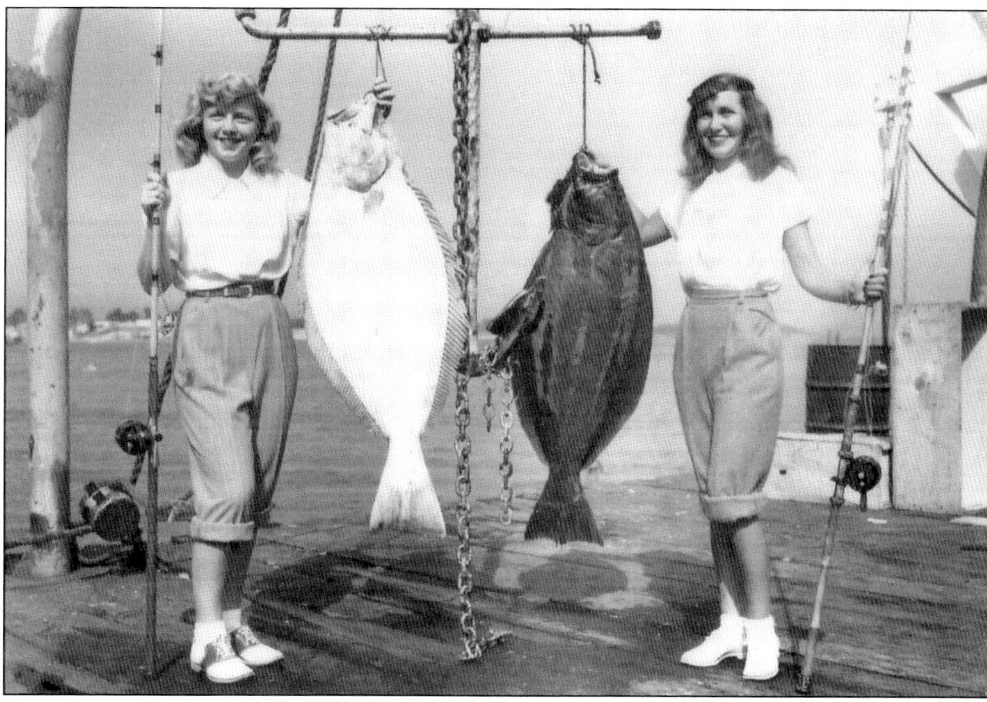

From the very beginning, the wharf supported commercial activities other than the dominant shipping and commercial fishing industries. As early as the 1920s, a variety of tourist-oriented enterprises operated on the wharf, most notably sportfishing operations, restaurants, trinket shops, and even an aquarium. For several decades, maritime industries provided a colorful cultural backdrop for visitors to the wharf. Here, a pair of performers with the Shipstad and Johnson Ice Follies displays two large halibut caught in Monterey Bay. With the opening of the Santa Cruz Small Craft Harbor at what was formerly Woods Lagoon (one of the Twin Lakes) in 1964, the wharf fully transitioned into a prime tourist destination for a variety of visitor-oriented businesses and activities. (Author's collection.)

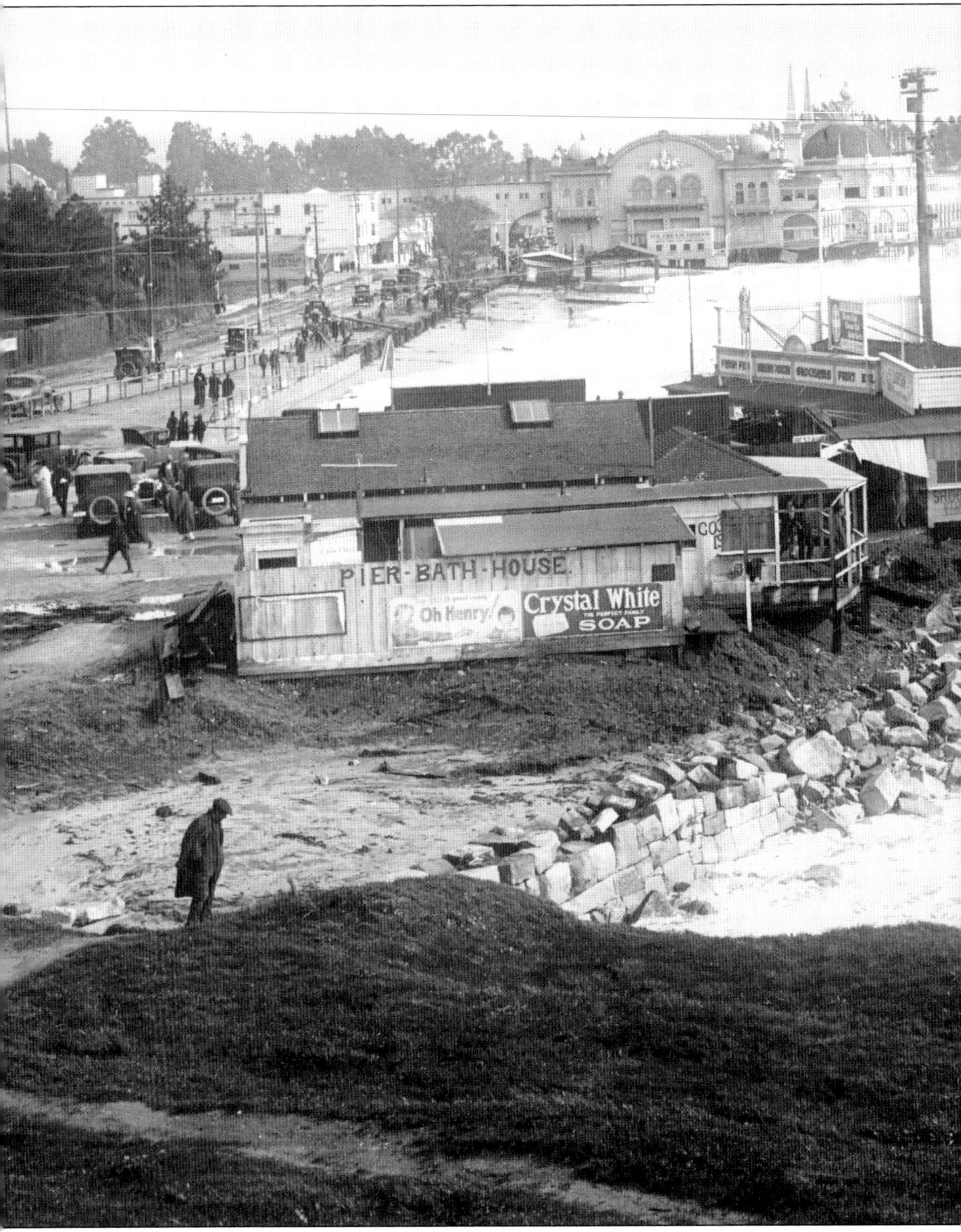

This never-before-published picture of the wharf was taken during a series of storms in February 1926. Many of the early businesses at the front of the wharf can be seen, including the Pier Bath House, Goebel's, and the Ideal Fish Restaurant (with walls washed away by waves). Also showing

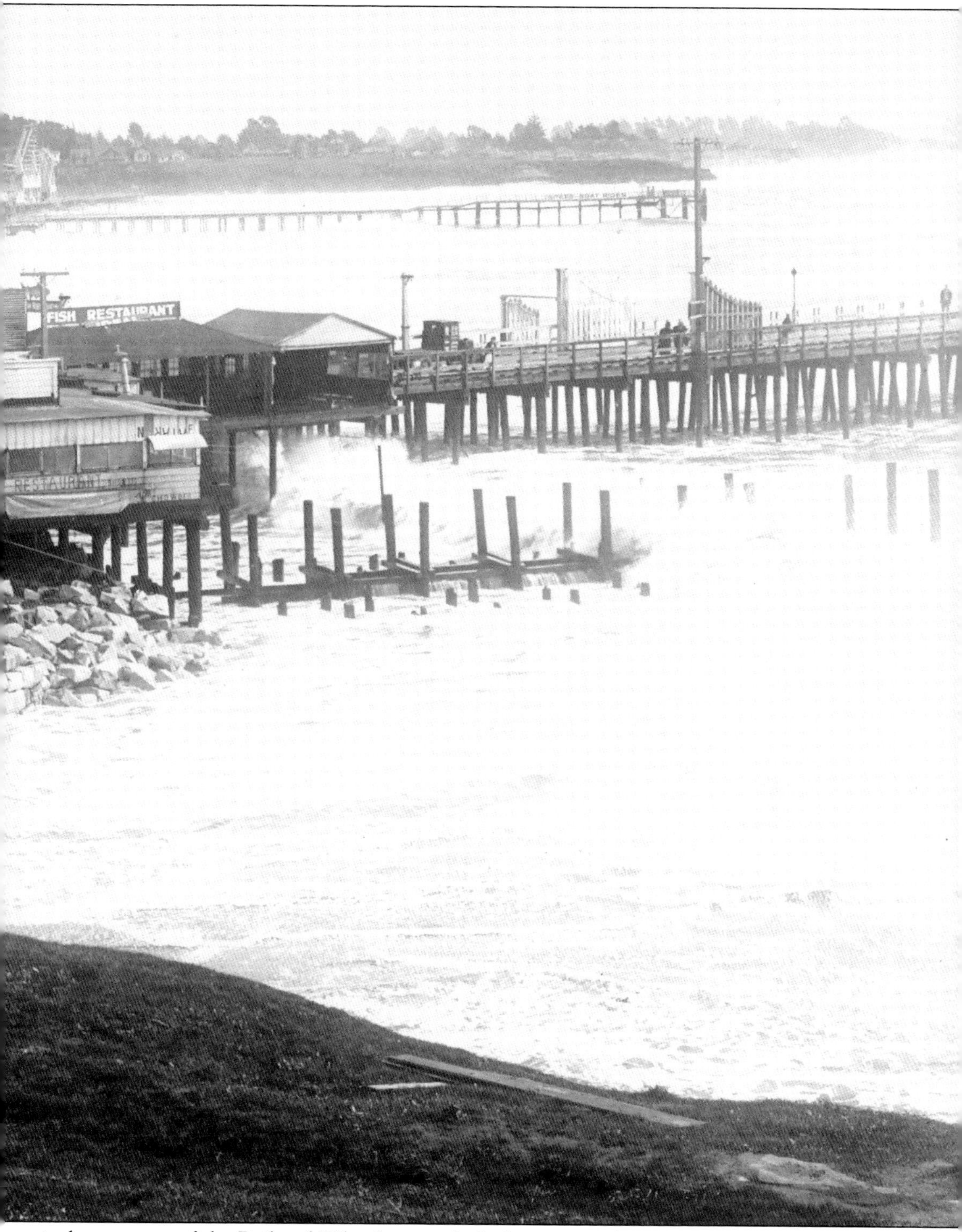

is the remnant of the Railroad Wharf, most of which was torn down in 1922. By mid-March, reconstruction of the buildings was in full swing. (Shelly Pearson.)

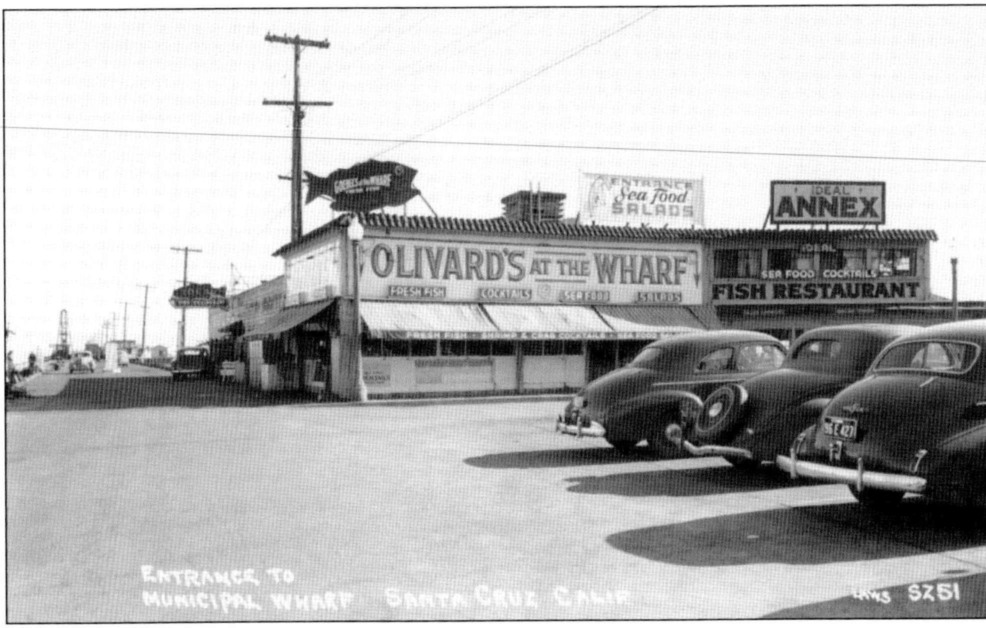

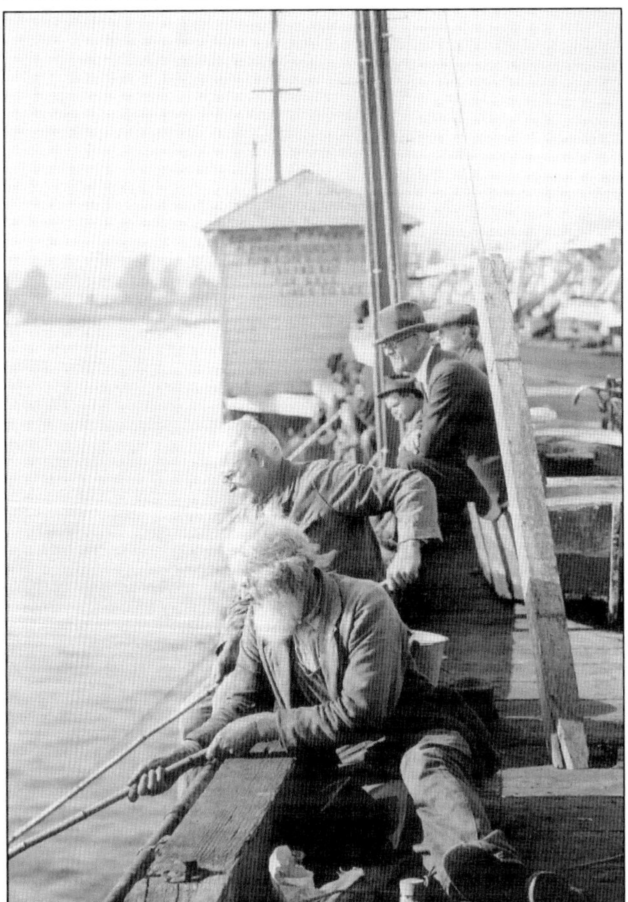

The entrance to the wharf is pictured in the late 1940s. Recent arrivals to Santa Cruz often marvel at the number of business establishments that once greeted visitors at the entrance of the wharf. Note that the fish sign at the top of the building proclaims "Goebels at the Wharf," while the sign on the facade announces "Olivards." In 1946, George Goebel sold the establishment to Tom Edwards and Joe Olivieri, who combined their surnames to rechristen their business. They were the owners of the Ideal Fish Restaurant. (Author's collection.)

Once the steamship lines stopped docking at the wharf, more of the structure was opened up to sportfishing. Local seniors went out daily to ply their hands at catching more than 20 different species of edible fish that could be caught from the wharf. It remains a popular activity to this day. (Santa Cruz Seaside Company.)

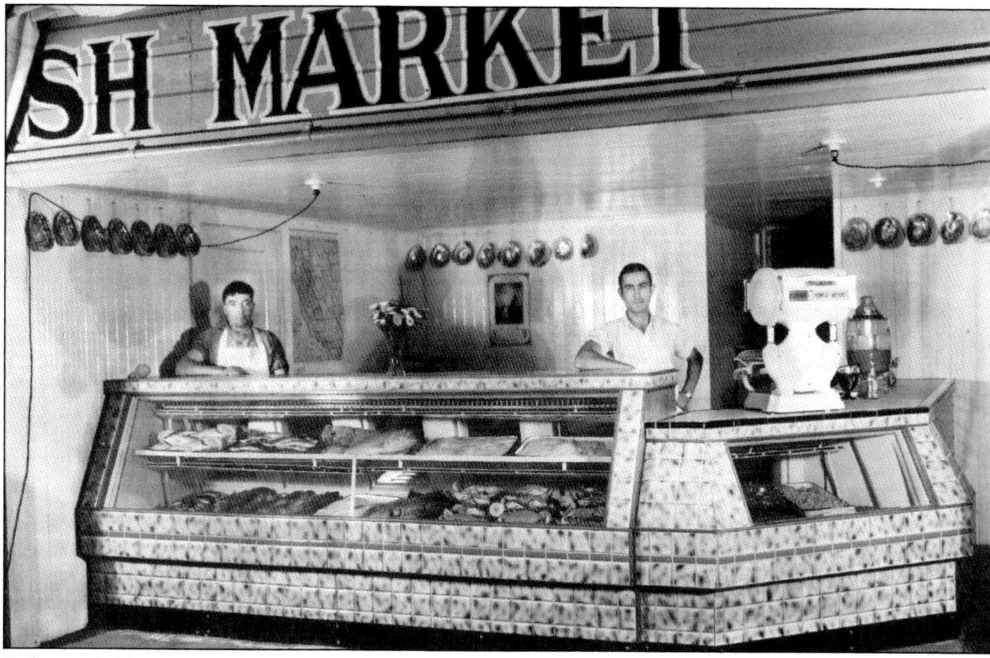

Urbani & Company Fish Market opened up on the east side of the wharf in the 1930s and was operated by Giuseppi "Joe" Urbani. It was one of the few establishments ever to be located on the leeward side of the pier. John Stagnaro (no relation to the Cottardo Stagnaro family, but whose parents were also natives of Riva Trigoso), worked for Urbani in his teens and later bought into the business. (Santa Cruz Museum of Art & History.)

The Urbani business became known as Urbani and Stagnaro in 1936, and then as Stagnaro and Stagnaro in 1937, when John and his younger brother Ernest bought out the entirety of Urbani's interest. The name was later shortened to Stagnaro Brothers Sea Food Company, as it is known to this day. The first lease in 1938 was actually issued by the city to Teresa Stagnaro, mother of the two brothers. (Author's collection.)

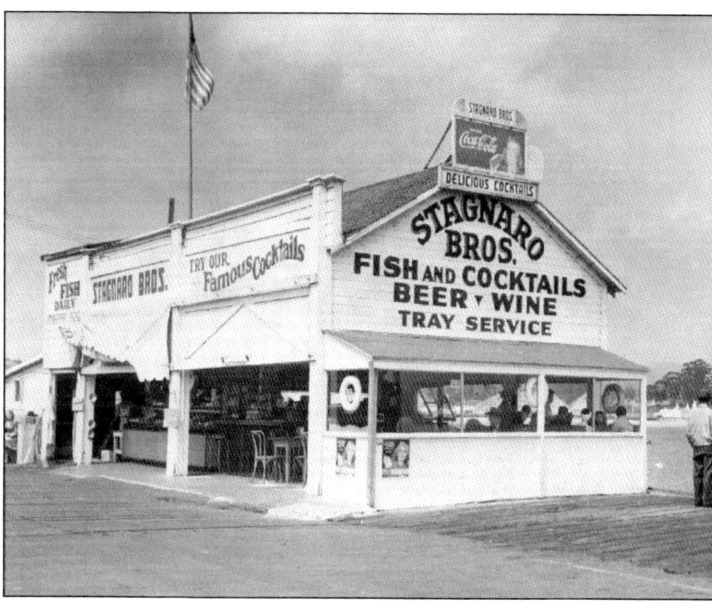

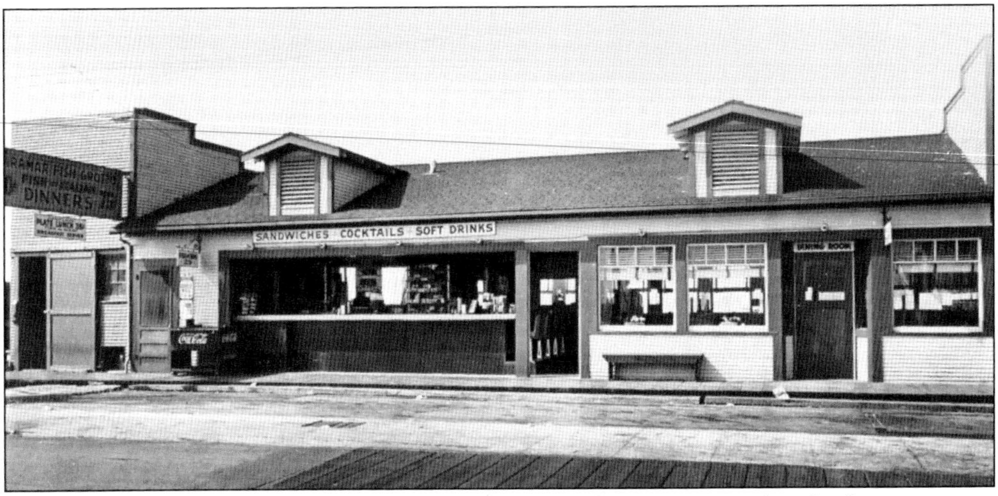

The legendary Miramar Fish Grotto was opened in 1937 by Mary Carniglia, the first woman to own and operate a business on the wharf. (Author's collection.)

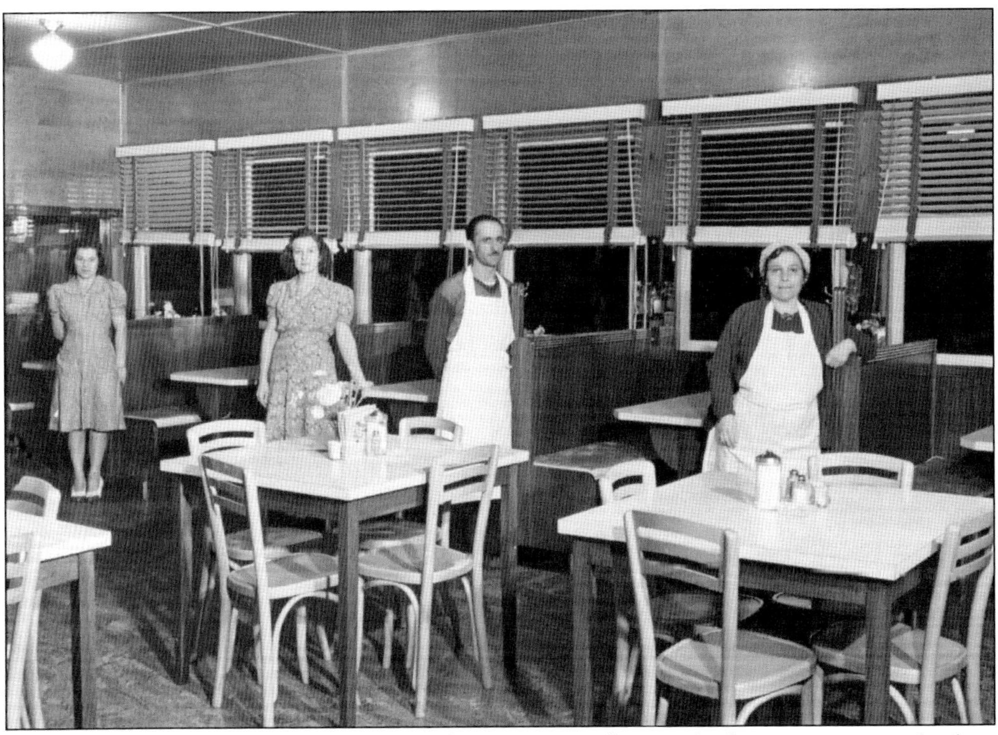

Mary Carniglia also served as head chef at the restaurant. She was also known to run a tight ship. To her left is Gino Ghio, who was an Italian prisoner of war in the United States during World War II; and at far left is Mary's daughter Lorraine Carniglia Canepa. The woman second from left is unidentified. (Carniglia family.)

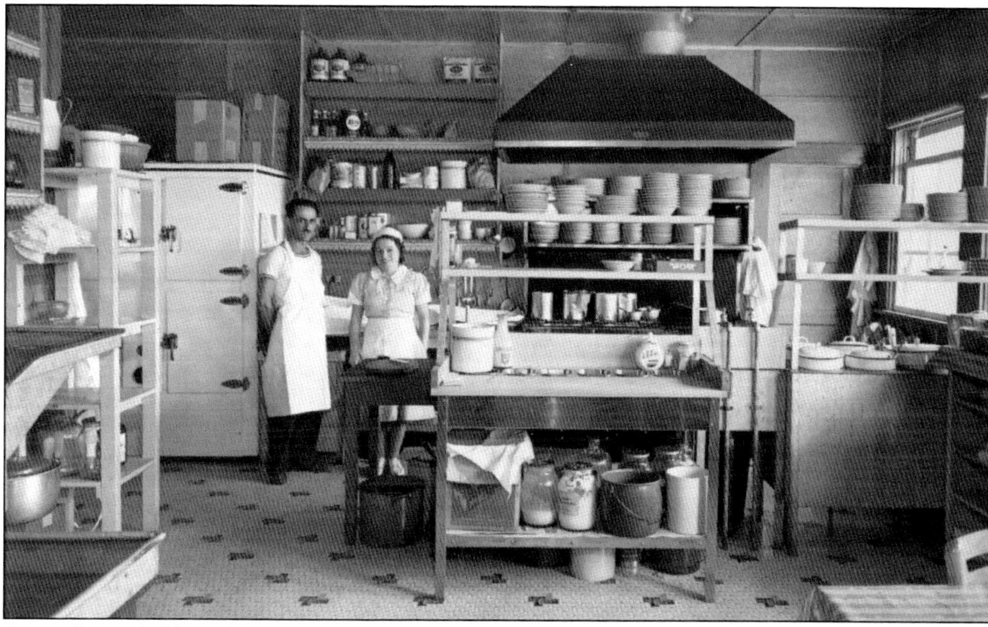

Carniglia prided herself on the cleanliness of her kitchen. Shown here are Gino Ghio and Lorraine Carniglia. The Miramar featured a seven-course fish dinner for 75¢. (Author's collection.)

Barbara Lusby, with a pair of California white sea bass, was featured in a national advertisement for the Santa Cruz Seaside Company supporting local tourism in 1942. Lusby was a competitive swimmer, model, and ballet dancer as well as a star in the annual plunge water carnivals held at the boardwalk. This picture appeared as far away as the *Pittsburgh Post-Gazette*. There was a bit of a controversy when it was revealed that Lusby was only 14 years old at the time the photograph was taken. She competed in the Pacific Association AAU swimming championships that summer. She died in 1971 at the age of 44. (Santa Cruz Seaside Company.)

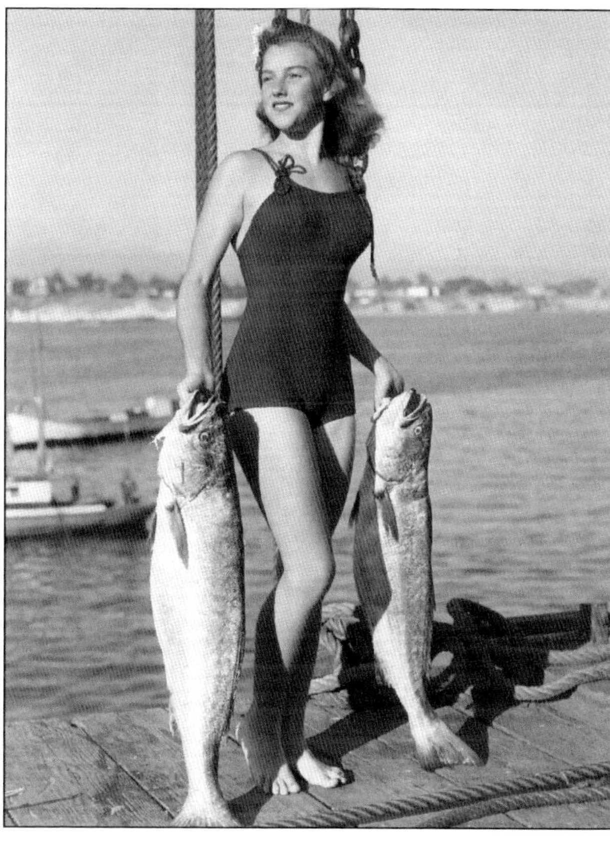

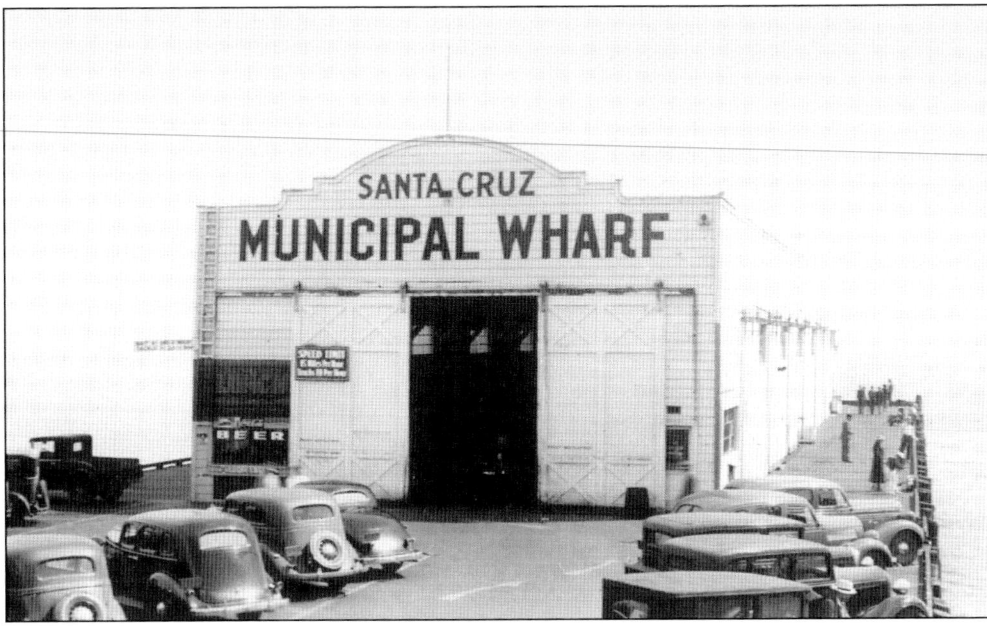

Slowly but surely, the large steamship warehouse at the end of the wharf was converted to uses unrelated to the steamship lines. At the northeast corner is Cartwright's Lunch Counter, which sold Lucky Lager beer, a regional favorite on the wharf that was originally made in 1934 by General Brewing Company in San Francisco and shipped down to Santa Cruz on the steamship lines. Its slogan in the 1950s was "It's Lucky When You Live in California." (Author's collection.)

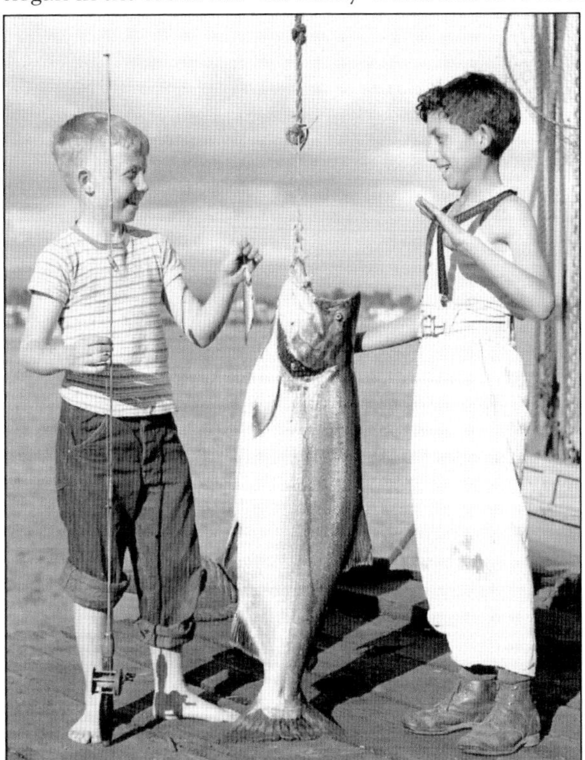

James "Jimmy" Van Houten (left) holds an anchovy and Robert "Big Boy" Stagnaro proudly displays a 40-pound salmon in 1940. Both young men were scions of waterfront families: Van Houten is the grandson of James R. Williamson and son of Wendel Van Houten; both older men served on the board of directors of the Santa Cruz Seaside Company. Van Houten became a founding member of Watsonville Wetlands Watch. Stagnaro was the youngest son of Cottardo Stagnaro II. His lifelong nickname came from being born prematurely at one and a half pounds. (Santa Cruz Seaside Company.)

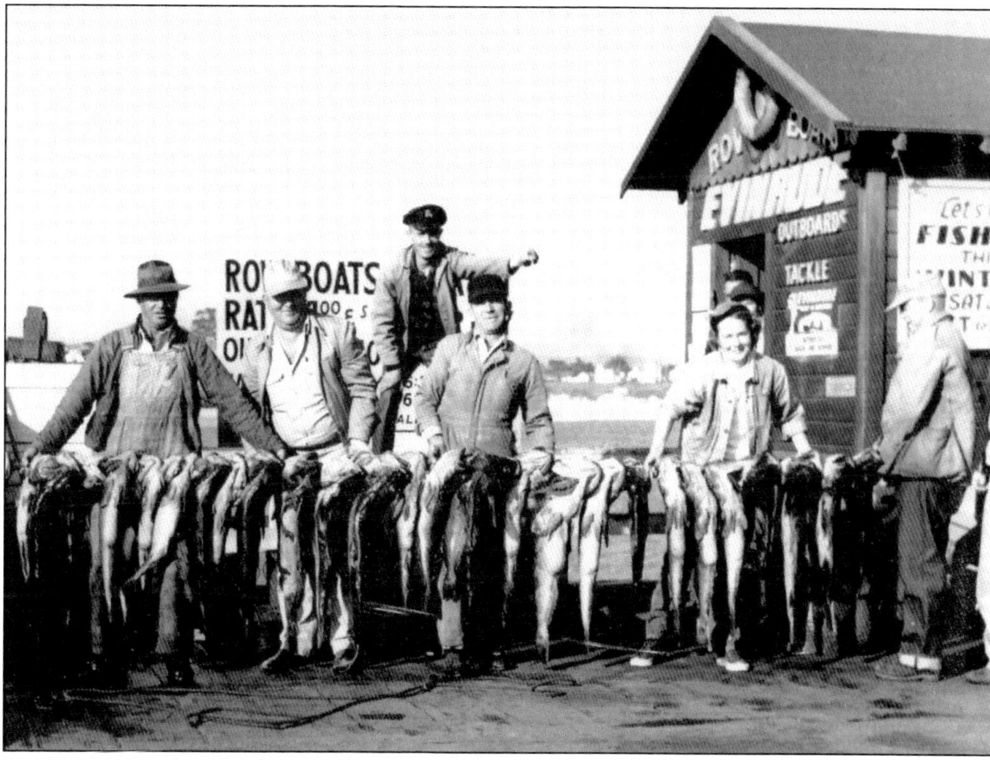

In 1946, Ed Twohig (back, center) opened Santa Cruz Boat Rentals on the wharf, which featured skiffs with oars and also outboard motors for rent. Here, fishermen and -women display a typical catch of rockfish and lingcod caught in local waters. The skiff rentals provided a more intimate and mobile fishing experience than the larger deep-sea barges. They operate on the wharf to this day. (Twohig family.)

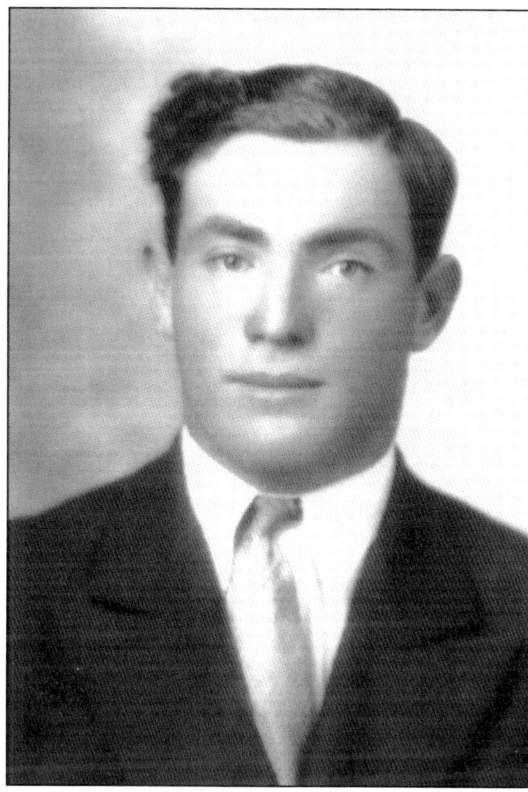

Louis Joseph Bassano, a member of the local fishing family, was one of the few fatalities on the wharf when he was killed in March 1930. While his boat was being hauled up by a hand davit, Bassano slipped and hit his head on the side of his boat. He was 22 years old. (Lynn Bassano Allegre.)

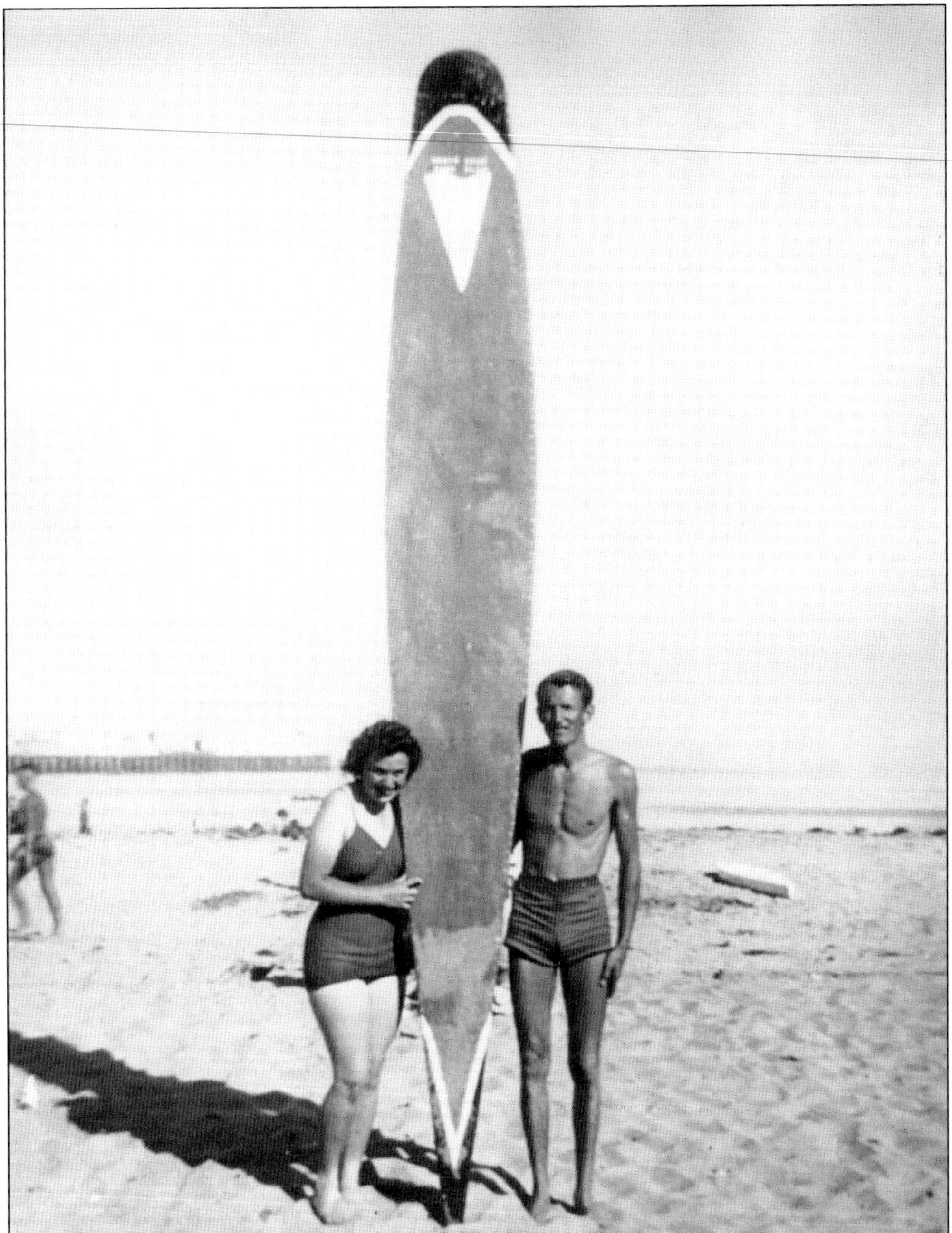

The Santa Cruz Surfing Club usually gets credit for popularizing surfing locally, but here, Andy Caviglia, who was raised in the Santa Cruz Italian fishing colony, displays his surfboard that he made at Santa Cruz High around 1936. He said he was an "independent" surfer. During World War II, he served in the Navy in the Pacific theater, sailing from Panama to the Philippines. Caviglia was a 60-year member of the Sheet Metal Workers Union. He died in 2014 at the age of 98. With rare exception, the first three generations of Santa Cruz Italian fishermen did not surf; their parents felt it was a waste of time. The fourth generation did. (Caviglia family.)

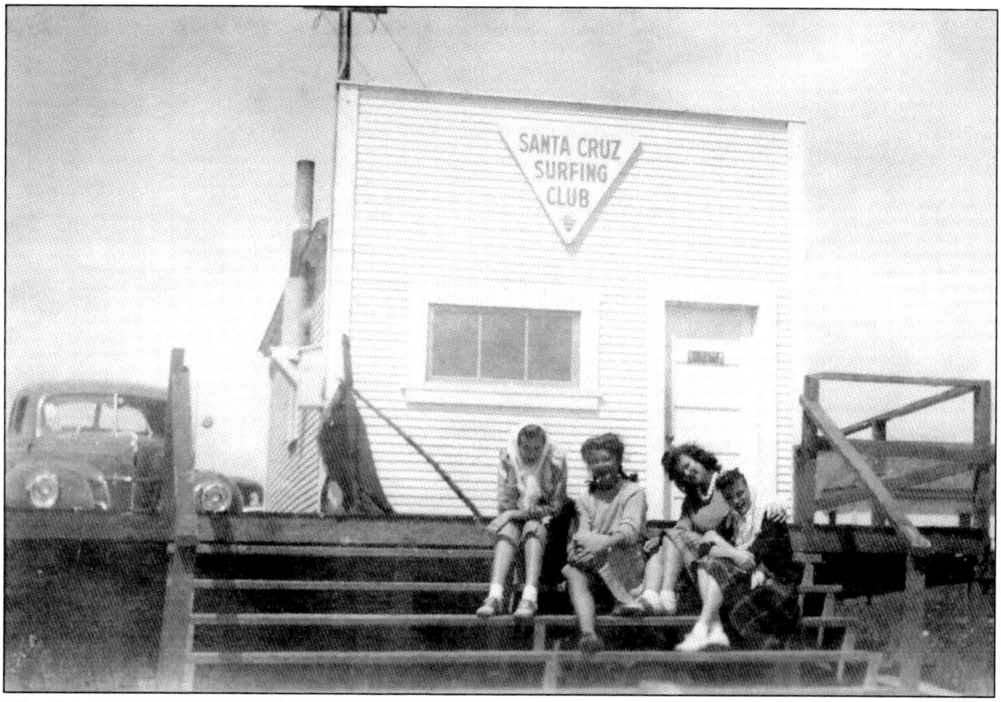

The Santa Cruz Surfing Club was founded in the late 1930s (the date of origin varies from 1936 to 1939) and eventually leased space just west of the wharf for its clubhouse. Wharf records from March 10, 1941, indicate that surf club president Harry Mayo and secretary-treasurer Stuart W. Corey rented out the space for $18.50. The legacy of the club is now honored by the Santa Cruz Surfing Club Preservation Society, which provided this photograph and which operates the Santa Cruz Surfing Museum at Lighthouse Point. (Santa Cruz Surfing Club Preservation Society.)

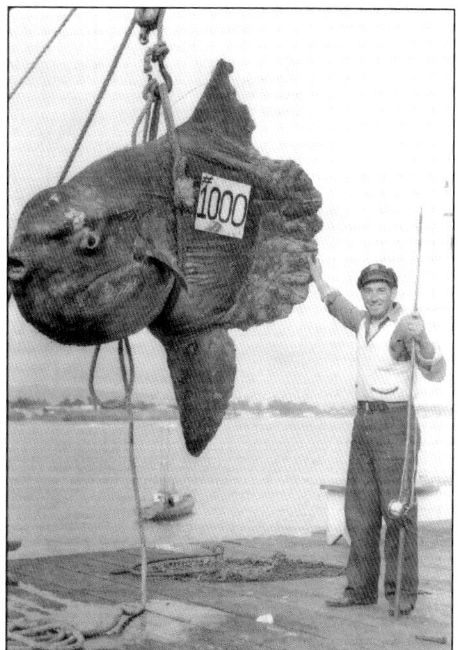

The real fisherman who caught the sunfish on the cover of this book was Sam Pennington, who skippered the Stagnaro fishing barge *Marie*. Although the fish was taken on March 17, 1939, the photograph appeared on the front page of the *Santa Cruz Sentinel* on April 9, 1940, under the headline "Last Sunbath for Mola Mola." The "barnacle-hulled monster," according to the article, was actually "shot through the head" by Pennington before being brought to the wharf for display. The fishing pole in Pennington's hand was merely a prop. (Author's collection.)

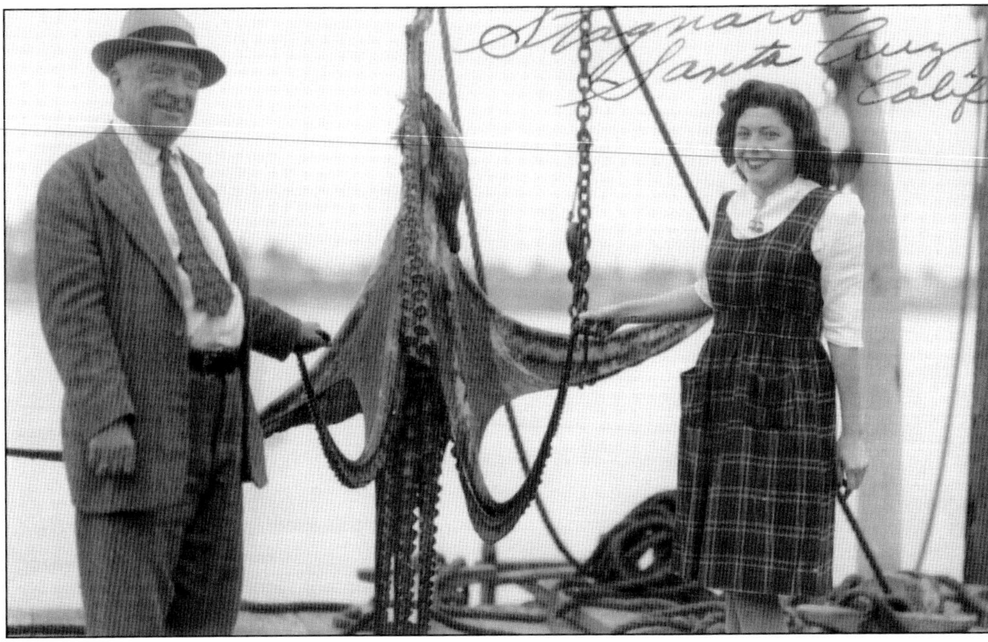

Legendary waterfront journalist Ernest Otto (left) was one of the most respected newspapermen on the Pacific coast. He originally wrote for the *Santa Cruz Surf* and later for the *Santa Cruz Sentinel* for a combined total of more than 70 years. He was a beloved figure in the last Santa Cruz Chinatown and at the wharf. He is pictured here with a large octopus and Betty "Sinatra" Stagnaro (Lamb), the youngest daughter of Cottardo Stagnaro II and a star swimmer in the Plunge Carnivals and Waterfront Follies in the 1940s. (Author's collection.)

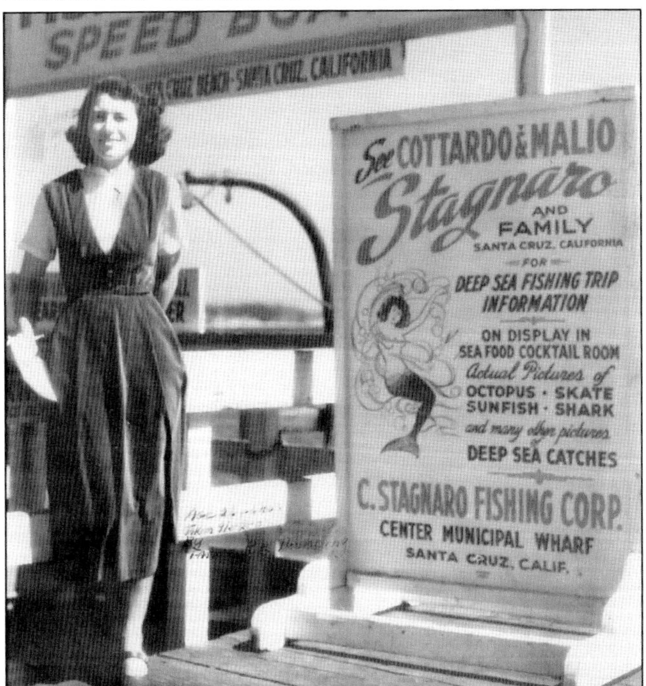

Another beloved fixture on the Santa Cruz waterfront was Gilda Jenny "G.J." Stagnaro, who is pictured here in September 1950 in a photograph taken by Fr. R.H. Boehning. Stagnaro worked in the family business for 60 years in a variety of capacities. Here, she is taking notes for California Fish and Game on the catches coming in on the sports boats. She died only a few feet from where this photograph was taken. (Author's collection.)

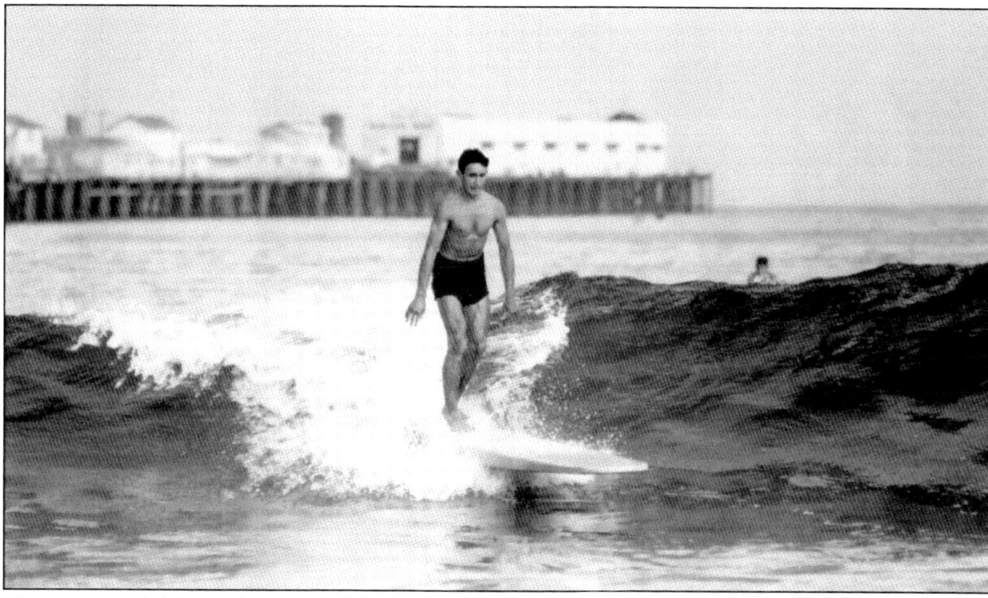

The immortal Alexander "Pinky" Pedemonte rides a wave at Cowell Beach with the Santa Cruz Wharf in the background around 1940. In addition to being a founding member of the Santa Cruz Surfing Club, Pedemonte was a legendary quarterback at Santa Cruz High and played on Army teams during World War II. He also served on the front lines in France and Germany. Pedemonte died in 2010 at the age of 86. (Harry Mayo collection.)

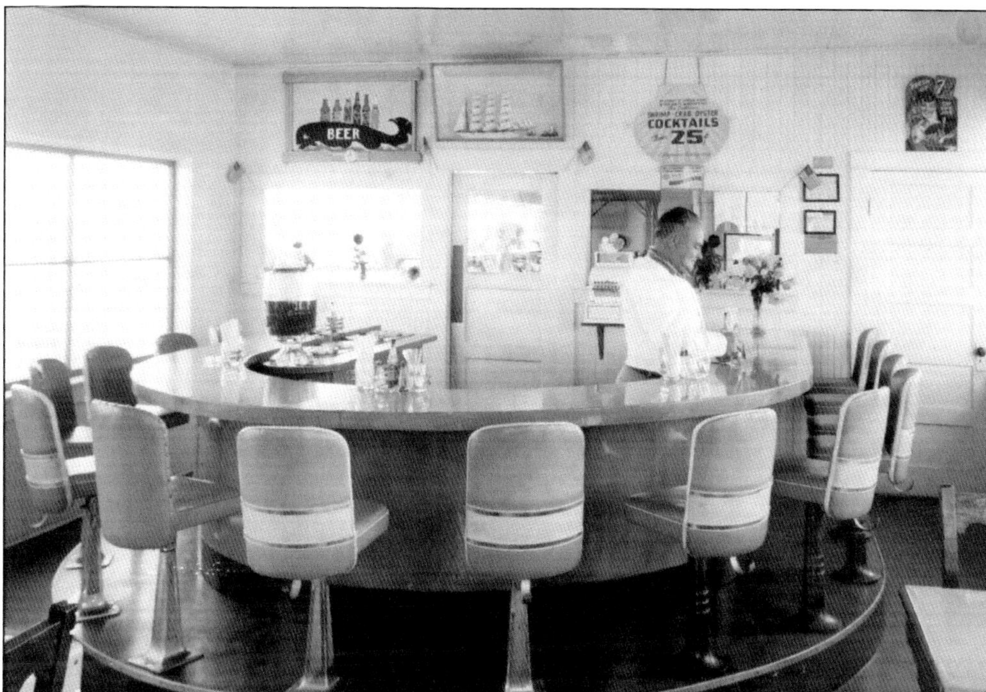

Pictured is the interior of the Stagnaro Sports Fisher Restaurant, adjacent to the family fish market. The swinging door between them allowed fresh fish, crabs, shrimp, and other seafood to be delivered directly from the market to patrons. (Author's collection.)

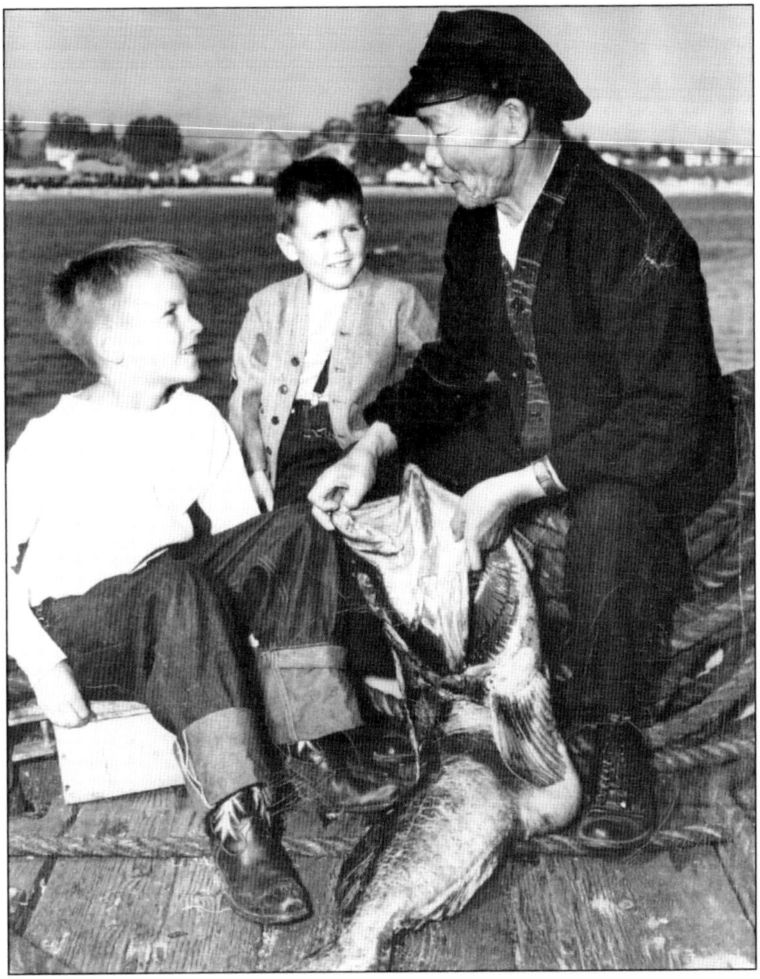

Ah Fook was a legendary fisherman who was written about extensively in local newspapers by Warren "Skip" Littlefield and Ernest Otto. Here, in a promotional photograph, Ah Fook is shown opening the mouth of a large lingcod for two young visitors to the wharf. In a cover story appearing in the September 28, 1941, *Sentinel News*, Littlefield identifies him as "Cheung Ah 'Mangia' Fook." According to Littlefield, Ah Fook's father worked with Frederick A. Hihn in securing labor to build the local railroad in the 1870s. (Author's collection.)

One of Santa Cruz's early artists was William Lemos (1861–1942). A native of New York, Lemos reputedly began his career by wandering the streets of New York City doing paintings by request. In the 1880s, he moved to the West Coast and opened up a studio at the Miller's Neptune Bath House. From 1904 until his death in 1942, he operated a studio on the Boardwalk, often painting on redwood slabs for souvenirs. During his later years, he went blind and would fish in front of the C. Stagnaro fish market, where members of the family would help bait his hooks. Lemos said that he originally moved to Santa Cruz "because of the fishing." (Santa Cruz Seaside Company.)

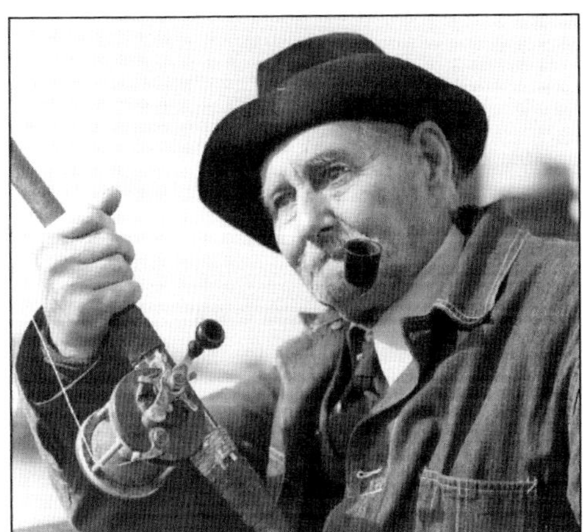

The annual Cottardo "Babe" Stagnaro Old-Timers Fishing Derby brought hundreds of fishermen and -women to the wharf each year. In 1972, Shirley Brown (center) of Stockton captured the queen's crown with a 27-pound, 13-ounce lingcod, besting the king's catch by Henry Marshall, also of Stockton, by six pounds. Fourteen-year-old Leta Stagnaro (between Malio and Brown) overlooks the coronation. In 1965, Brown caught a record 193 lingcod throughout the season, which she donated to charities. (Author's collection.)

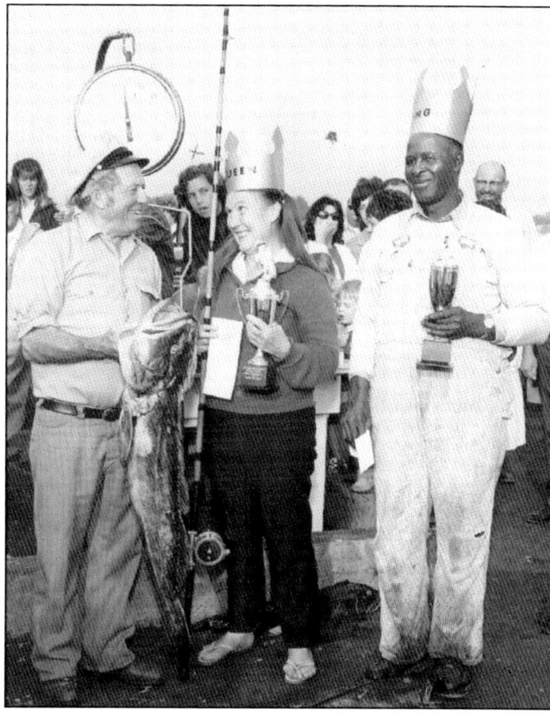

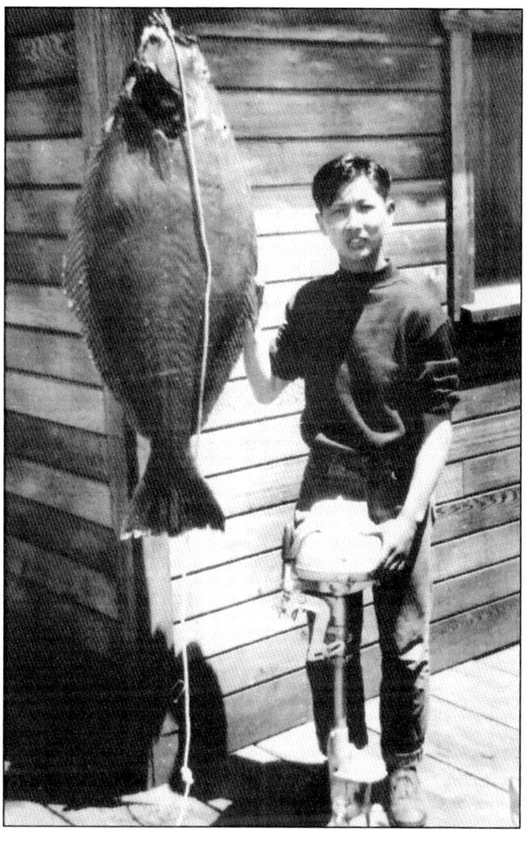

Teenager Young Lee is pictured with a 20-plus-pound petrale sole caught off a Santa Cruz Boat Rental skiff around 1947. Lee, who was raised in Santa Cruz's Chinatown, and his brother Wee Lee were inveterate fishermen and often went out with their community elder Ah Fook. Young Lee drowned in a tragic accident while fishing below Weitchpec, in Humboldt County, near the juncture of the Klamath and Trinity Rivers in October 1948. He was wearing oversize waders that filled with water and was swept away to his death. (Twohig family, Lois Van Buren.)

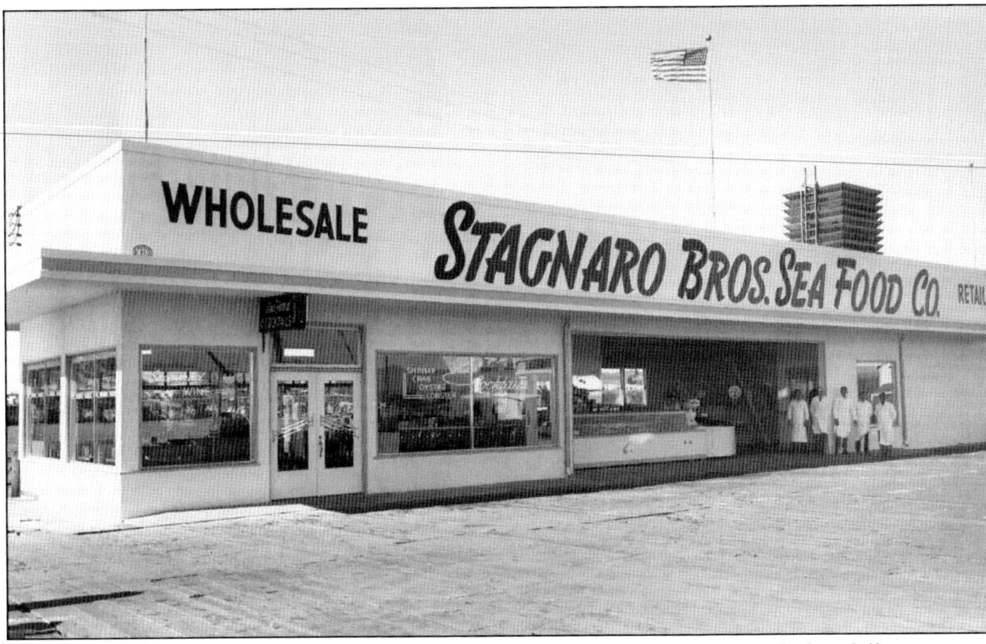

Stagnaro Brothers Sea Food Company expanded its operation in 1947 to include a full restaurant, retail fish market, and wholesale fish operation on Washington Street (a short distance from the wharf). This building served the family until it was torn down in 1986 to make room for their two-story restaurant, which remains open to this day. More than a dozen members of the family still remain in the business. (Stagnaro Bros.)

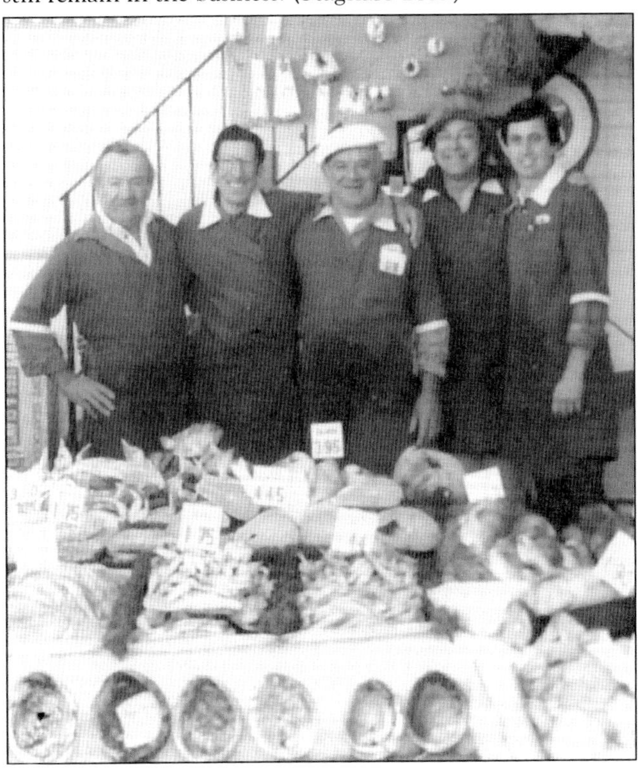

The "last of the Mohicans" are, from left to right, Giovanni "John" Stagnaro, Steve "Ghighi" Ghio, Ernesto "Ernie" Stagnaro, Bob McPherson, and Larry Bryson—pictured back when salmon was only $3.95 a pound. This portion of the Stagnaros' open-air market is featured in the Clint Eastwood film *Sudden Impact*. (Stagnaro Bros.)

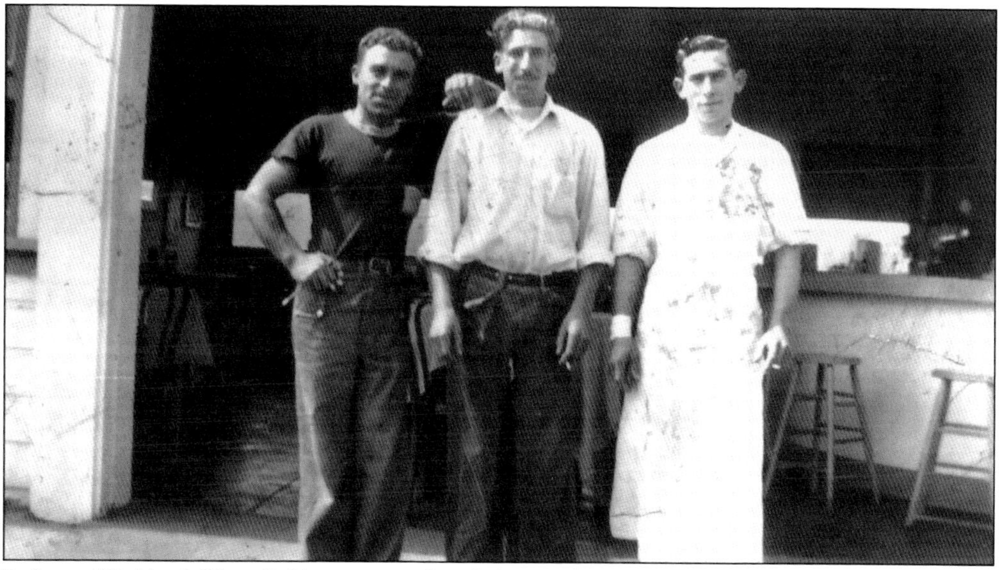

Roberto "Robbie" Ghio (left) is pictured with his nephews Steve "Ghighi" Ghio (center) and Victor Ghio in the 1940s in front of the old Santa Cruz Fisheries. Robbie and Ghighi worked their entire lives on the wharf, while Victor went to work on his own fishing boat, the *Catherina G* (named after his mother). The film *Maddalena Z (Voyage of the Heart)* is based on his life. (Author's collection.)

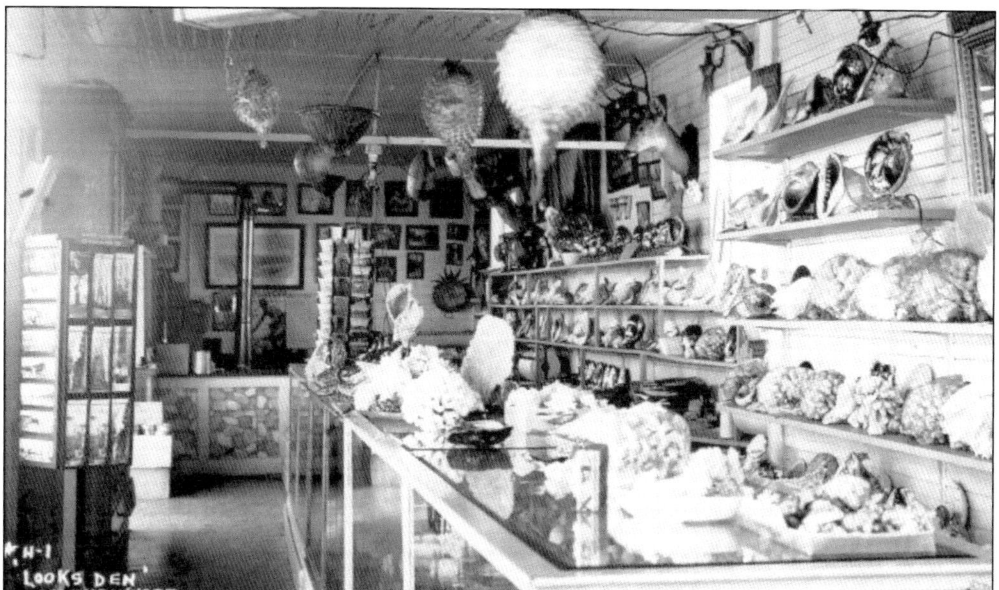

As it gradually shifted from a working wharf to a more visitor-oriented one, Charles R. Look opened a small bait and tackle stand, aquarium, and curio shop on the wharf in 1935, at the site of the Western California Fish Co. Looks Den featured nautical and maritime memorabilia. Look was a prominent grocer in Santa Cruz, operating the Package Grocery on Pacific Avenue until 1920. He collected curios from all over the world and placed them on exhibit (or sold them) in his shop. Look ran the business until his death in 1943 at the age of 93. This was a favorite haunt of the author in his youth. (Author's collection.)

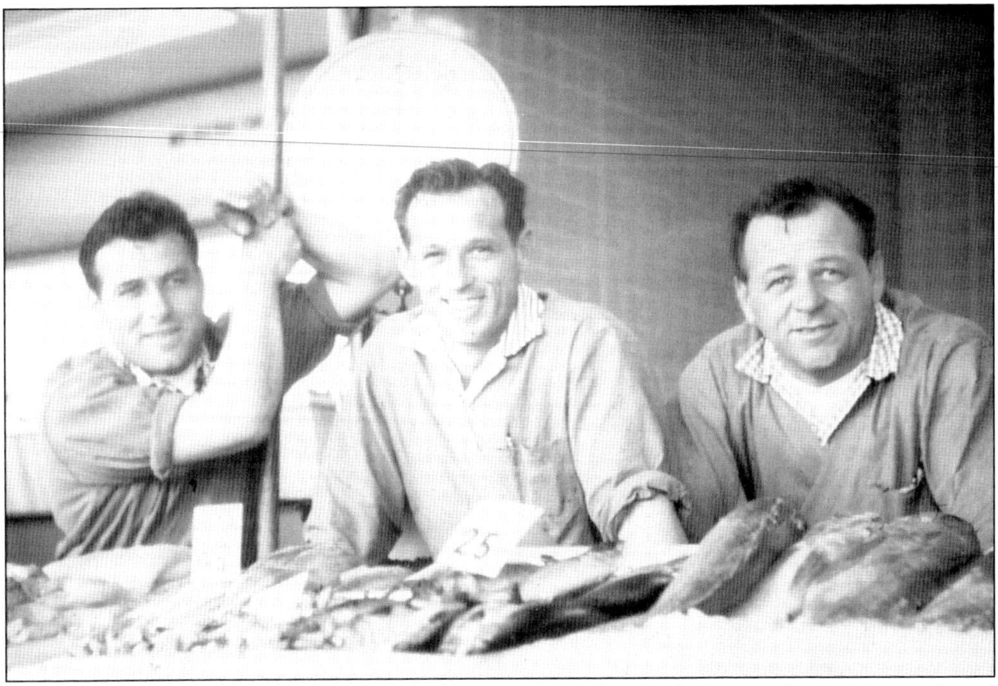

Three Carniglia brothers are pictured in the 1950s—Marco (left), Batista "Jocko" (center), and John. The eldest sons of Mary and Marco Carniglia, the three bothers operated the Carniglia Brothers Restaurant and Fish Market on the wharf beginning in 1953. John's son Stefano operated a high-end restaurant, Carniglia's, until 2012. (Donald Carniglia.)

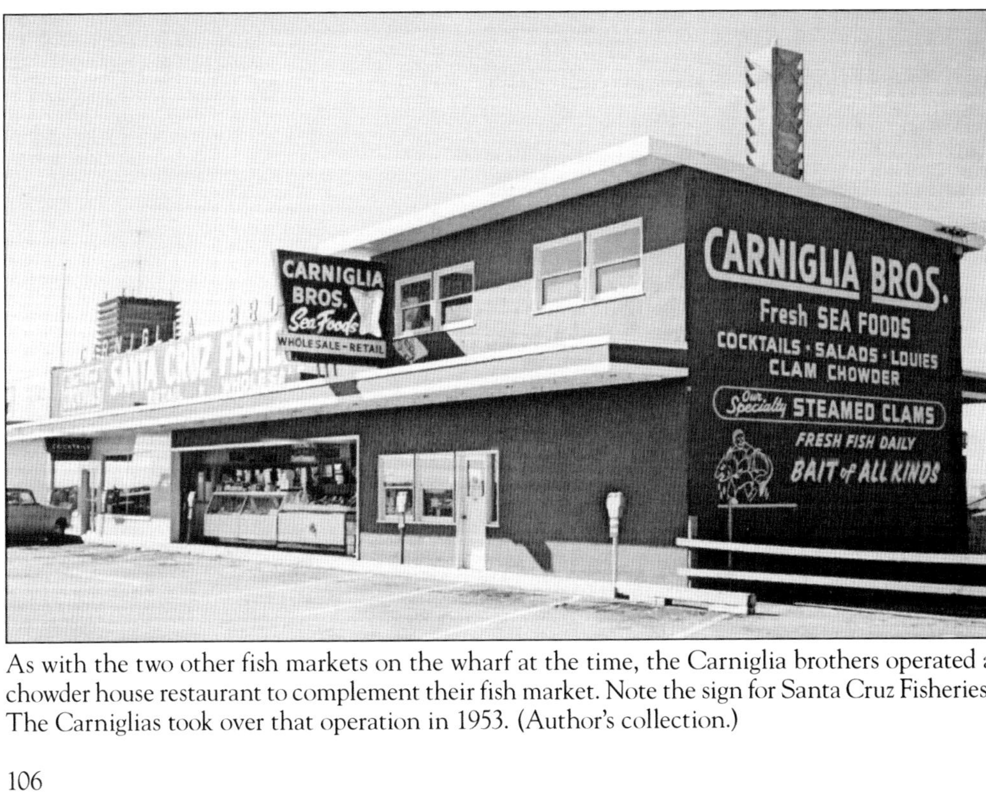

As with the two other fish markets on the wharf at the time, the Carniglia brothers operated a chowder house restaurant to complement their fish market. Note the sign for Santa Cruz Fisheries. The Carniglias took over that operation in 1953. (Author's collection.)

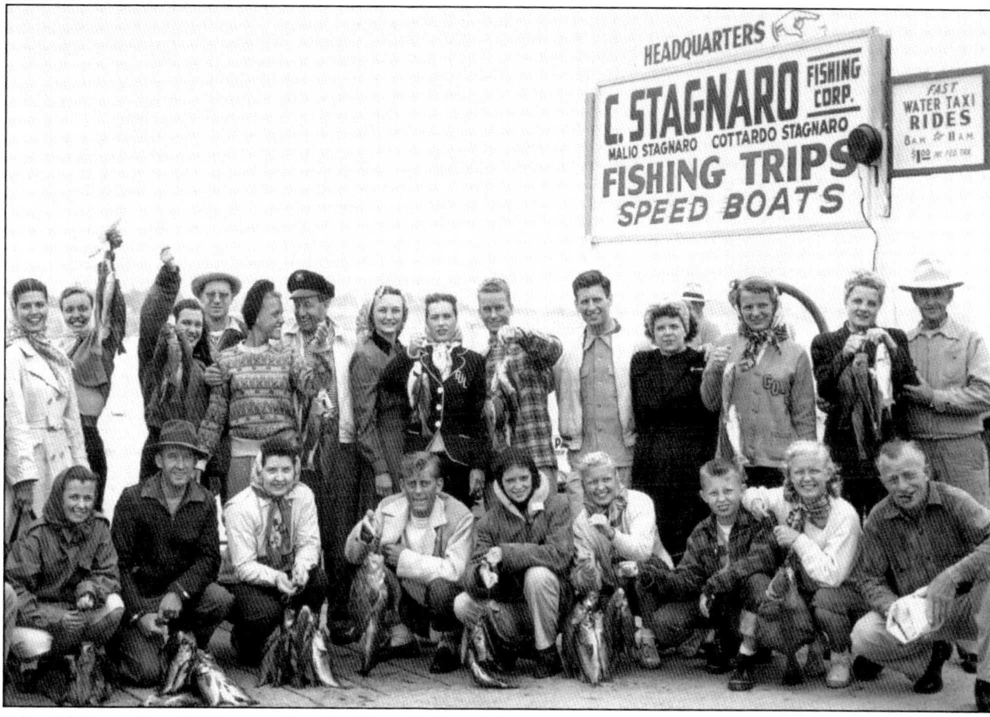

The Shipstad and Johnson Ice Follies made monthly trips to Santa Cruz during their runs in San Francisco, chaperoned by journalist Todd Powell (sixth from left in the back row), the nationally known *San Francisco Chronicle* journalist who often promoted the Santa Cruz waterfront. The famed Scotvold twins, Joanne and Joyce, can be seen in the bottom row, at right. (Author's collection.)

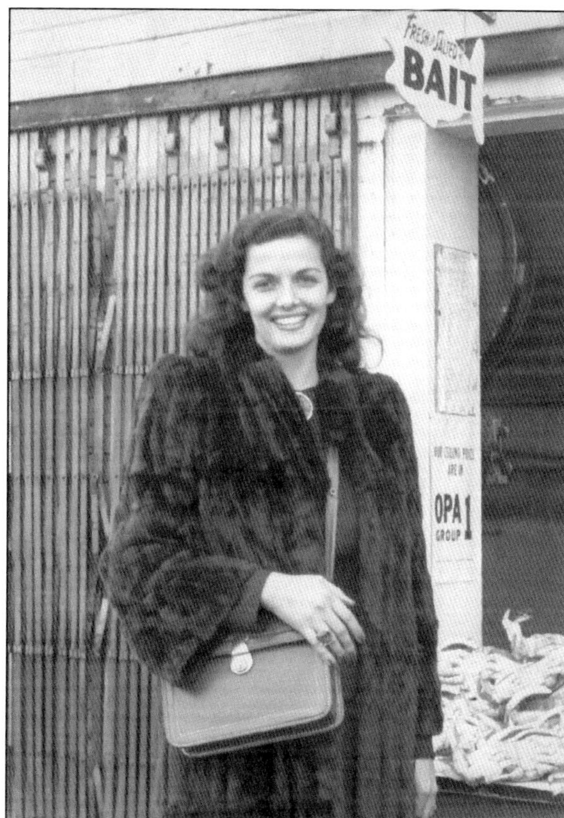

Glamourous star Jane Russell visited the Santa Cruz Wharf in December 1944, the year after her sexually provocative role in Howard Hughes's *The Outlaw* caused a public sensation. Russell was married to her high school sweetheart Bob Waterfield, then a football star at UCLA. They were visiting Northern California for college football's annual East-West Shrine Game played in San Francisco the following day. The West's coach, Babe Hollingbery, spent his summers in Santa Cruz. Russell reportedly enjoyed her visit. (Author's collection.)

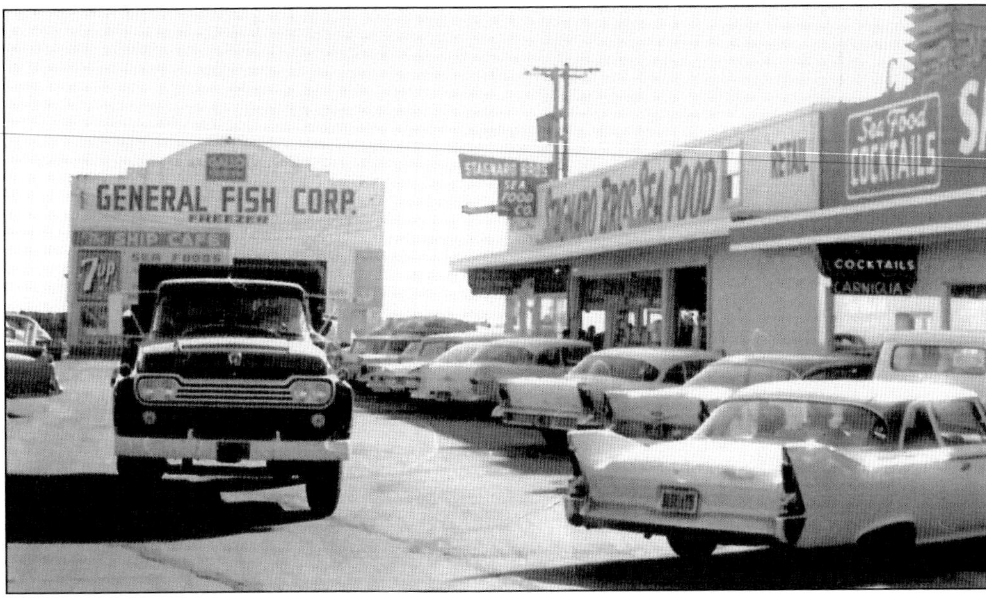

The steamship warehouse at the end of the wharf eventually gave way to fishing. In 1939, brothers "Tisto" and "Monk" Loero opened the General Fish Company, located first in Santa Cruz and later in Monterey. According to a 1941 article by Ernest Otto in the *Sentinel*, "The Loero brothers are believed to be the youngest men in the whole-sale fishing business in the state." (Author's collection.)

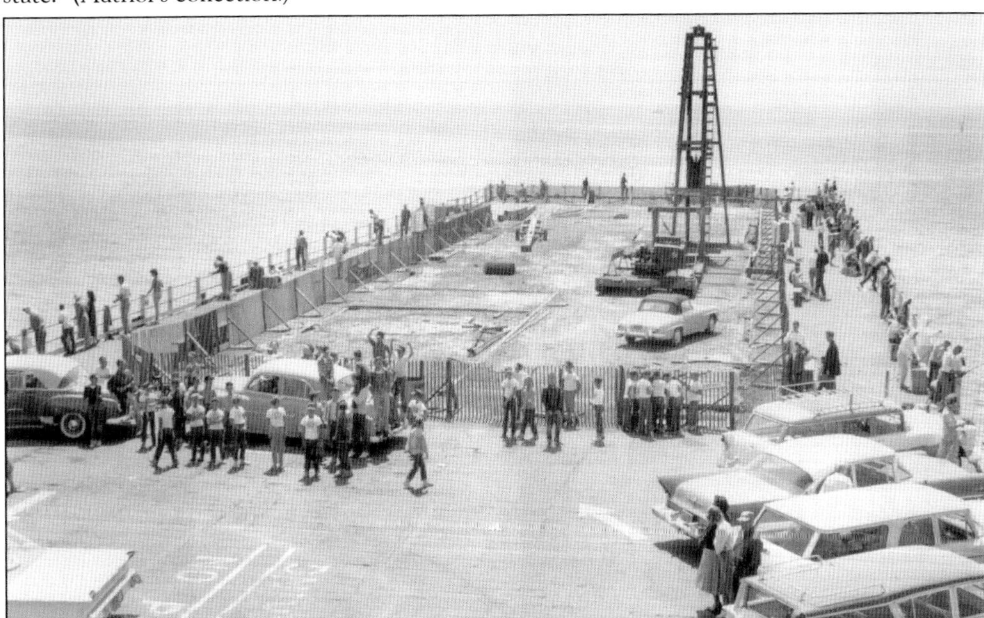

By 1959, deteriorating conditions at the end of the wharf forced the city to demand that General Fish vacate the premises. Demolition of the warehouse took place the following year. For several months, there was heated debate throughout the state about whether the wharf could be saved. A report issued in June 1960 indicated that it could. By September, led by city recreation director Carl Bengston, a $49,500 grant from the California Wildlife Conservation Board was secured for repair of the wharf and the creation of a public fishing section at its end. (City of Santa Cruz.)

The plaque and totem pole were erected in January 1961 marking the completion of the California Wildlife Conservation Board project. The official dedication took place on Saturday, January 19, with roughly 150 in attendance. More than 1,180 linear feet of space was created for recreational activities. The totem pole was made by Ralph Gallagher, who is of Cherokee descent. (Santa Cruz Seaside Company.)

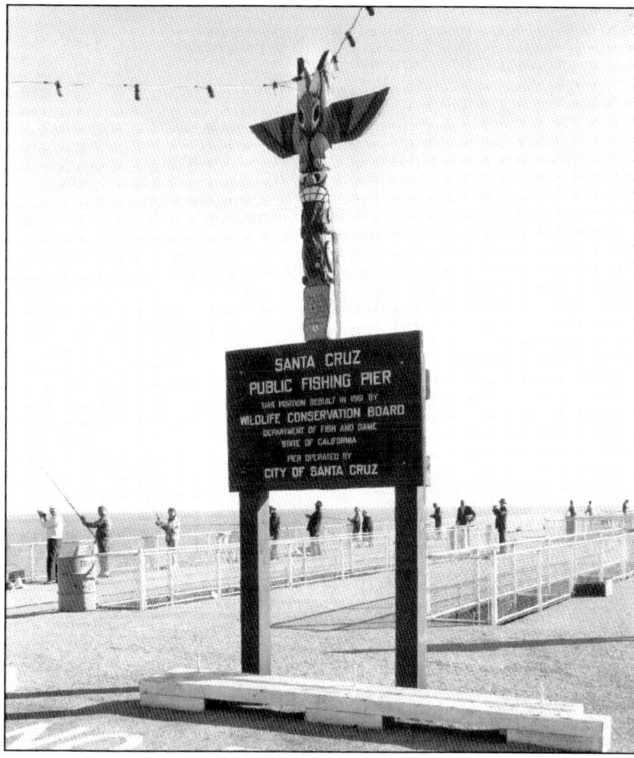

Fisherman Joe Loero and his daughter, Stella Loreo (Bible), bait longlines on the wharf in the 1940s. (City of Santa Cruz.)

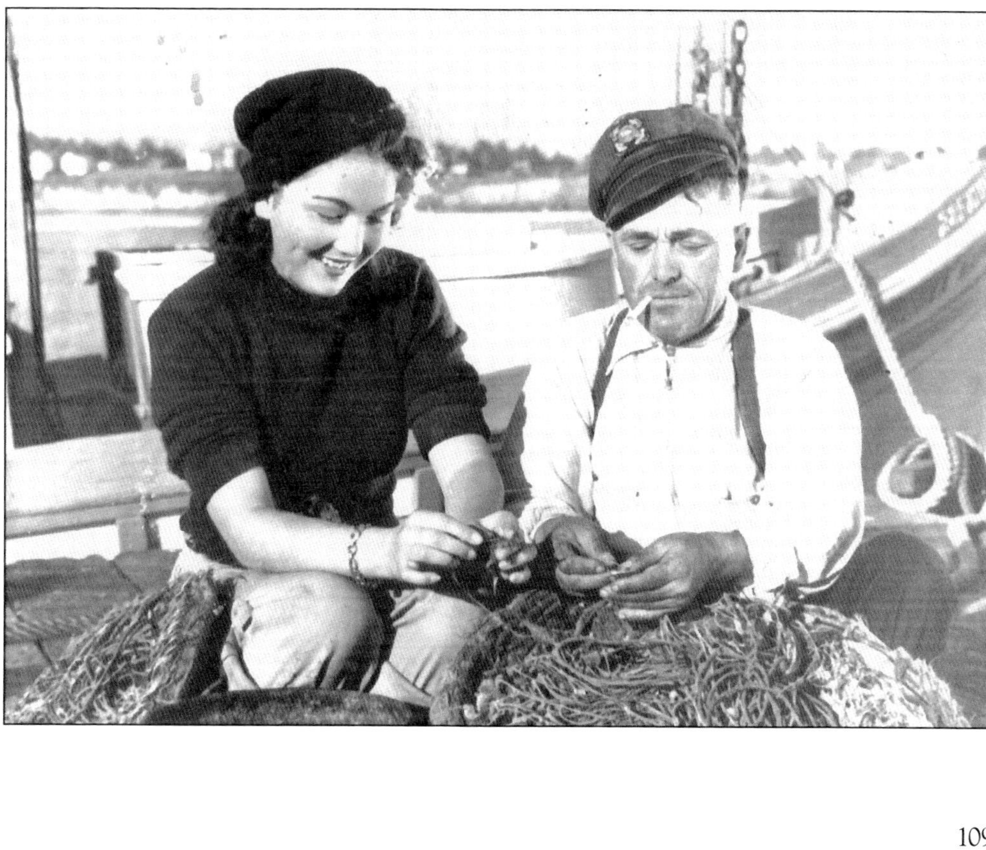

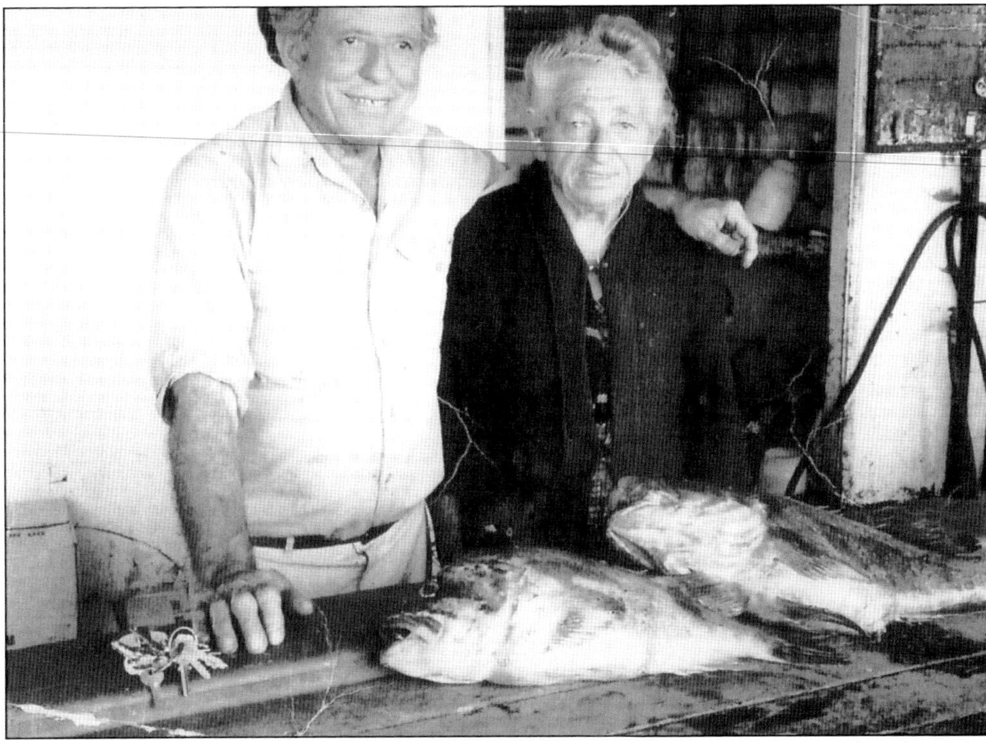

One of the first photographs ever taken by the author, in the summer of 1968, this shows his great-uncle Malio Stagnaro (left) and his grandmother Batistina Stagnaro with a pair of white-belly rock cod in front of them. Not only were the two Stagnaros brother- and sister-in-law, but they were also first cousins. Batistina lived in Santa Cruz for nearly for more than 70 years without needing to learn English. The fish market's on-site icehouse can be seen behind them. (Author's collection.)

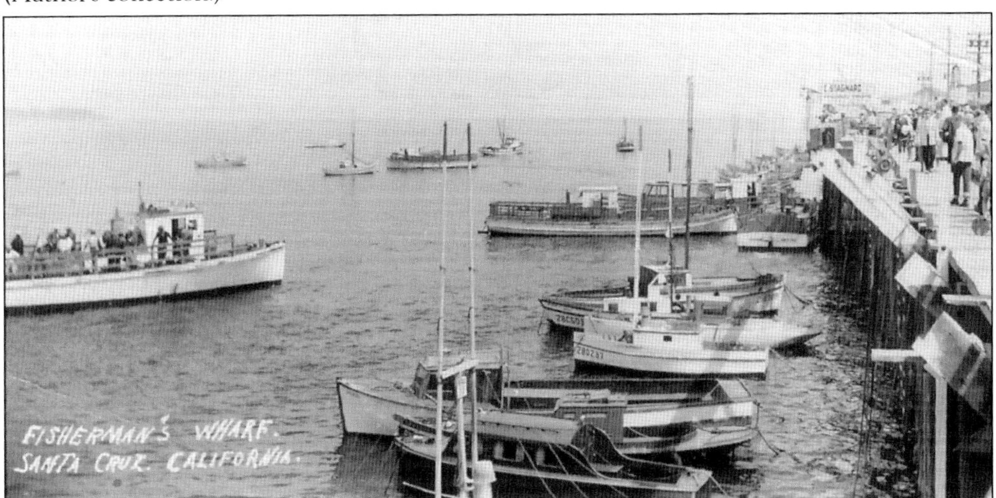

During various stages of its history, the wharf was dubbed "Fisherman's Wharf," echoing similar nomenclature in San Francisco and Monterey. Into the 1960s, it was lined with fishing boats. Here, the Stagnaro No. 1 fishing barge awaits clearance to dock at the Stagnaro landing at the center of the wharf. (Author's collection.)

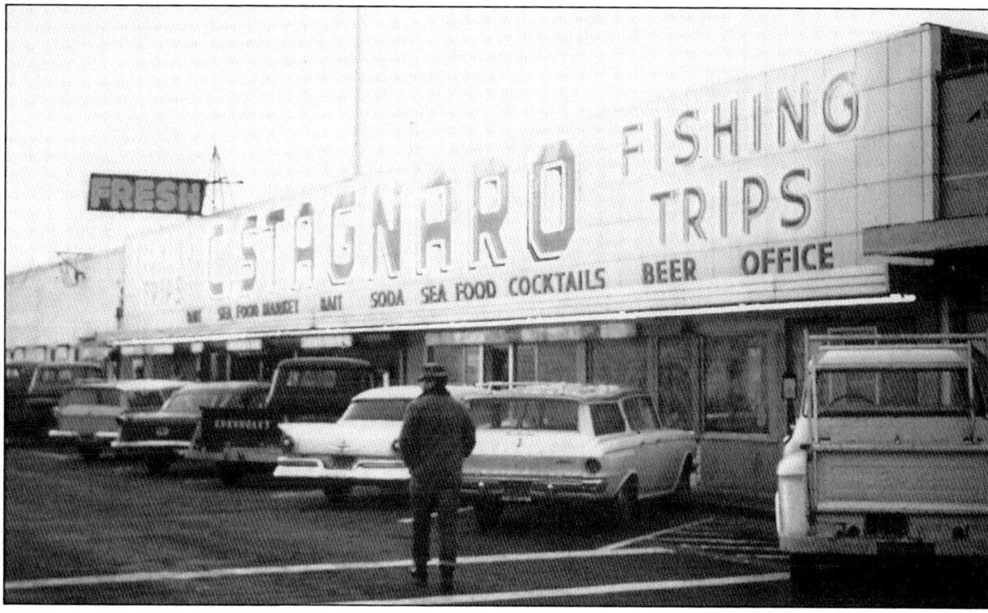

A grey day on the wharf is pictured in the early 1960s. During the months from Labor Day to Memorial Day, the wharf was often a quiet place, without the bustling crowds of the summer months. It was also covered in neon. The C. Stagnaro signs were blue and red and could be seen all the way to Twin Lakes beaches. The neon sign perpendicular to the fish market used to flash: "Fresh . . . Fish . . . Bait." (Author's collection.)

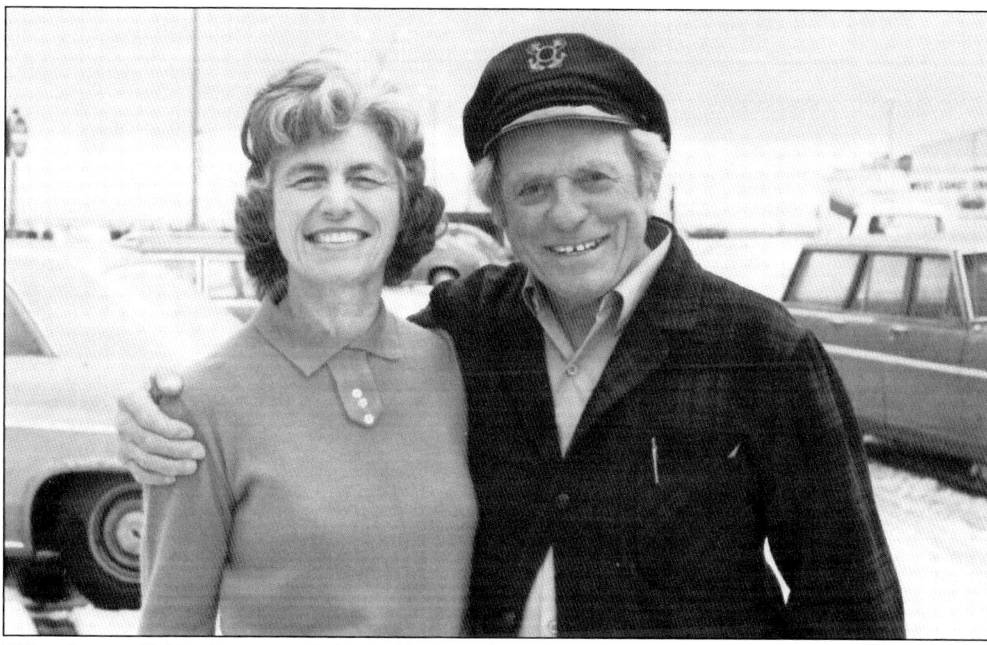

Wharf icons Gilda Stagnaro (left) and her uncle Malio Stagnaro enjoy a rare snow cover on the wharf on February 5, 1976, in a photograph taken by the author. Malio's station wagon (right) could not find traction on the slick surface, so he drove off in the author's Volkswagen van (with a rear engine). Malio was quoted in the *Sentinel* declaring that it was the most snow he had seen on the wharf in his lifetime. Gilda made snowballs. (Author's collection.)

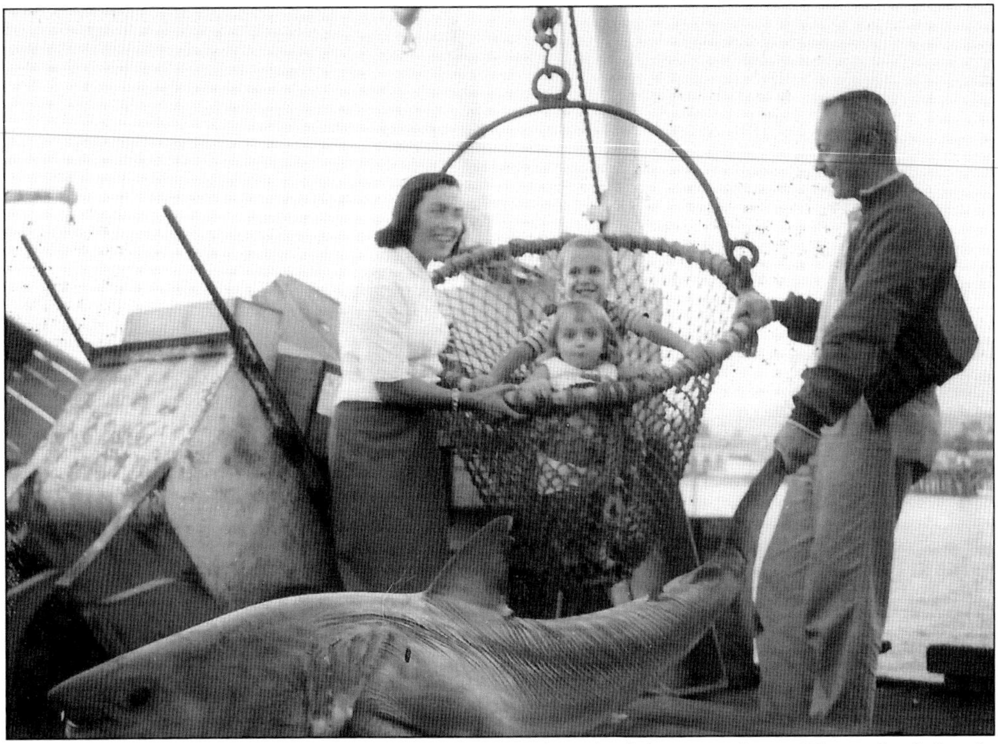

Families often spent evenings on the wharf enjoying the colorful surroundings. The author's family was no exception. Lindy Stagnaro Dunn (left) and Frank Dunn (right) check out the large shark while their kids, Geoffrey and Peggy, ride in a fish basket in 1959. The Pleasure Pier can be seen in the background. (Author's collection.)

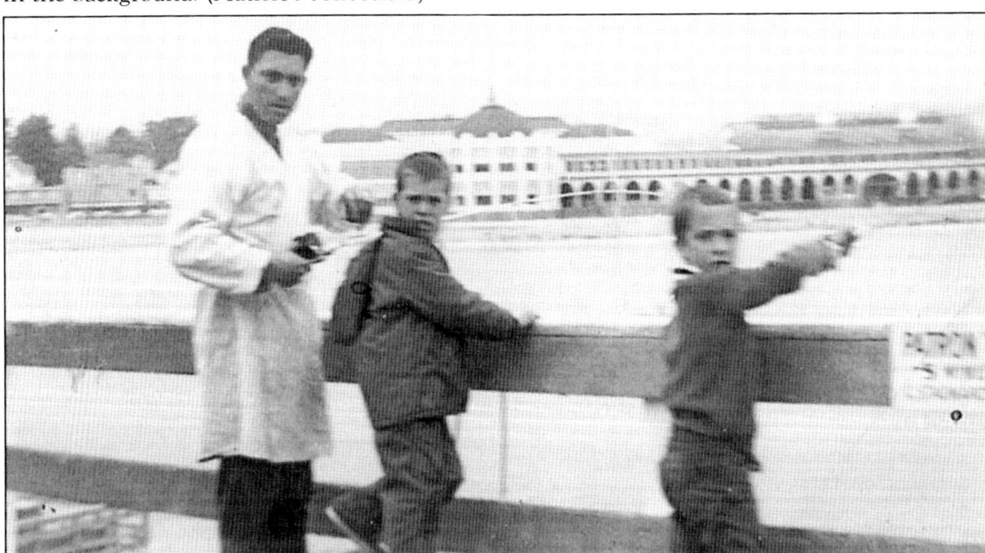

This is a portrait of the artist as a young fish boy. Robert "Big Boy" Stagnaro, with his son, Bill Stagnaro, and nephew Geoffrey Dunn, fish from the wharf in 1962. "Big Boy" is fixing a backlash on his son's reel. His eldest son, Malio, must have been camera shy, as the trio was generally inseparable. (Author's collection.)

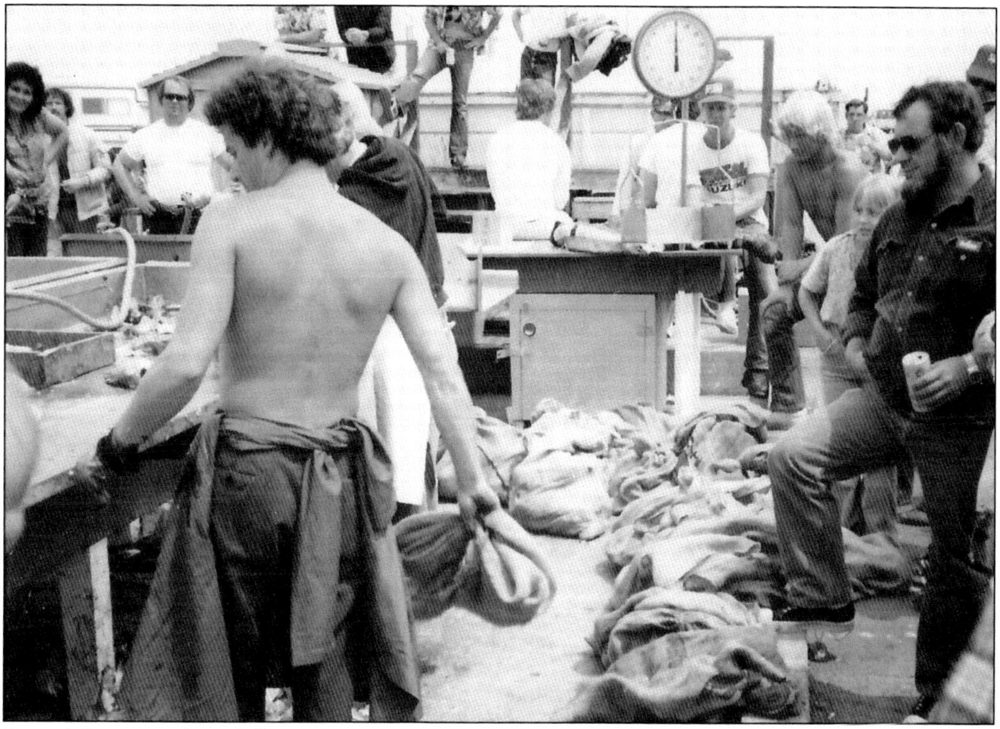

Sportfishermen aboard the Stagnaro party boats used to line up around the cleaning tables to have their fish filleted before they departed for home. Some days, several tons of fish were cut. Estrella Stagnaro used to bark out to tourists about the "art of filleting fish." Her nephew, author Geoffrey Dunn (left, with shirt off), cut fish for the party boats every day on the wharf until 1985. (Author's collection.)

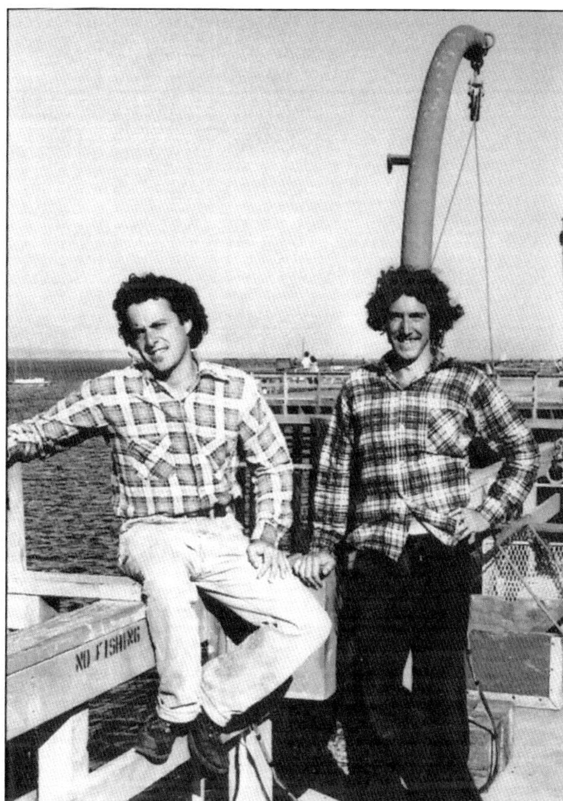

Cousins Geoffrey Dunn (left) and Bill Stagnaro are pictured together in 1979. The pair did dry-dock work on the family party boats in the late 1970s and early 1980s. (Author's collection, photograph by Leta Stagnaro.)

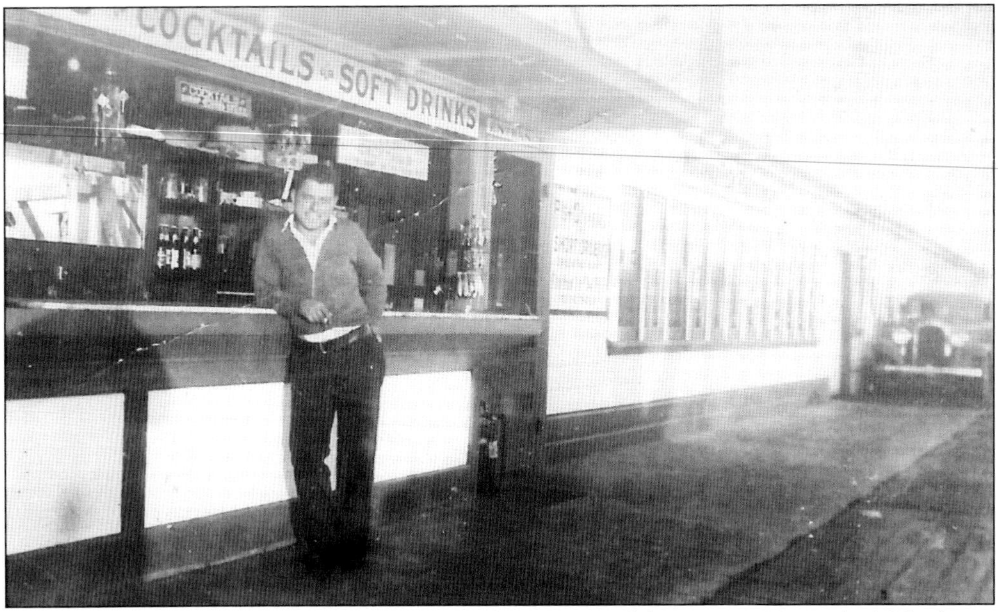

Batista J. "Dodie" Stagnaro enjoys a break at the Miramar fish counter. He worked 364 days a year in the family fish market, taking only Christmas Day off. Dodie was named vice president of the family corporation in 1950. He died of a heart attack on the wharf in 1968 at the age of 54. (Author's collection.)

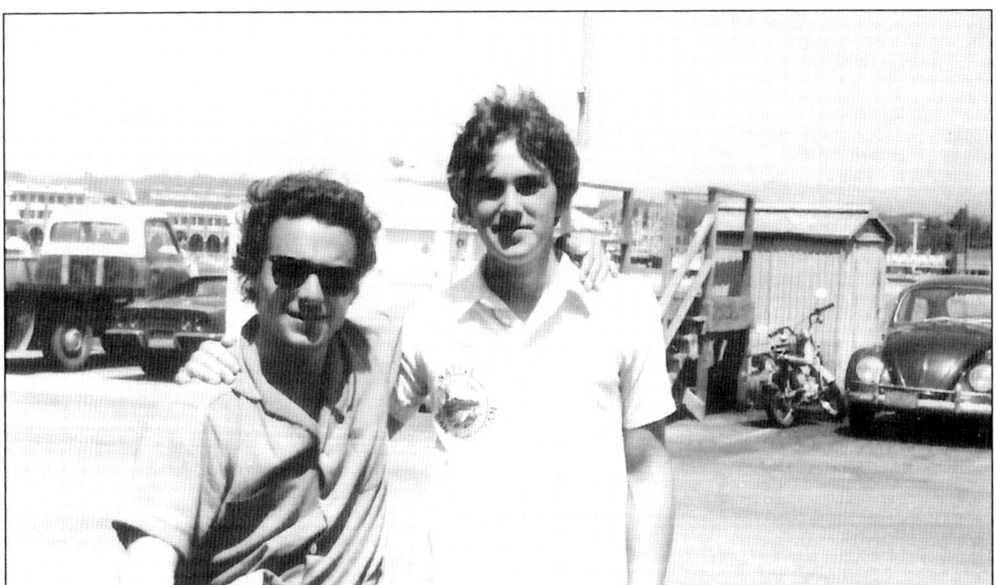

Pictured here are Geoffrey Dunn (left) and his longtime fish-cutting partner, James "Jimmy" Umland, sporting his Native Santa Cruzan sports shirt, enjoying a quiet moment after work around 1982. Umland began working as a deckhand on the C. Stagnaro fishing boats at the age of 10. He loved being around the boats. He later became a long-haul truck driver. (Author's collection.)

Seven

THE WHARF TODAY . . . AND TOMORROW

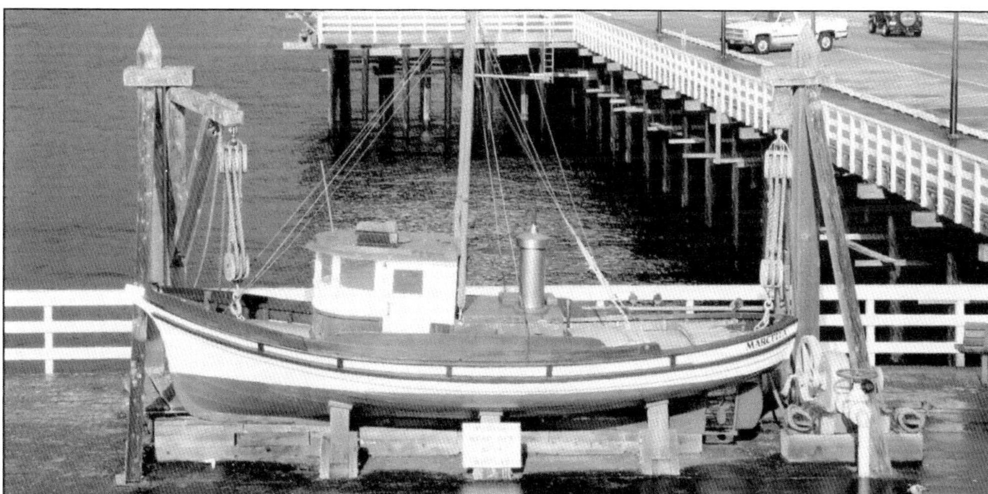

In December 2014, the Santa Cruz Wharf celebrated its centennial with a series of events that marked its economic and cultural contributions to the greater Santa Cruz community. Thousands of local and national dignitaries participated in the yearlong festivities. With some 4,528 wooden piles treated with creosote, the wharf continues to be maintained by the City of Santa Cruz and hosts upward of four million visitors annually. Presently 2,745 feet long, it remains the longest wharf of its kind in both the Pacific Ocean and along the continental United States. The *Marcella*, on davits here, was donated to the City of Santa Cruz in 1994 by the late Robert Podesta in memory of the double-ended fishing boats that once graced the wharf. It was formerly the *Cella Bessie*, built for Joe Loero in 1916. (City of Santa Cruz.)

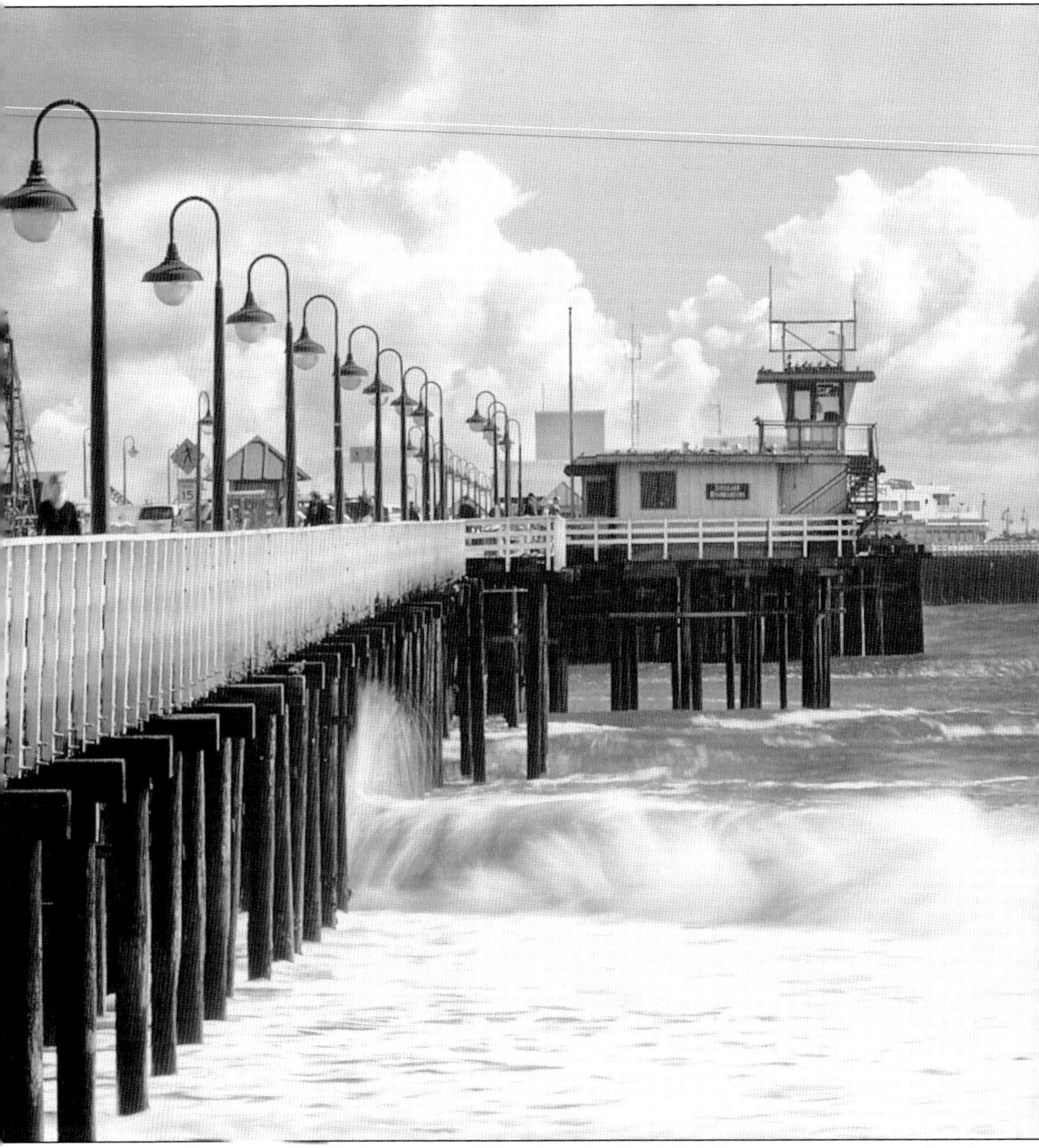

A series of tsunamis hit the Santa Cruz Wharf in March 2011 following a massive earthquake in Japan. Little damage was done to the wharf, but the Santa Cruz Yacht Harbor was hit hard by the surging waves; one dock was completely destroyed and more than 300 boats were ripped from their berths. (City of Santa Cruz, photograph by Anthony Solis.)

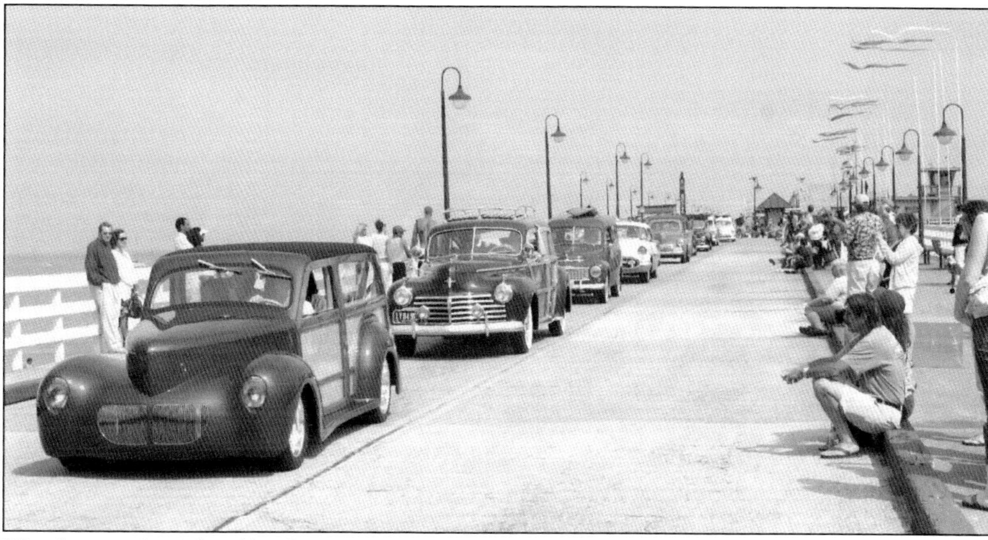

Woodies on the Wharf has become an annual institution in Santa Cruz and the largest event of its kind featuring pre-1952 wood-bodied cars. Founded in 1993 by the Santa Cruz Woodies Club, with Don Iglesias serving as president with an assist from Lisa McGinnis of the parks and recreation department, the showcase is now one of the largest and most popular woody events in the world, bringing in more than 200 beautifully refurbished vehicles each year. (City of Santa Cruz.)

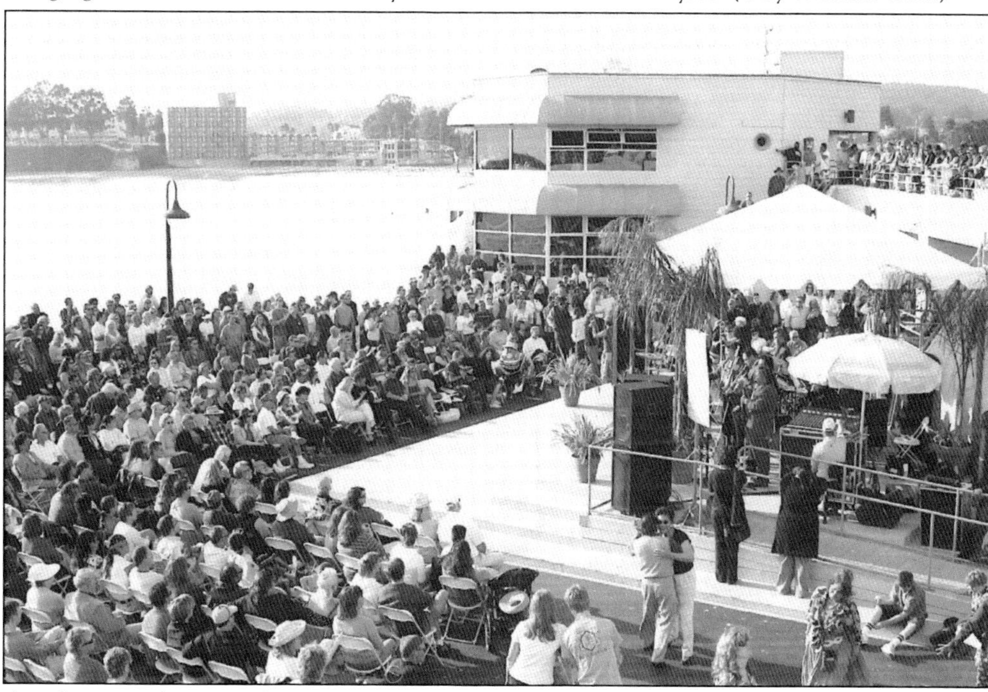

Another popular annual event sponsored by the parks and recreation department is Jazz on the Wharf, where bands perform both outside on the wharf stage (pictured) and inside various restaurants. A potpourri of jazz styles is represented each year (usually in the spring), including classical, Dixieland, Latin, New Orleans, Chicago, big band, Latin, Gypsy, blues, and various other renditions of what is truly an American art form. The music is always great and the views unsurpassed. (City of Santa Cruz.)

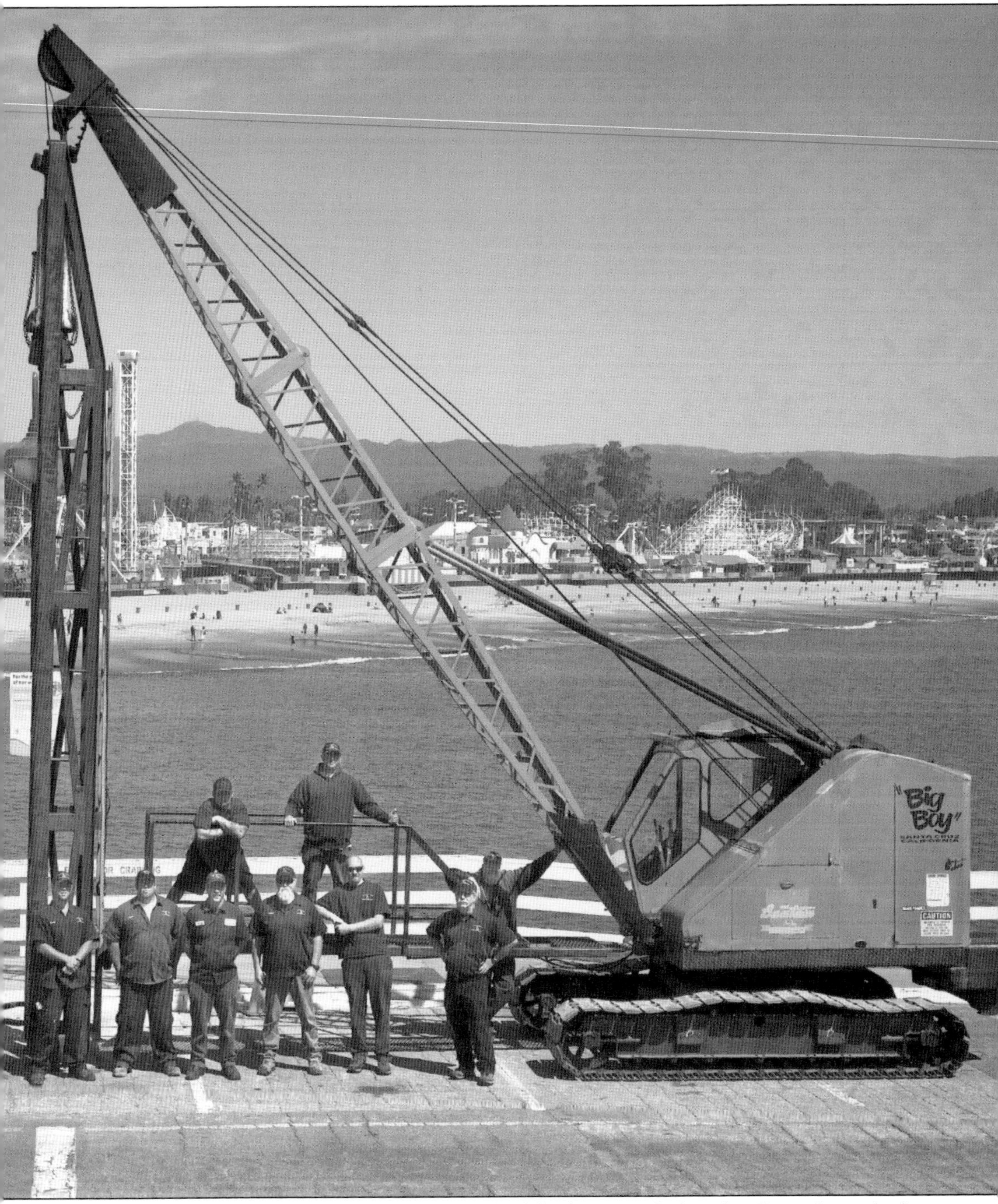

The wharf maintenance crew is featured in the fall of 2010 with the wharf's resident pile driver, "Big Boy," a 1959 Bantam C 350-A crawler crane reconfigured as a pile driver in 1998. From left to right are (first row) Marco "Sparky" Palermo, Garth Taylor, Britt Hoberg, Michael Duckett, Brad "Buck" Arbsland, Jon Bombaci, and William "Earl" Rue; (second row) Josh Riggins and Mike Brumett. (Jon Bombaci, City of Santa Cruz.)

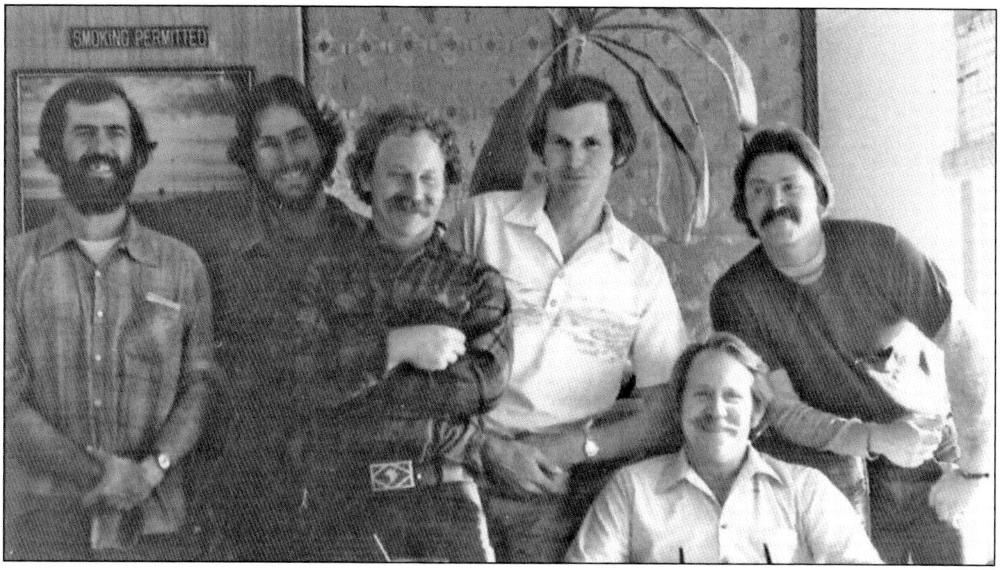

Wharf superintendent Bill Eisle (seated) oversaw maintenance of the wharf during the critical decades from 1973 to 1993. He is widely credited with putting all of the logistics in place with respect to security, staff, and infrastructure (crew structure, security, and infrastructure upgrades) that are the groundwork for the stability the wharf enjoys today. Behind Eisle in 1982 are, from left to right, Dan Buecher, Gilbert "Gib" Hettman, Rob Langdon, Jack Harrell, and Tom McAuliffe. (Dan Buecher.)

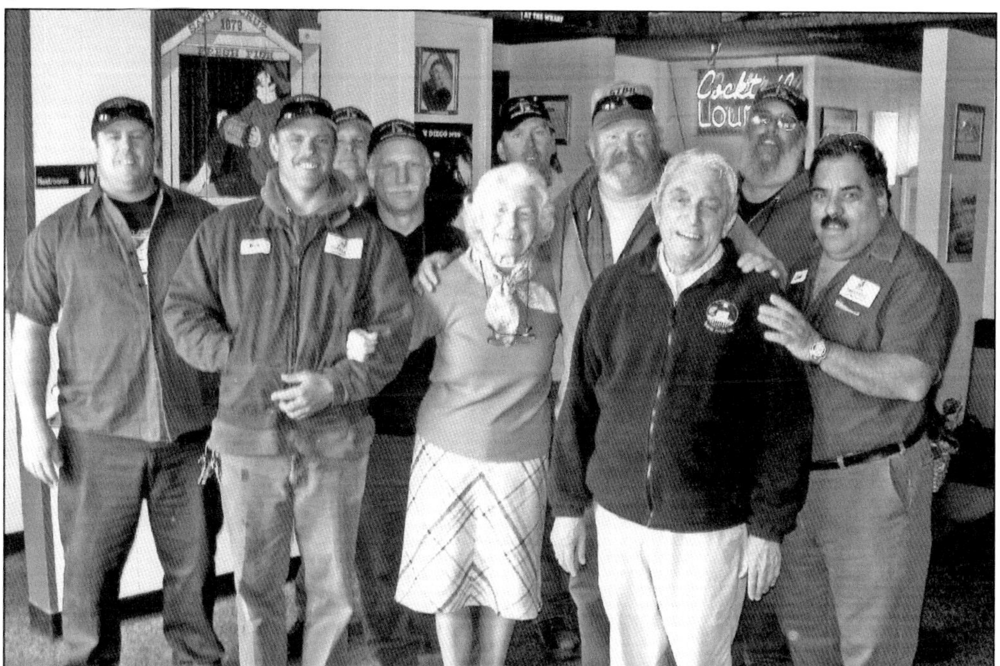

There has always been a close relationship between the wharf crew and the wharf business community. Here, celebrating Gilda Stagnaro's 81st birthday with her brother Robert (center) in 2005 are, from left to right, Garth Taylor, Brit Hoberg, Cam Kinder, Jon Bombaci, Dan Hill, William "Earl" Rue, David Maruska, and Hank Aranda. (Dan Buecher.)

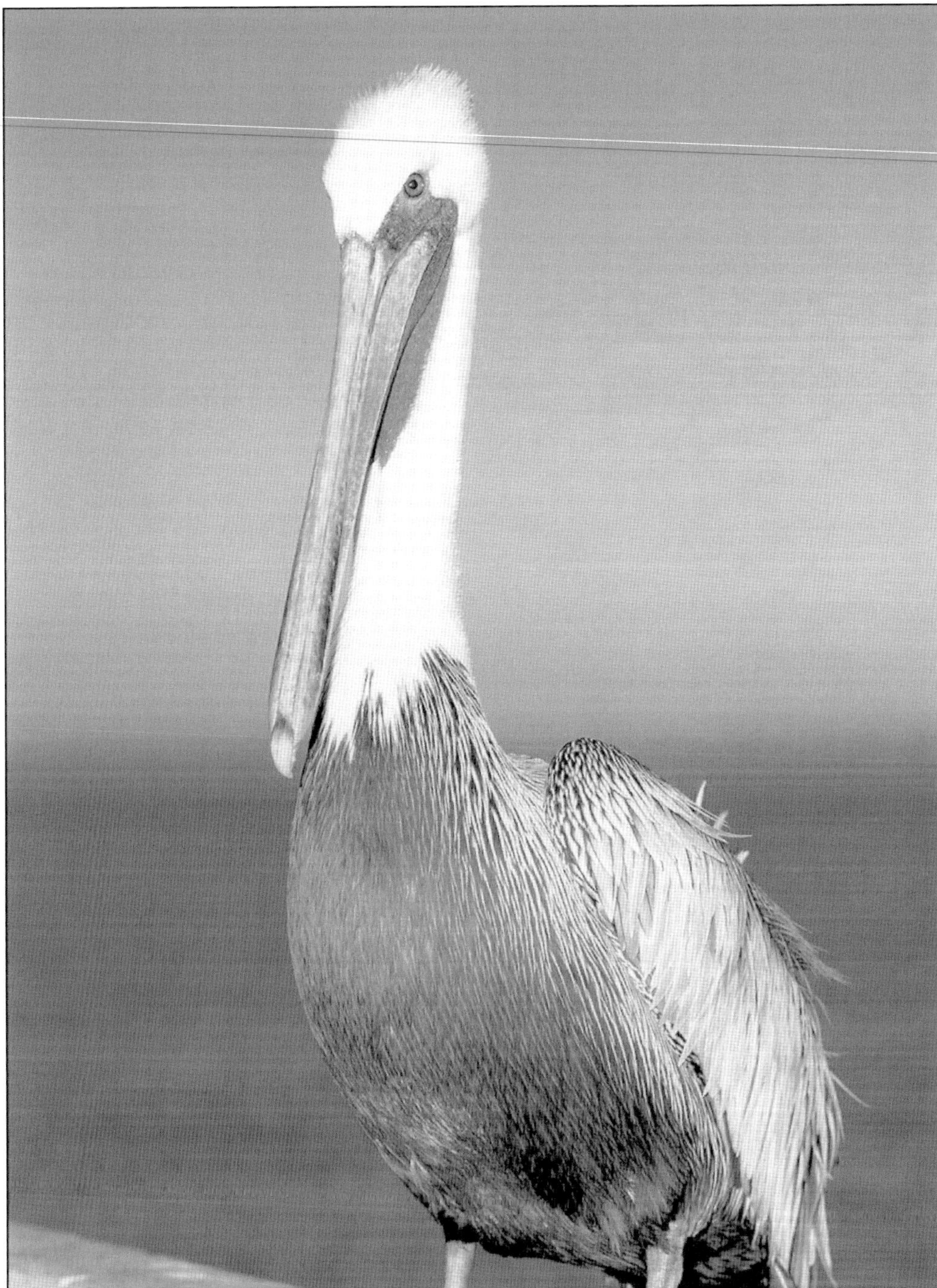

One of the more beautiful visitors to the wharf annually is the California brown pelican (*Pelecanus occidentalis*), which is today plentiful in numbers but was nearly wiped out in the 1960s by the pesticide DDT. It was declared a federally endangered species in 1970 but was removed from the list in 2009. With wingspans of more than six feet, they can be seen diving for small migratory fish—sardines, anchovies, and mackerel—that arrive in the Monterey Bay in the warmer summer months. (City of Santa Cruz.)

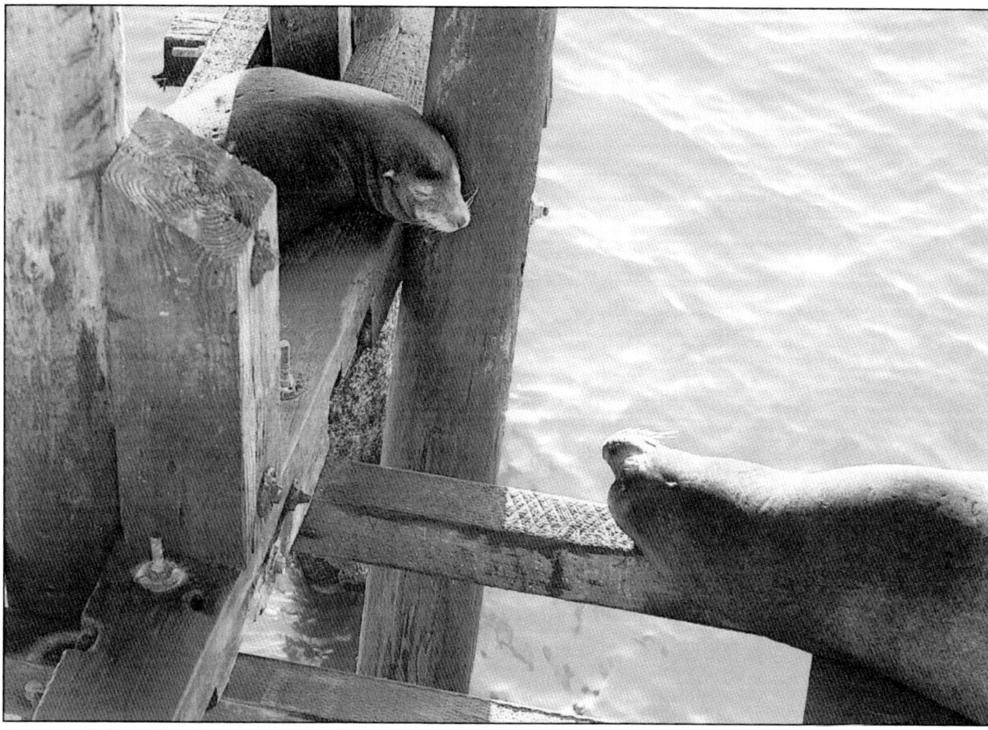

Some of the wharf's most popular—and clamorous—inhabitants are the California sea lions (*Zalophus californianus*) who have claimed many of the wharf's landings, cross beams, and catwalks as their habitat. Males are up to eight feet long and can weigh 800 pounds and more; females are roughly six feet and average 220 pounds. They have made a remarkable comeback in recent decades. In 1950, the population was approximately 10,000; today, it exceeds 300,000. (City of Santa Cruz.)

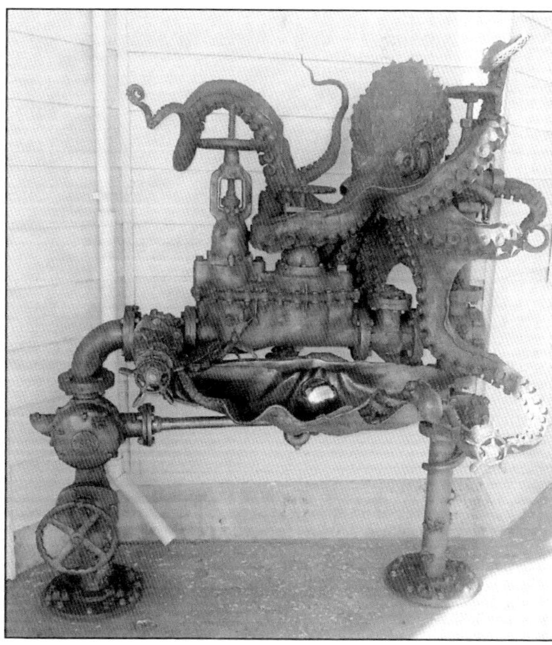

One of the most recent artistic additions to the wharf is this ornate octopus drinking fountain located outside the restaurant Splash. Created by talented local artist Sean Monaghan, owner of the studio and foundry BronzeWorks, the wharf fountain, entitled *Pearl Diver*, is the third octopus-themed drinking fountain created by Monhaghan since the 1980s. Monaghan also provided bronze work for the Three Princes plaque at Lighthouse Field. Splash opened in June 2016, replete with a rotating bar. (City of Santa Cruz.)

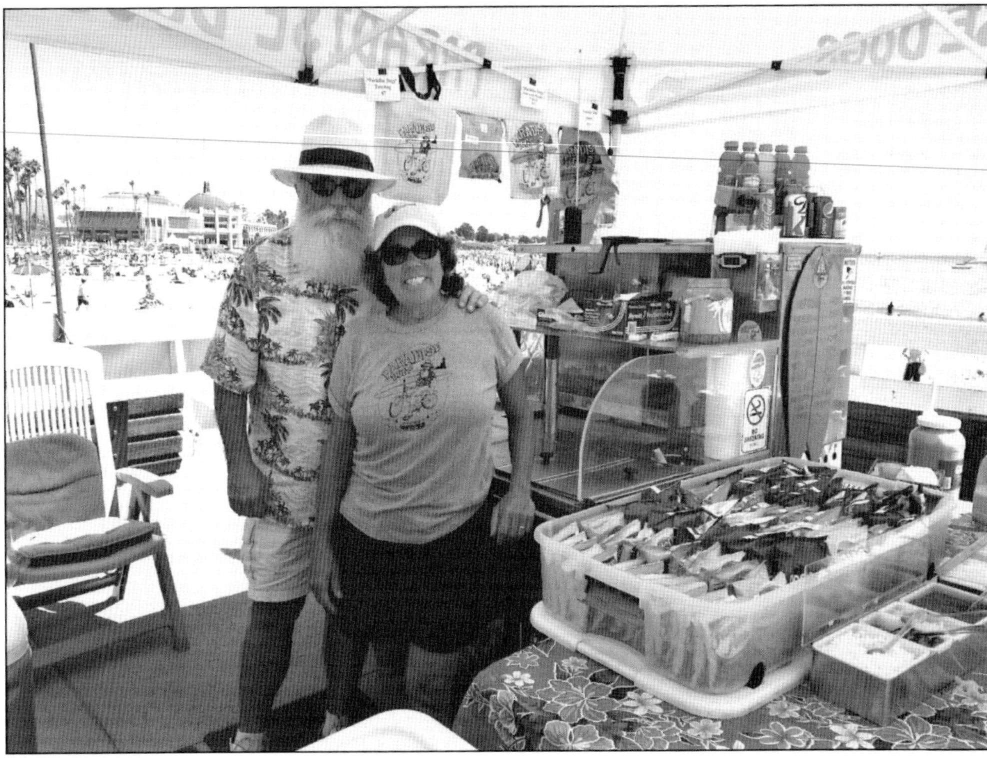

Two of the more popular figures on the wharf are Vince and Margie Tuzzi of Paradise Dogs at the beginning of the wharf. Vince was always intrigued by the idea of selling hot dogs al fresco on the waterfront and purchased the existing vendor stand in the early 2000s. The Tuzzis' talented daughter Gina designed the logo that graces their T-shirts and tote bags, which they also sell at their stand. (Vince Tuzzi.)

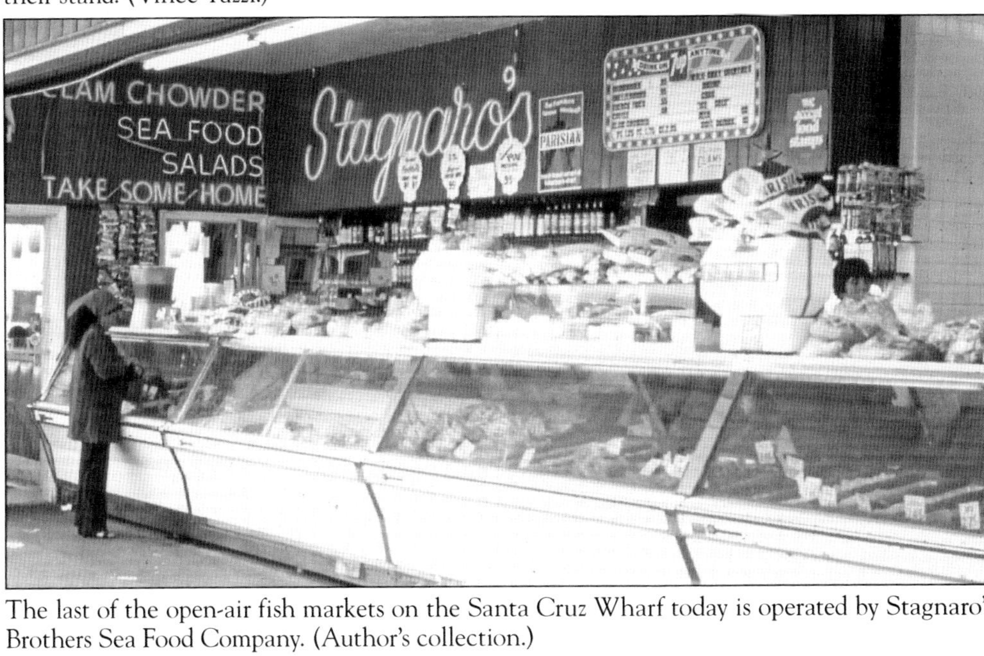

The last of the open-air fish markets on the Santa Cruz Wharf today is operated by Stagnaro's Brothers Sea Food Company. (Author's collection.)

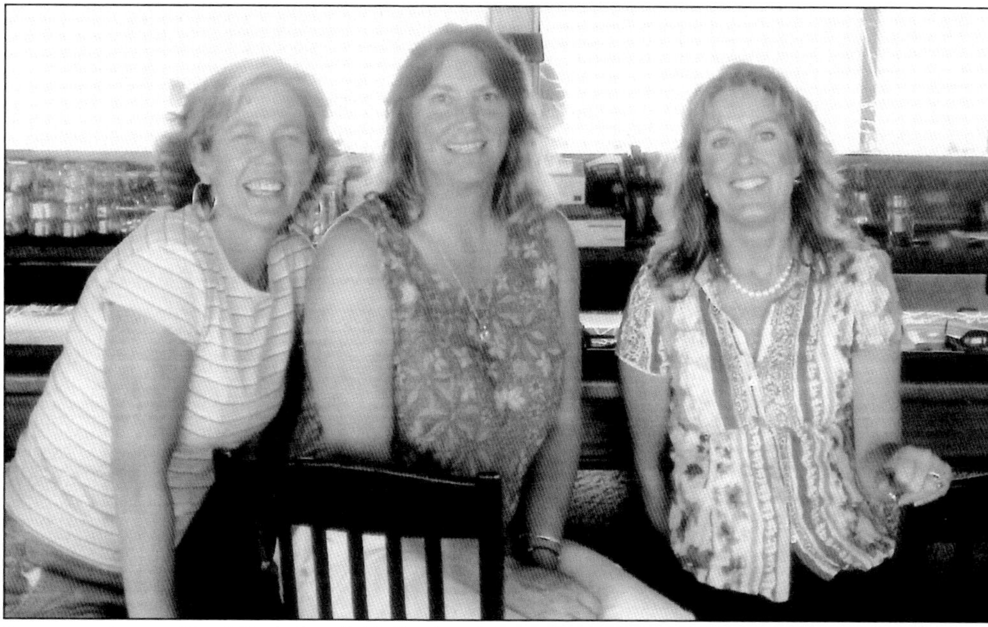

Longtime friends Carol Brubaker (left), Darlene Enrico (center), and Melissa Mobley enjoy a moment of relaxation at Gilbert's on the wharf in the 1990s. Santa Cruz native Brubaker is now a manger of Woodies Café at the wharf, while Mobley, who has worked at the wharf for more than 30 years, now joins her husband Mark Gilbert in a number of wharf enterprises. (Mark Gilbert.)

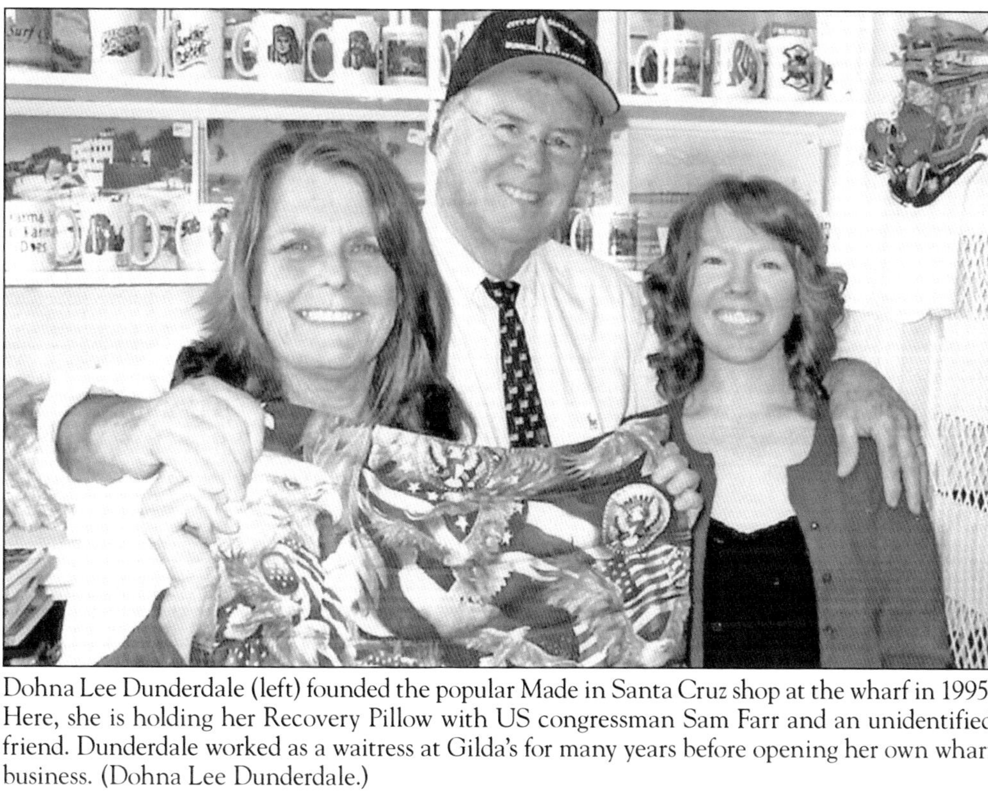

Dohna Lee Dunderdale (left) founded the popular Made in Santa Cruz shop at the wharf in 1995. Here, she is holding her Recovery Pillow with US congressman Sam Farr and an unidentified friend. Dunderdale worked as a waitress at Gilda's for many years before opening her own wharf business. (Dohna Lee Dunderdale.)

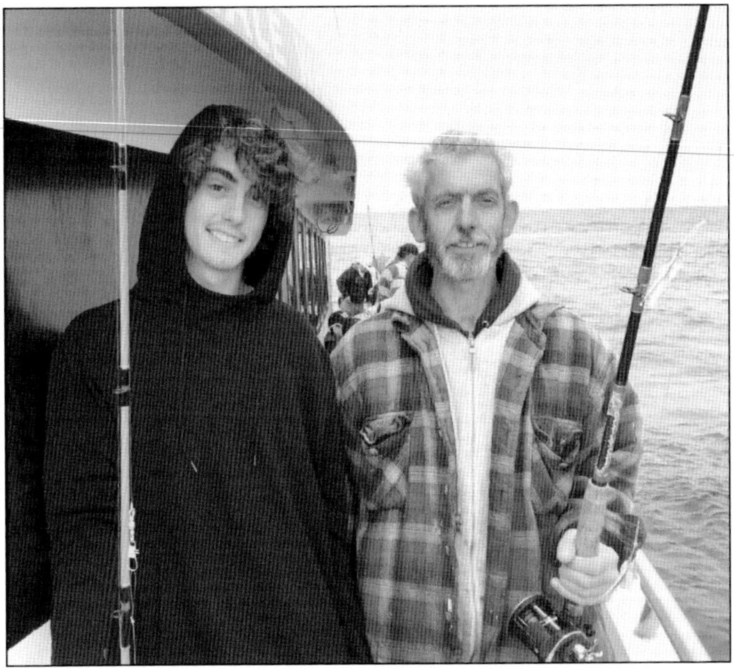

Robert "Dino" Stagnaro, right, is pictured with his son Zachary aboard the 60-foot *Velocity* of the Stagnaro Sport Fishing, Charter, and Whale Watching Cruises, which Dino runs with his cousin, skipper Ken Stagnaro. Dino and his brother Malio operate Gilda's on the wharf, the fourth generation of the family to do so; Zachary, who also works at the restaurant, marks the fifth. (Laura Paz, photograph by Trinidad Paz.)

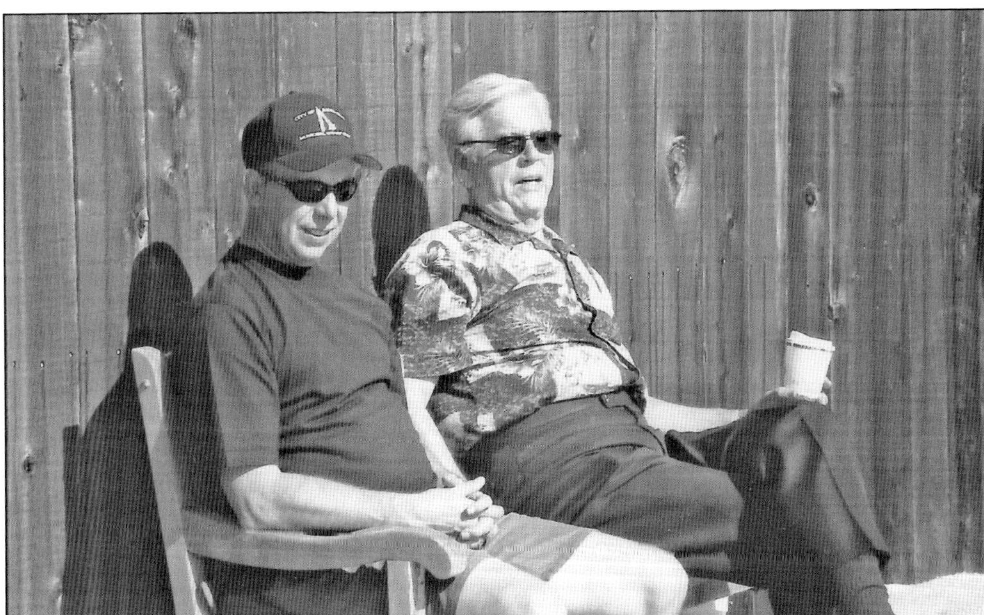

Wharf mavens Mark Gilbert (left) and his father, Jim Gilbert, enjoy a quiet moment away from their family businesses. Jim had been a longtime restaurateur on the Monterey Waterfront when he purchased the Ideal Restaurant in 1977 and Malio's (later to become Gilbert's) in 1980. His son purchased the latter and quickly became the most successful wharf entrepreneur of the new millennium, with a trio of successful restaurants—Firefish Grill, Woodies Café, and the Dolphin—and Woodies Gift Shop. He recently purchased the Miramar restaurant and plans to transform it "in the next few years." (Mark Gilbert.)

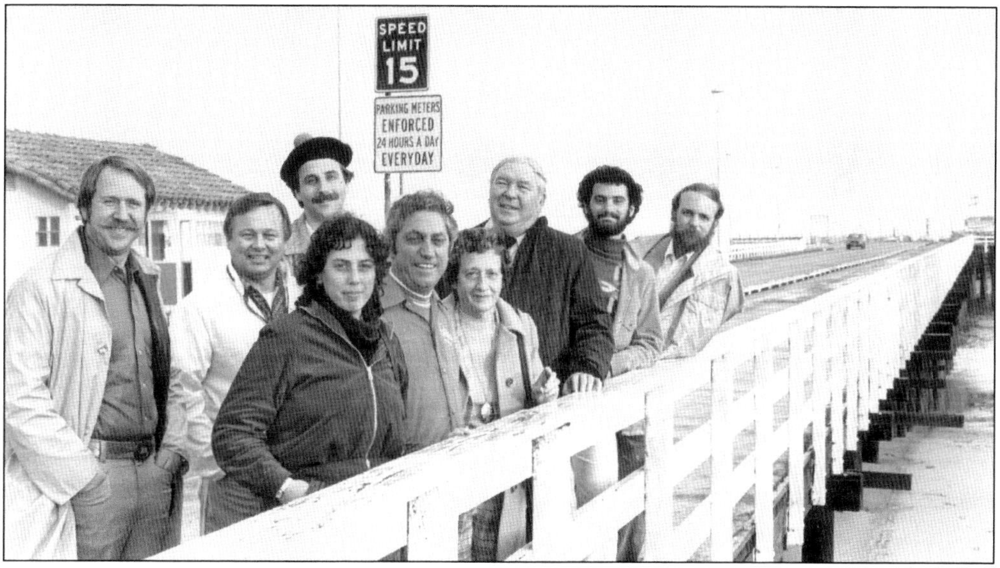

The California Italian American Arts Organization (CIAO) initiated a community-based research project on the local Italian fishing community in the late 1970s and early 1980s. The project resulted in a series of photography exhibitions, festivals, oral histories, magazines, and a documentary film, *A Day on the Bay*, that played on PBS. Pictured, from left to right, are wharf supervisor Bill Eisle, longtime wharf business leader Ward Noland, CIAO founder Ricco Gaudino, Lorrie Berman, Robert "Big Boy" Stagnaro, unidentified, unidentified, filmmaker Mark Schwartz, and UCSC advisor Dr. Michael Orbach. (City of Santa Cruz.)

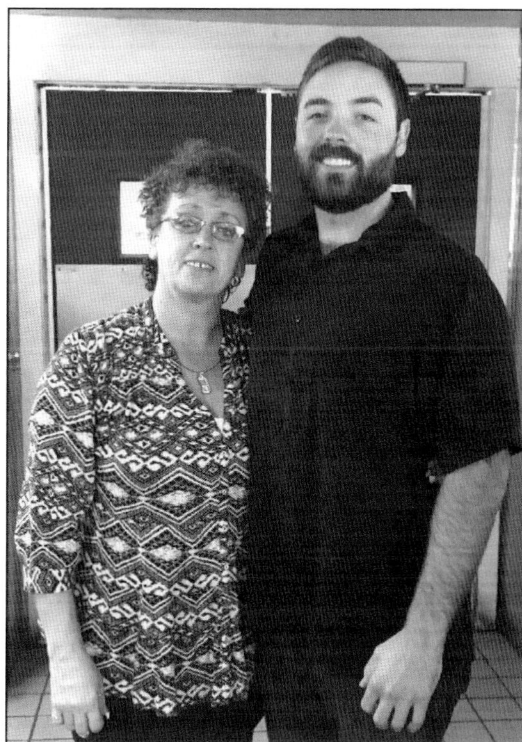

Mother and son Suze and Austin "Bubba" Towne are pictured in the kitchen at Gilda's. Suze has worked on the floor of Gilda's for more than 25 years, while Bubba started as a busboy there at the age of 14. Many families are represented by multiple generations of employees in wharf businesses. (Austin "Bubba" Towne.)

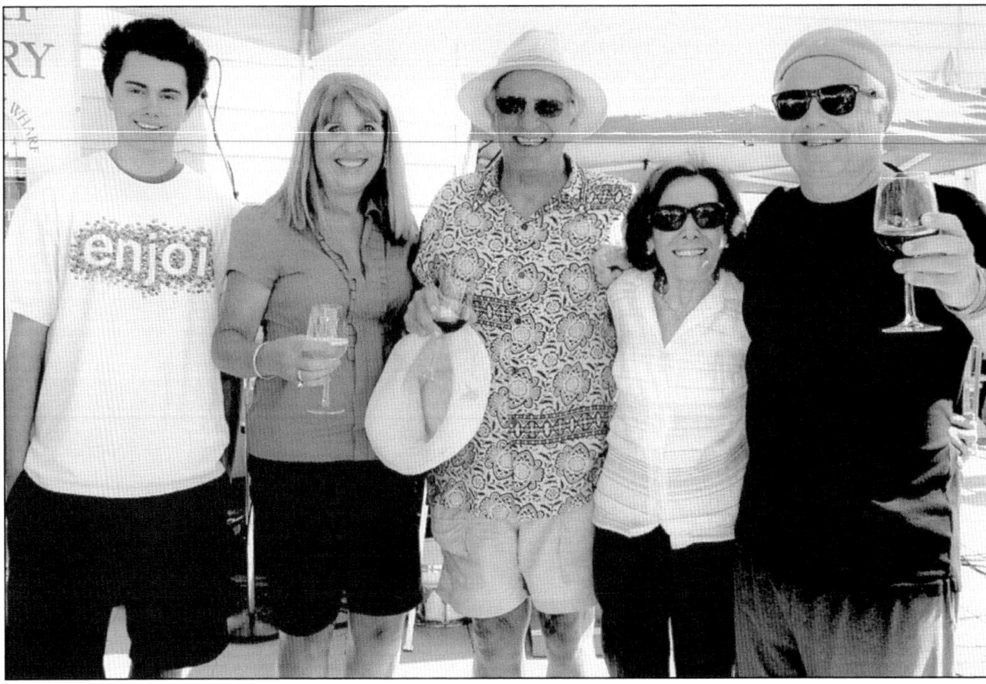

Three generations of Santa Cruz Italian fishing families celebrated the wharf's centennial in October 2014. From left to right are Dylan Dunn, Lynn Bassano Allgre, Wayne Bassano, Lindy Stagnaro Dunn, and author Geoffrey Dunn. (Author's collection.)

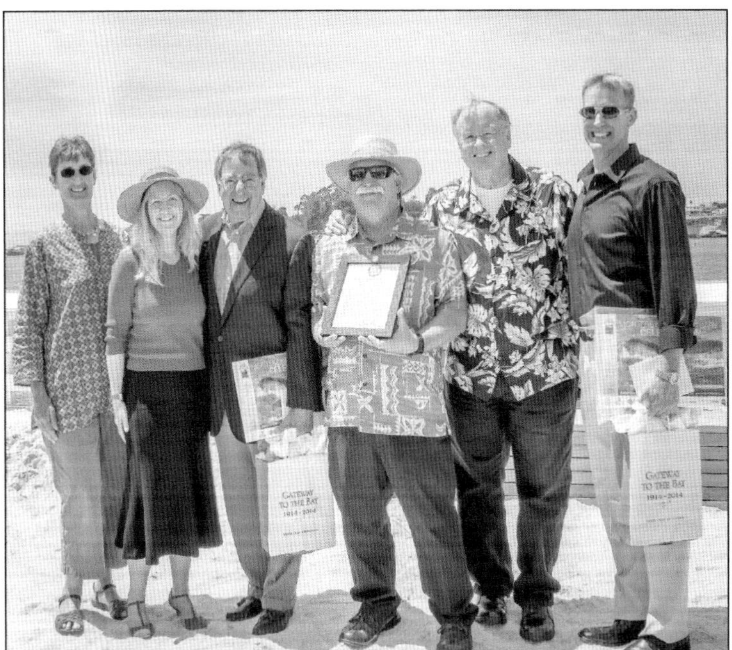

Pictured here at the centennial celebration of the Monterey Bay Sanctuary on May 17, 2014, are, from left to right, former and current mayor Cynthia Mathews, former mayor Lynn Robinson, former secretary of defense Leon Panetta, wharf supervisor Jon Bombaci, Congressman Sam Farr, and Monterey Bay Sanctuary superintendent Paul Michel. (Jon Bombaci, City of Santa Cruz.)

The Wharf Centennial Commemoration, with permanent plaque, took place on December 5, 2014. Pictured here, from left to right, are city manager Martin Bernal, Dave Rosener, retired wharf supervisor Dan Buecher, John Young, wharf supervisor Jon Bombaci, Joel Braga, Britt Hoberg, Marco "Sparky" Palermo (far back), Kory Kvenild, Hank Aranda, Annalise Bryant, then-mayor Lynn Robinson, Frank Hunter, and parks & recreation director Dannettee Shoemaker. (Jon Bombaci, City of Santa Cruz.)

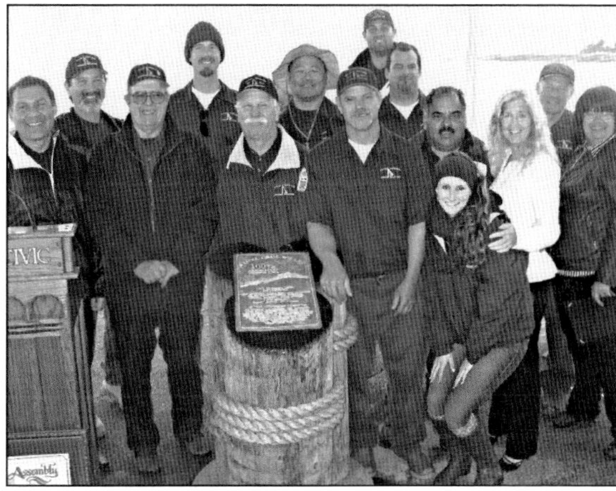

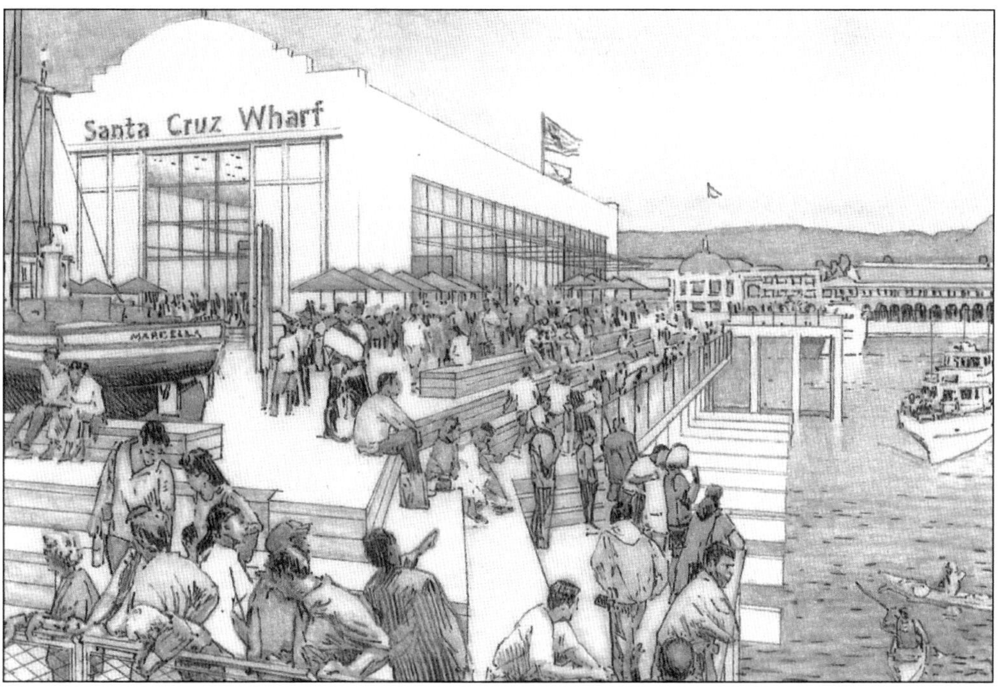

In October 2015, the Santa Cruz City Council adopted *The Santa Cruz Wharf Master Plan and Engineering Report*, which encompasses a 2.5-acre expansion for public access, recreation, and engagement with the Monterey Bay National Marine Sanctuary. Prepared by ROMA Design Group, the plan proposes expanding the wharf on both the east and west sides, adding additional walkways. The new buildings would include a welcome center, a landmark center, and an indoor/outdoor event center (pictured in this rendering) at the end of the wharf. (City of Santa Cruz.)